(07957603680)

An analytical and critical study of
ISLAMIC HISTORY

THE RISE AND FALL OF MUSLIMS

From The Pious Caliphs to Abbasid
Spain and Moghal Dynasties

Maulana Saeed Akbar Abadi

Adam Publishers & Distributors
New Delhi-2 (India)

ALL RIGHTS RESERVED

This Book is copyright under the Berne Convention. Apart from any fair dealing for the purposes of private study, research, criticism or review, as permitted under the copyright law, no portion may be reproduced without written permission. Enquiries should be made to the publishers.

Adam Publishers & Distributors
Exporters & Importers
1542, Pataudi House, Daryagunj, New Delhi-110002
Ph.: (O) 23282550, 23284740, 23267510
Fax.: 23267510 (R) 95120-2413957
E_mail : apd@bol.net.in
www.adambooks.com

Edition - 2004
ISBN 81-7435-293-7
Price

Printed & Bound In India
Published by
S. Sajid Ali
Adam Publishers & Distributors
1542, Pataudi House, Daryagunj, New Delhi-110002

End of Khiljis	221

Chapter 10
THE TUGHLAQ DYNASTY	226
Sultan Ghias-ud-Din Tughlaq	227
Waywardness and cynical attitude	231
Sultan Feroze Shah Tughlaq	234
Amir Taimoor	238
The Sadaat Dynasty (1414 A.D. – 1450 A.D.)	239
Lodhi Dynasty	240
Sultan Sikandar Lodhi	240
Sultan Ibrahim Lodhi	241
Advent of Babar and the Mughal rule	241
The character and perfection of Babar	242
Humayoun	243
Sher Shah Suri and his family	244
Successors of Sher Shah Suri	246

Chapter 11
THE REIGN OF MUGHALS	248
Jalal ud Din Muhammad Akbar	248
Religious innovations of Akbar and the downfall of Islamic vlaues	249
The last days of Akbar	250
Noor ud Din Saleem Jehangir	251

Chapter 12
THE EAST INDIA COMPANY	254
Death of Jehangir	254
Emperor Shah Jahan	254
Aurangzeb Alamgir	256
Education and training	257
Administration of law and justice	258
Moral and administrative reforms	258
Codification of Islamic laws	259
Bravery and fearlessness	259
General conditions of India at Alamgir's death	262

Contents	9
Muslims burnt alive	177
Massacare of Muslims	177

Chapter 7
RISE AND FALL OF MUSLIMS IN INDIA	179
Attack on Sindh By Muhammad Bin Qasim	180
Sad end of Muhammad Bin Qasim	182
Acceptance of Islam by Hindu Rajas of Sindh	184
Sindh under the Abbaside Caliphate	185
Amir Sabukta-Gin	186
Sultan Mahmood of Ghazni	187
Sultan Mahmood attacks Punjab	187
Sultan Mahmood attacks Multan	188
Battle at Peshawar and conquest of Nagar Kot	188
Siege of Nagar Kot	189
Conquest of Thanseer	189
Attack at Kashmir	189
Conquest of Qannouj	190
Conquest of Som Nath	190
Sultan Mahmood's death	191
Life and character of Sultan Mahmood	191
Decline of the Ghazni State	194
The Ghauri Dynasty	194
The Slave Dynasty	197

Chapter 8
SULTAN SHAMSUD DIN ALTAMASH	199
Raziyya Sultana	201
Nasir Ud Din Mahmood	202
Successor of Balban	207
The Khilji Dynasty	208

Chapter 9
ALAUDDIN KHILJI	213
Arrogance and egotism of Alauddin	214
Respect for Hazrat Sultan Nizam Ud Din Aulia	218
Public reforms	219

Sea power of the Ottoman Turks	129
Suleman the Great	129
Justice and good administration	130
Military preparations and equipment	130
Works of public welfare	131
Two distinct periods of Ottoman Rule	131
Comparison of Banu Abbas with the Ottomans	131
Fall of Ottoman power	133
Causes of Deterioration	133
Institute of heir-apparent	136
Royal marriages with foreign women	137
Rebellion in the army	138
Disloyalty and corruption of civil chiefs	139
Economic deterioration	140
Inactivity and lassitude of religious scholars	140
Awakening in the rivals	141
Rebellion of the Arabs (Hidjas)	142
End of institute of Khilafat	142
Existing world of Islam	143

Chapter 6
ANDULUSIA (SPAIN)
THE RISE AND FALL OF MUSLIM RULE

ANDULUSIA (SPAIN)	144
Exploits of the Muslims in Spain	146
Different eras of the Muslim governments in Spain	150
Ali Bin Hamood	152
Qasim Bin Hamood	153
The last days of Banu Umayyads in Spain	154
Murabiteen	156
Yousuf Bin Tashifein and battle of Zalaka	156
Domination of Spain by Yousuf Bin Tashifein	159
Al-Mowahhidoon	160
Ibne Hood	161
Kingdom of Granada	163
Death of Abu Abdullah	173
Repression and Tyranny of Granada Muslims	173
Burning of books on Islam	176

Contents

Rationalism or dogmatic theology:	93
A doubt and its satisfaction	94

Chapter 4
CRUSADES AGAINST ISLAM

CRUSADES AGAINST ISLAM	96
Crushing defeat of Crusades	98
Sultan Noor-ud-Din Zangi	98
Sultan Salah-ud-Din Ayyubi	98
Death of Sultan Salah-ud-Din Ayyubi and after	99
Saljuqis	101
Banu Hamdan	102
The attacks by Tartars and defence of Muslim leaders	103
Malik Zahir Babris	104
Annihilation of Batnia sect	104
Repeated successes against Tartars	104
Conversion of Tartars to Islam	106
Hero of the Abbaside Caliphates	107
Conduct of Mansoor as well wisher of Islam and Muslims	107
Re-establishment of Abbaside rule (Caliphate) in Egypt	110

Chapter 5
AAL-E-USMAN (THE CHILDREN OF USMAN)

AAL-E-USMAN (THE CHILDREN OF USMAN)	114
Character of Usman Khan-I	114
Continuos conquests and entering of Islam into Europe	115
Sultan Murad-I	116
Sultan Ba-Yazid Yaldram	117
Crusaders alliance	119
The battle of Angora	120
Effects of battle of the Angora on Islam	122
The Revival of the Usmani Empire	122
Sultan Murad-II	123
Sultan Muhammad Fateh	124
More conquestes by Sultan Muhammad	125
Sultan Salim-I	126
Transfer of Caliphate	126
Service to the Holy Places of Islam	127
Respect and regard for the Shariat law	128

Oppression of government functionaries	57
Prejudices of Banu Omayyah	57
Mal-administration of national treasury:	58
Dissension and disunity:	58
Soundness of religious tenets:	59
Services of Abdul Malik Bin Marwan:	59
Extirpation of the Kharijites:	59
Mischief of Mukhtar:	60
Tawwabeen:	60
Agitation in Iraq:	60
Walid Bin Abdul Malik:	62
Repeated attacks on Constantinople:	62
Period of Sulaiman Bin Abdul Malik	64
Causes of Muslims' failure:	66
Hazrat Umar Bin Abdul Aziz	68
Yazid Bin Abdul Malik	73
Hisham Bin Abdul Malik	74
Caliphs of Banu Omayyah after Hisham Bin Abdul Malik	75
Walid	75
Yazid Bin Walid	76

Chapter 3
PERIOD OF THE RULE OF BANU ABBAS

	79
Harrowing tales of Tyranny	79
Contrast in speech and action of Saffah	80
Fatal effects of nominating successors	82
Transfer of authority to Turkish slaves:	83
Two phases of the Abbasides Caliphate:	84
Period of decline and deterioration:	84
Corruption at ministerial level:	86
Division of Khilafat into pieces	87
Severe repression of hanbalities:	88
End of Abbaside Caliphate of Baghdad:	89
Development of knowledge and arts under Abbasides and its effect on the decline of Muslims	89
Quranic principles of education	91
Line of reasoning adopted by philosophy:	92

Contents

Preface ... 12

Chapter 1
THE RISE AND FALL OF MUSLIMS ... 13
Wisdom and philosophy: ... 14
"Tauheed" (Monotheism): ... 17
"Itteqa" (Piety): ... 19
Collective effects of "Tuheed" and "Ittiqa" ... 21
Simple living and life style of the Khalifas ... 23
Protection of the Bait-Ul-Mal (National Treasury) ... 24
Justice and equality ... 25
Selection of the Caliph ... 26
Supervision and accountability of the Governors ... 26
Prophecy of the Holy Prophet ﷺ: ... 31
Martyrdom of Hazrat Usman ؓ: ... 33
The Caliphate of Hazrat Ali ؓ ... 33
Opposition of Hazrat Ali ؓ: ... 38
The attitude of Amir Mo'awiya ؓ ... 39
Event of arbitration: ... 40
Comments on the rulership of Hazrat Ali ؓ: ... 42
The causes of the failure of Hazrat Ali ؓ: ... 43
Re-appearance of tribal prejudices: ... 43
Differences in spiritual status: ... 46
Example of Amir Mo'awiya ؓ: ... 46
Effects / influence of Non-Arab Muslims on the Islamic polity ... 47
Asceticism and solitude of the elite companions of the Holy Prophet ﷺ: ... 48

Chapter 2
REIGN OF BANU OMAYYAHS ... 50
The effects of monarchy: ... 52
Bai'at (pledge of loyalty) for Yazid: ... 53
Comments on the regime of Banu Omayyah: ... 54

THE RISE AND FALL OF MUSLIMS

This book presents, detailed account of the wonder-inspiring rise of the Muslims and their pathetic fall. It embodies the stories and assessments of the very first "Khilafat-e-Rashidah" (the well-guided government of the immediate successors of the Holy Prophet of Islamﷺ, the Muslim governments in the succeeding periods of history, their political strategies, their collective and social events and conditions in the cultural and administrative scenarios. The factors and events leading to the rise of the Muslims and their faults and shortcomings resulted in their horrible downfall, have been critically analysed. It is in fact an astonishing long tale, which spread over a span of hundreds of years of the History of Islam.

Contents

Successors of Aurangzeb	262
Muhammad Shah	264
Attack of Nadir Shah	265
Battle of Panipat	266
Siraj Ud Daula	267
Deewani rights for East India Company	268
Hazrat Shah Wali Ullah of Delhi	269
The family of Hazrat Shah Wali Ullah	271
Hazrat Syed Ahmad Shaheed	273

Chapter 13
REVIEW OF THE PAST AND PRESENT AND CAUSES OF THE RISE AND FALL OF MUSLIMS — 274

Reformatory activities of Muslim scholars	274
Reformatory activities of mystics	280
Blessings of Islamic government	280
Final comments on rise and fall of Muslims	281
Index	283

PREFACE

In October, 1941 A.D. the compiler of this book delivered a speech under the heading: "The factors of the Rise and Fall of the Ummah" under auspicies of the "Anjuman of Islamic History and Culture" in the Muslim University, Aligarh. Later, it was published in the Monthly "BURHAN" with suitable additions.

The subject was touched upon in a simple but impressive manner. The readers of "BURHAN" were deeply impressed by it. Every body liked and appreciated the narratives and some literary critics suggested the need of its publication in the form of a book. After a few months, the essay assumed the shape of a full-fledged book after suitable changes and additions. When it was introduced in the market it was felt that some most important aspects of the history of Muslims had been omitted and left over.

The next Edition of the book which appeared in August, 1947, included the important events of the Muslims, rise and fall in Spain and Bharat (India), raised the number of pages from 329 to 368.

It is now felt that this book has become presentable as a Research document. May Allah benefit the readers.

Mufti Atiq-ur-Rehman Usmani
Manager, Nadwatul-Mussannifin
Delhi: 27 August, 1947 A.D.

THE RISE AND FALL OF MUSLIMS

It is an astonishing feature of human history that the world saw the rise of the Muslims to the pinnacle of glory and other nations submitted to their supremacy and rule. After few centuries the decline and fall of the Muslims started and reached its abysmal depths. Now the Muslim nations of the world present a picture of total disintegration. There are no more any gatherings of Muslims to discuss science and literature and various other branches of knowledge in which other nations of the world are far surpassed. The numerical strength of the Muslims now is far more than former period of history. But, unfortunately they stand at a miserably low level of knowledge, character, and spiritual and moral strength.

A student of history knows very well that, after the sad demise of the Holy Prophet ﷺ, the Muslims left the Arabian Peninsula and spread in the different corners of the world. They kept winning success upon success and within the first century of Islam, they had conquered Sind, Chinese Turkistan and Andaloosia (Spain) despite the hardest oppositions and concerted military forces of the non-Muslims. Besides acquiring political and military power, the Muslims successfully converted plenty of non-Muslims to Islam and blessed other nations with teachings of Islamic Truth and the supreme culture and civilisation of the Muslims. Except a few countries, all the conquered lands of the world took up the colour of Muslim civilisation, moral system, art and culture, scientific inventions and knowledge in various fields. Histories are unanimous in acknowledging that the Muslim contribution to the sum total of human knowledge, culture and civilisation is colossal.

Unfortunately the scenario has altogether changed. In every department of life the Muslims are presenting a woeful picture. They have become uncultured, ignorant and careless horde of human beings who are aimlessly following the nations of the world without understanding.

The unprecedented degeneration has naturally urged the Historians to think over and analyse the causes of the decline fall of the Muslims. This metamorphosis has not taken place without valid and significant causes. Before pin-pointing the causes of the Muslims' decline, it appears to be necessary to recount the factors and circumstances which combined to make the Muslims a strong and progressive nation.

After comprehending the factors which combined to push the Muslims to the apex of glory, we have to study that, with the passage of time, internal and external forces of disintegration combined to create gradual disintegration and degeneration of the Muslims so that, after few centuries, the deterioration of the Muslims began to touch the abysmal falling point of her national life. Men of heart and wisdom among the Muslims learnt the misfortunes of the Muslims and many of them have shed tears of blood over their existing unfortunate condition.

It is difficult in the following pages to narrate the long tale of a thousand years in detail. But a cursory viewpoint has to be presented to understand the pros and cons of this case. As students of history, we shall now proceed to narrate, discuss and analyse the various factors and circumstances which will make the unfortunate fall of Muslims intelligible from the view point of a Historian.

Wisdom and Philosophy:

Scholars of human nature know that man has two inherent qualities, the intellectual power which enables the man to know and understand the reality of things which he views and the power of action. This power gives him the quality of discerning between good and bad, useful and useless and the things worthy of selection and rejection. After having selected a course of action, the inherent power of action comes up to play its role. Both the inherent qualities – belong to the human self. One is the source of comprehension and the other is the source of activity. Besides these two fundamental qualities, there are many other complementary and additional forces which are derived from the fundamental qualities of discrement and activity. Th philosophy of human moral is based on these qualities and the whole subject deals with good engendering good morals and bad morals due to the moderate or excessive indulgence of these qualities. What we call "Wisdom" in moral philosophy is the name given to these two fundamental qualities. It is the "Wisdom" which makes the human individual a master piece of God's creative art. The success and progress of the humans depends on the soundness and health of these two qualities, and their moderate use. Just as an individual is a combination of the inherent qualities of discernment and activity, so have the nations collectively a distinct power of discernment and a power of activity. Thus a nation's collective quality of action and discernment is a clear reflection of the individual qualities. When a nation works on these qualities, a uniformity and concord becomes conspicuous in her aims, objectives, beliefs and actions. The collective performance of the nation will be healthy and fruitful, yielding valuable results for itself and the humanity at large if the collective nature of the nation is healthy and has not become perverted. Such a nation will successfully fight and conquer the forces of evil and disintegration, and the forces of virtue and goodness will come out and prevail the social order.

After the above introduction, we should study the teachings of Islam to discover that these are based on human belief and human action. Belief is based on the ideology entertained by men and human conduct and human actions are based on the potential of activity. Islam has fixed the limits of both these qualities within which human duties and human obligations are to be performed. This is a kind of charter for the day-to-day human activity and human thought which gives him the power to make distinctions between good and bad, between virtue and vice and between likes and dislikes. This charter of Islamic teachings makes possible and easy for a Muslim to decide what he may do and what he may not do. The basic charter of human activity, as contained in the Holy Quran, explains and manifests the limits and the values of human thought and human activity. The aim of the Islamic teachings is to make every believer well versed in Truthful knowledge of ideology and to shape him for righteous and useful activity so that his conduct in life proves that he is the best among the created things — "Ashraf-ul-Makhlooqat".

Allah, the Exalted, has impressed upon mankind that the appearance of His Prophet ﷺ is His greatest gift for the human beings. He says:

$$\text{لَقَدْ مَنَّ اللهُ عَلَى الْمُؤْمِنِيْنَ اِذْ بَعَثَ فِيْهِمْ رَسُوْلًا مِّنْ اَنْفُسِهِمْ يَتْلُوْا عَلَيْهِمْ اٰيٰتِهٖ وَيُزَكِّيْهِمْ وَيُعَلِّمُهُمُ الْكِتَابَ وَالْحِكْمَةَ وَاِنْ كَانُوْا مِنْ قَبْلُ لَفِيْ ضَلٰلٍ مُّبِيْنٍ}$$

"Allah has surely been gracious to the faithful in sending to them an apostle from among themselves to purify them, and to instruct them for before that they were in monstrous error."

It is the "wisdom" which has been expressed in the Holy Quran as:

$$\text{وَمَنْ يُّؤْتَ الْحِكْمَةَ فَقَدْ اُوْتِىَ خَيْرًا كَثِيْرًا}$$

"He gives wisdom unto whom He will, and he unto whom wisdom is given, he truely has received abundant good."

Since "Wisdom" has been called "abundant good", the scholars of human psychology have unanimously stated that "Wisdom" is not a name for man's abundance of knowledge; it definitely includes human conduct. This is so because knowledge, which does not produce virtuous action, is only a burden. This fact has been elaborately impressed in a Tradition of the Holy Prophet ﷺ which says: 'Knowledge without suitable action is a burden and action not based on truthful knowledge is misguidance."

The Holy Quran has granted mankind a charter of human conduct which includes tenets to be believed and actions to be performed. When human ideology and human force of activity are properly guided under the teachings of Islam, a faithful Muslim is the gift of wisdom. Such a person will live a life which leads him to success in this world and in the Hereafter. The collective observance of the teachings of Islam will make the Muslim nation the highest nation of the world. This is not a mere claim or a slogan. There is a vast series of arguments to prove its authenticity.

It is not possible to narrate all types of Islamic tenets and rules of conduct which combine to create "Wisdom: in the followers." However salient points of belief and human conduct will be usefully explained in the following paragraphs to impress that they have played the basic role in the progress of Islam and the Muslims.

"Tauheed" (Monotheism):

Monotheism is a faith, an ideology, a spiritual view., All the tenets of Islam are based on monotheism i.e., there is no deity (Worthy to be worshiped) except Allah Who is one and unique. This belief calls upon a man that man should guard against any partnership or sharing with God in His Unique Oneness of Essence (Zat: Self) or in His Attributes which are many and various. A faithful Muslim must firmly believe that all profit and loss, benefit or harm accrues from God Who is our Creator and we are His creation whose foremost duty it is to obey Him, to serve Him and to worship Him. We are a dignified creation and we must learn not to bow our heads before aught except Allah because our sustinance, life, death, honour, dishonour, success and failure, prosperity and poverty — are all determined by the bidding of God. No human being, however big or high he may be, possesses any power or capacity to grant any thing or to withhold any thing for the human beings. As such, it is God and God alone whom we should fear and love and with Him we should entertain our hopes. When we are needy, we must put up our needs to Him. All human beings are equal and no body has a right to rule over other human beings or to acquire authority over others. No human being has any right to formulate laws for the human beings. The system of Rules for the conduct of human affairs has been revealed by God and we human beings have only to understand and follow them with sincerity and assiduity. The differences among human beings in capabilities and status are the creation of God and they are intended for the proper administration of day-to-day life. Among human beings we find scholars and ignorant persons, rich and poor, rulers and ruled, judges and professors, merchant and skilled persons. This is all under Divine distribution of the functions of life. Inherently all human beings are equal. We are parts of a big machine which runs the collective life of human beings.

All good and salvation belong to those human beings who are fortunate in acknowledging the greatness of Allah and make them subservient and obedient to His orders and who have no aims, no intentions, no likes and no dislikes of their own. Their mutual relations are only for the pleasure of God. Their love, hatred, likes, dislikes, prosperity, knowledge and wisdom are all for the pushing of the Divine mission and for wishing the pleasure of God. Their day-to-day activity is not for their own benefit or gain. It is only for the pleasure of God.

As against the God-fearing people, there are a vast multitude of human beings who are disobedient to God and who have rebellious and arrogant attitude towards the divine teachings and the principles laid down for life. Their similitude is like a stone which hinders the passage on a highway and does not permit smooth running of vehicles. If the stone is small in size, the high speed of the running vehicle will push it aside. If the stone is heavy and big like a rock, its removal will call for hard struggle. The engine of collective life requires smooth and co-ordinated function of all the parts for its proper running as also the clearness of the road which should have no hurdles and hindrances.

The tenet of Monotheism (TAUHEED) is an effective force for onward push of collective life. The holder of this belief cannot live under subjugation of negative Satanic forces. The early Muslims of the golden era of Islam had correctly understood their individual status as a reflective force of the Divine forces which control and move the cosmos. This faith gave them high vision and courage and defeatable urge to live and die for Divine purpose. They lived to obey the command of Allah, to avoid His prohibitions and to diffuse and propagate the mission of Islam. They were not intimidated or cowed down by the biggest political powers of the world. They had one centre for collective life activity which gave them power and courage for performing highest good deeds. They had built up such noble characteristics which made them work out miracles to the surprise of all mankind.

"Itteqa" (Piety):

From perusal of the preceding paragraphs the reader will have been ensured that, by virtue of the doctrine of monotheism (TAUHEED), human beings have been granted a most moderate ideological strength. This doctrine gives man a power of distinction between right and wrong.

The doctrine of monotheism has given mankind an ideal, a goal for life which is work and thought for the pleasure of God who is the Deity, the Creator, the Sustainer and the Resurrector. It enlarges the vision of man and makes him acquainted with his whence and whither. The teachings of Islam lay down a complete set of good deeds which can win the pleasure of God. It is worthy of notice that the injunctions and prohibitions of Islam are moderate and do not touch the extreme limits of human conduct.

Piety is the foundation of all Islamic actions and conduct. Piety seeks to prepare man to discharge amicably and sincerely his relation with God, his Creator and with human beings, His creation. All human actions and conduct aim at earning the pleasure of God and obeying His orders in all situations. If a father spends money on the welfare of his son and a son respects and obeys his father, their intention in such normal conduct should be to obey God and earn His pleasure. Iqbal, poet of the East says:

> *"By every action which you perform you should have one single aim of earning the nearness of God. If you do so, the effulgence and glory of God will be reflected on you."*

Self pleasure or self-appeasement is a negative value and it should not be the aim of a right thinking Muslim person. Common social relationship and international relationship should be considered under the influence of Islamic ideology.

The spirit of piety works out a miracle in human actions and human conduct. The ideology of monotheism and piety (which is fear of accountability before the Tribunal of God) relieve human ego of the evil of tribal prejudices, and evil bias of colour, race and creed, social status and wealth, selfishness and pride, self-worship and jealousies. These moral curses can be totally got rid of at individual and collective levels. The effect of the removal of these moral and psychological evils from the life conduct of individuals and groups will doubtlessly make the human society an amicable social order and give them good chance for peaceful, amiable life.

It will be useful to study the Islamic code of injunctions and prohibitions in the light of the science of psychology. Islam has neither placed any embargo or shackles on human activities nor has it given all faculties of human conduct any free hand to function without let or hindrance. Natural limits for human conduct have been laid down to make human activities useful and pleasant. Moderation in human actions and conduct has made it attractive for human beings.

To appreciate the beauty of Islamic teachings we may study two of the basic human faculties namely lust (or desire) and anger. Human lust or desire seeks to acquire every desirable and lovable thing whereas human anger seeks to ward off all dangerous things and guards or protects the human life stature. Islam has taught, and taught with sound reason, what is desirable and covetable and the lawful means to reach or obtain the objects of desire as also the reasonable limits of acquisition for things of desire. Similarly it has taught human beings the occasions for the correct use of the faculty of anger. It has taught us what is harmful for human interest and to what extent it is harmful. It has also taught the reasonable and sensible means for defence and the proper ways for warding off all chances of danger and the effects of harmful things. This universality of the teachings of Islam has made them acceptable to all opinions and for all times and environments.

Collective Effects of "Tauheed" and "Ittiqa" (Monotheism and Piety):

After knowing the spirit of the doctrines and code of conduct taught by Islam, it will be easy to understand and appreciate that a society who acts on those doctrines and code of conduct will certainly emerge as the most civilized, most cultured and most active and motivated nation of the world. They shall have no ill-will, no grudge against any individual or nation. They will be a righteous people, firm and steadfast in their support for every righteous cause and fearless to defend cause of justice and fairplay. In their eyes all rich and poor, black and white, Arabs and non-Arabs shall be equal. They shall treat all human beings dispassionately and do even-handed justice to every body. They will have no enmity or grudge against any individual or nation. They will be free from any passion for aggrandizement and political high-handedness. Their aim and purpose of life will be to save humanity and do every thing possible for the welfare of society.

An important aspect of the character of such a nation will be its full and complete faith in God. Firm in their belief for the Divine support, it will care for no opposition, however strong, and will undertake and complete every task of national importance or welfare. The leader of such a nation shall have all the noble qualities of leadership. He will be wise, social, amiable in disposition, selfless in his service, meek and humble in his treatment of general public. He will look upon his position and wealth as gifts from God which he will use for the service of the needy persons. Such people will have a sense of dignity and self-sufficiency. Their contentment would be reflecting on their faces. In spite of need and poverty they would have monarchical majesty. They would love God and God would love them. Armed with invisible Divine support, they would fight with forces of evil and disintegration even without proper arms and defence equipment. Land or sea, they would fight everywhere against the Satanic forces and fill all lands with the blessings of justice, fairplay, love and sacrifice as taught under the teachings of Islam. A student of history would do well to find out if any group of people other than the companions of the Holy Prophet of Islam, had such noble qualities of character and such dedicated love and service for the welfare of humanity.

Whatever has been stated above is not poetic exaggeration. It is manifestation of truth and historical facts. Students of history know very well that Rustum and Sohrab were most brave heroes of the Persian people. But, can they be compared with Hazrat Ali ؓ (a companion and successor of the Holy Prophet of Islam S.A.W) who gave up control of the vanquished opponent who had (out of grudge and enmity) spat at the face of Hazrat Ali who was sitting over his body, holding full control to kill him. The infidel was not killed but left away. He was left free because Hazrat Ali ؓ did not wish to avenge his personal grudge which had been arousd due to the spitting of the infidel on his face. Before this unexpected incident, Hazrat Ali ؓ wanted to kill him because of the infidel's enmity of God and his opposition to the mission of God.

The stories of many a just rulers have been narrated in the pages of history. But no nation can put up before humanity a person of the status of Hazrat Umar ؓ who was not only a just and fair Ruler but whose personal life was a monument of simplicity, deprivation and self-sacrifice. He put on clothes with patches stitched there. He sat on bare ground to take decisions of national importance. He moved about incognition to find the needy orphans and widows and did not hesitate to carry on his own back loads, of food and victuals to relieve hunger and deprivation.

Every nation has heroes of national status who sacrificed in a marvellous way for the uplift of the nation. But the person of Hazrat Usman ؓ (companion and third successor of the Holy Prophet of Islam) stands unique in his sacrifices for Islam and his steadfastness in the face of most deterring circumstances, he gave away millions and millions of his wealth for the welfare of Islam and Muslims. When miscreants and evil-mongers surrounded his house under a nefarious plan to kill him, he did not allow any of his bodyguards to use their swords in his defence. His action was far-sighted as he knew that use of the sword in his personal defence would open the doors of unending mischief and bloodshed for the whole nation of Muslims.

The above precedents of noble qualities of character are most un-common in the annals of mankind. Political power and power of authority has spoiled many a great ruler in history. But the Muslims displayed equality of treatment, justice and fair play for all, meekness and courtesy in places where others displayed arrogance, haughtiness and high-hardedness to quell and vanquish their opponents without caring for the merits or the demerits of a situation.

Leaving aside the period of prophethood, the 30 years rule of the successors of the Holy Prophet (S.A.W) (Commonly known as KHILAFAT-E-RASHIDA i.e., well-guided rule of successors) is most prominent period of human history as also the golden period of the history of Islam during which mankind saw the most immaculate model of rulership which has always been praised and quoted by the leaders of mankind including Bernard Shaw, Carlayall, Toynbe and Mahatma M.K. Gandhi. Some of the prominent features of the period of <u>KHILAFAT-E-RASHIDA</u> may be usefully narrated here under:

(i)   **Simple Living and Life Style of the Khalifas (Caliphs of Islam):**

The well-guided caliphs of Islam lived a most simple life in their life-style there was no ostentation or display of the vanity of rules. Before embarking upon the office of "Khalifat", Hazrat Abu Bakar ؓ (the first caliph) used to milk the cow of a poor girl who said: "Now that you become our ruler, who will milk our cow?" he replied: "The office of Khilafat cannot prevent me from personal services of the people." The life-style of Hazrat Umar ؓ has become proverbial and world history has failed to quote a precedent of his like. The Muslim armies under Hazrat Umar ؓ had toppled the Sasani government of Persia whose erstwhile Rulers used to shudder and tremble with awe when Hazrat Umar ﷺ was mentioned to them. Military Generals of proven calibre like Amir Mo'awia and Khalid-bin-Walid were taken to task under orders of Hazrat Umar ﷺ and they submitted to his orders with utmost humility and respect. Despite such level of authority, Hazrat Umar ﷺ used to wear a shirt with patches and a turban which was old and partially torn. His footwear was simple and common. He had no palace to live in, and no sumptuous tentage for meetings. If sleep over-powered him, he slept underneath the shade of a tree. He had no chamberlain on his door of Khilafat and any body could see him at any time without let or hindrance. He was so conscious of his responsibility that he inquired and looked after the needs of the poor, the widows and orphans, whose houses he personally visited and rendered them service. He was never shy of visiting market places for the purchase of his personal needs and those of the needy people who could not visit the market for valid reasons.

Once Hazrat Ali ﷺ (the fourth caliph of Islam) visited the market place during the period of his authority. He bought some fruit and was carrying them home. Some body on the way suggested that he might hand over the fruit to some one else to carry them home. He said: "The family man is more deserving of carrying his burdens for his family."[1]

(ii) Protection of the Bait-ul-Mal (National Treasury):

Due to selfless dedication to the injunctions of Islam, sincerity of purpose and fear of God, the well-guided caliphs of Islam jealously guarded the "Bait-ul-Mal" (National Treasury) which they looked upon as a Valuable Trust of the Muslims. They were so conscious of accountability on the Day of Judgement that they spent every pice of the Treasury with care. They never spent any thing from the Bait-ul-Mal for their personal comfort or the comfort of their families. They took bare minimum for their basic human needs which they rightly took for performance of stately duties.

---

1. Ibne Aseer, Vol. 3, P. 160

Hazrat Umar ؏ once fell ill and was advised by his physician to take honey which was available in the Bait-ul-Mal. For this, he came to the mosque, sat on the pulpit and made a formal request to the Muslims for permission to take honey from the Bait-ul-Mal for his personal use.[1]

During the regime of Hazrat Ali ؏, Abu Rafey (a slave of the Holy Prophet) was incharge of the Bait-ul-Mal. Once Hazrat Ali ؏ saw his daughter wearing a jewel which actually belonged to the Bait-ul-Mal. On inquiry he was told that the jewel was given to the daughter by himself. On this Hazrat Ali ؏ told him: "When I married Hazrat Fatima (Radhi-Allahu-Anha) I had nothing in my possession except a goat skin. We both slept on it and, during the day, I used to put the fodder on this skin for my she-camel. I had no one to support Hazrat Fatima (Radhi-Allahu-Anha) in her household which she carried out all done."[2]

Meticulous care was observed in the expenses from the state Treasury. Similarly great care was taken in the collection process to avoid un-called for coercion in the revenue collection and to ensure that no collector indulged in unfair means and oppression on the tax-payers.

(iii) Justice and Equality:

In the administration of law, there was no distinction between commoners and favourites. Every one was treated strictly in accordance with the demands of Law (Shariat). Family ties and affiliations were not allowed to stay in between the impartial execution of justice. When Abu Shahma, a son of Hazrat Umar ؏ took wine, penal action was immediately taken and Hazrat Umar ؏ personally inflicted lashes on his son who expired.[3] A brother-in-law of Hazrat Umar ؏, Qadama Bin Mazoon was convicted of the same crime (drinking) and Hazrat Umar ؏ did not in the least

---
1. Tabqat-e-Ibn-e-Saad
2. Ibn-e-Aseer, Vol.3, P.159 and Tabri, Vol.6, P.90
3. Moarif Ibn-e-Qataiba, P.81

hesitate to inflict 80 lashes on him.[1] When a Qibti citizen of Egypt personally complained to Hazrat Umar ؓ about the oppressive attitude of Hazrat Amr Bin Aas ؓ (who was then the governor of Egypt), Hazrat Umar ؓ at once called him and inflicted the usual punishment on him.[2]

Beauty of the conduct of the ruling caliph of Islam is that, if he had a complaint against any one in his subjects, he would lodge a formal plaint and appear before the Qazi (Judge) as an aggrieved party. The judge would decide the case purely on merit without considering the status of the complainant. Once armour of Hazrat Ali ؓ, the fourth caliph of Islam, fell down on the way and a Christian picked it up. He filed a suit in the Court of Law. The judge asked the caliph to produce a witness which he could not do and the decision of the court was pronounced against the caliph.[3]

Hazrat Umar ؓ was well known for his high dignity. Once he had a difference with Obai Bin Ka'b and a complaint was lodged with Zaid Bin Thabit (who was the acting judge). When he went to the court, the judge stood up in reverence and vacated his seat. Hazrat Umar ؓ said: "This is the first injustice which you have done." Saying this, he sat side by side with the other party.

(iv) Selection of the Caliph:

The caliph of the Muslims was selected through an open vote cast by men of sound understanding and opinion who represented the ground public. There was no rule of succession to transfer the authority to a son or a nephew of the ruling caliph nor was it permissible for a caliph to leave a will or a recommendation for any one to succeed him as caliph.

(v) Supervision and Accountability of the Governors:

The rightly guided caliphs of Islam personally lived a life of

---

1. Tabqat-e-Ibn-e-Saad, biography of Qadamat.
2. Hussain-al-Mohazira, Vol.3, P.1
3. Inbe-e-Aseer, Vol.3, P.160

austerity and absteniousness. They wanted their governors and the officers of the state to live simple lives on their own pattern. Great care and caution was observed in the selection of government functionaries. After selection they were called upon to take a pledge that – (i) they would not ride a Turkish horse (which was a sign of austocracy); (ii) they would not wear fine (costly) clothes; (iii) they would not take food prepared from fine flour; (iv) they would keep their doors open for all complainants during day and night. [1] Besides this, the assets and expenses of all government officers were checked. If the assets and expenses of an officer were found to be in excess of his income, he was at once taken to task and half of his assets were taken away by the government and deposited in the National Treasury. Many incidents of this type have been narrated in the famous book: "Futuh-ul-Buldaan".

The above quoted rigid conditions were not laid down for declaring good food and good clothing as unlawful but for the purpose of inculcating habits of hardihood and simple-living in the government functionaries. Once white bread (made of fine flour) was served to Hazrat Umar on the dining cloth. He inquired: "Do all the Muslims eat such food?" The reply being in the negative, he declined to take the bread. [2]

Once Utba Bin Farqad-al-Salmi who was governor of Azarbaijan sent to Hazrat Umar certain peculiar and costly variety of "Halwa" (Sweets) as a gift. Hazrat Umar returned it and wrote to the governor: "Do you take such delicacies and niceties without the hard earnings by your parents or yourself? We shall not eat any thing except the items of food which common Muslims take in their homes. [3]

The virtuous life of the Muslims was not limited to the Caliphs of Islam. The entire body of Muslims who had been companions of the Holy Prophet displayed such high traits of

---

1. Tabri, Vol.5, P.21
2. Asad-al-Ghabba, biography of Hazrat Umar
3. Futuh-ul-Baldan, P324

character that the living humanity was astonished to see that a large gang of Arabian Bedouins who were illiterates, uncivilized and uncultured, were suddenly changed into the best models of humanity. By their thought and knowledge, actions and conduct, they were doubtless paragons of humanity who shone on the firmament of time as suns and moons.

The high altitude of human character which the Bedouins of Arabia had attained was by and large due to the doctrine of "Tauheed" which worked as running spirit in their temporal and religious activities. Under the law of "Survival of the Fittest", they had the unique right of superiority over the various groups of the then living humanity. They were, therefore, rightly addressed by their Lord Allah:

لَاتَهِنُوْاوَلَاتَحْزَنُوْا وَ اَنْتُمُ الْاَعْلَوْنَ

"Do not lose heart; do not be grieved because you will certainly rise to the heights of glory if you (continue to be) Mominin (faithful and loyal to Islam)".

Allah, the Exalted, was so much pleased with their conduct that He declared them to be His own confederates. He (the Exalted) said:

اَلَاَانَّ حِزْبَ اللهِ هُمُ الْمُفْلِحُوْنَ

"Hearken! Verily the confederates of Allah (alone) shall be successful."

Poet of Muslim Ummah, Iqbal has said:

"Firm and unflinching belief, constant action (in the right direction) and universal, conquering love; these indeed are the swords of (great) men for the struggle in life."

The qualities of success, as enumerated by Islam are peculiar to the Muslims who stood firmly by the doctrine of "Tauheed" (monotheism). Similarly constant action and conquering love are also of peculiar type. The universal love of the true Muslims was love for the entire humanity who were looked upon as the dear creation of Allah, the Exalted, Who wanted each human being to live a straight and virtuous life to earn evolution of the soul which may qualify them for entry into the Gardens of Eden. Even when Muslims fought with non-Muslim forces, their actual aim was not conquest of land, but amelioration and reformation of human beings, removal of injustice and inequality. The conquered nations were so well treated by the Muslims that they looked upon them as their saviours and well wishers. In the battle of Persia, as many as four thousand soldiers collectively accepted Islam and came on the Muslims side, to fight against the Persians. In the Battle of Madain and Jaloola, the Persian soldiers fought under the command of Hazrat Sa'd Bin Abi Waqqas ؓ and won the battle against infidels. Similarly Muhammad Bin Qasim conquered not only the land of Sind, he won the hearts of the people living there by his amiable and generous treatment. When Yazid Bin Abi Kabsha came to replace Muhammad Bin Qasim as governor under orders of the Central Government, the local population of Sind wept at the arrest and departure of Muhammad Bin Qasim out of sheer love and regard. They prepared a portrait of Muhammad Bin Qasim and kept as a memorial at Keeraj. This is what Historian Blazri has written in his famous boom "Futuh-ul-Buldaan".

The doctrine of Tauheed inculcated great moral and spiritual virtues which give the Muslims a great spirit of hardihood, love for humanity at large and to fight against the forces of evil. When they are in the battlefield, people with temporal pomp and show cannot stand against the undaunted spirit infused by Islam.

A deputation of the ambassadors of Islam visited the court of Iranian emperor Yazd Gard under the leadership of Hazrat Noman bin Moqran ؓ. The court was decently decorated for their reception. But the ministers of Islam entered the court with great indifference towards wordly grandeur, wearing their Arabian long coats, covered by Yemani sheets of cloth and holding their whips in their hands. The Emperor was over-awed at their behaviour and their gleaming faces shined with luster of faith and virtue.

Events of Divine support to the Muslims on the battlefields have been narrated by the author of "Futuh-ul-Buldaan". The grand father of Abu Raja Farsi (who later on embracedy Islam) stated that he was fighting on the side of Persia against the Muslims. In the beginning of the battle, the Arabs threw arrows at the Persian army in which soldiers of the Persian army said: "These are hardly arrows. These are insignificant sticks." But the self-same sticks thrown by the Muslims worked ruin in the Persian army. The sharp arrows which the Persian soldiers threw towards the Muslims got entangled in their clothes and did not injure the soldiers. But the arrows from the Muslim army, despite their inferior quality, tore through the steel armours worn by Persian soldiers and their heavy helmets.[1]

Another event narrated by Blazri also relates to the Persians. When the defeated army of Persia ran from Qadsia towards Mada'in, the Tigris river fell on the way. After crossing the river the army of Persia removed all the boats from the river and set the bridges on fire so that the victorious forces who were chasing them may not be able to cross the Tigris. But the Muslim soldiers fearlessly put their horses into the Tigris Waters and swam through the river safely to the opposite bank. On seeing their sight of bravery and courage, the Persian soldiers said among themselves: "By God, you are not fighting human beings; you are at war with the Jinns."[2]

Scholars of human psychology will agree that such events of abnormal courage and bravery cannot take place without very high moral and spiritual forces at work in the human beings. This was the great altitude of faith and virtuous deeds on which the Muslims had been elevated due to the doctrine of monotheism which forbids fear of aught except Allah, the Exalted.

---

1. Futuh-ul-Baldan, P.260
2. Futuh-ul-Baldan, P.263

Prophecy of the Holy Prophet ﷺ :

The golden era of Islam could not continue for long. It was unfortunate and perhaps it was in the nature of things that deterioration should creep in the body polytic of Muslims. The following prophetic words of the Holy Prophet ﷺ are significant. He said:

خیرامتی قرنی ثم الذین یلونهم ثم الذین یلونهم ثم ان بعدکم قوما یشهدون ولایستشهدون ویخونون ولایؤمنون وینذرون ولایفون ویظهرفیهم السن (صحیح بخاری)

"The best period for my Ummah (followers) is my period; it will be followed by a good era (of my companions) after which the third era (of the followers of my companions) will also be full of blessings. Thereafter a people shall come into existence who will give evidence without being asked for evidence. These people shall be full of deception and will not honour their trusts. They will vow to do certain good deeds but they will betray their own vows. They will put on flesh and will look fatty persons."[1]

---

[1] Hafiz Imad-ud-Din Ibne Katheer (who died in 774 A.H.) has narrated from Tabrani giving a clue to acquisition of governmental authority by sheer force. This explains the various changes and vicissitudes in the history of Islam from time to time. A brief picture of the coming events in the History of Islam has been drawn in the following words of the Holy Prophet: "The Government of Islam made a start with Divine blessings and prophethood. Then it will be blessings combined with Caliphate. Then it will change to a government by force. It will be followed by rebellious people who will spread terror and mischief in the land. Muslim monarchs will make silk and wine as lawful for them and will freely indulge in acts of lust and debauchery. They will be given a free hand by Providence till they will meet their Lord Creator. (Albadaiya-wan-Nahaiya, V.8, P20)

The Prediction of the Holy Prophet ﷺ clearly points to these distinct periods of the collective life of the Muslims. The first period is the period of the Holy Prophet's ﷺ own life time. The second period covers the life time of his illustrious companions; and the third period covers the life time of the great followers of the companions of the Holy Prophet ﷺ. All the three periods were blessed epochs of the Muslim history. But the volume of blessings and benedictions varied according to the distance of the period from the life-time of the Holy Prophet ﷺ. The best and the most blessed period was that of the life time of the Holy Prophet ﷺ. The Divine blessings and support to the Muslim cause was slightly reduced during the second period of companions. It suffered further decline in Divine support and blessings during the period of the followers of the companions when the pristine spirit of Islam kept dwindling in every thing till it disappeared with the culmination of the third blessed period. This point may further be explained by quoting the vicissitudes in the life times of a man. The period of youth encounters strength and all sorts of physical, moral and spiritual perfections. This was the Prophet's ﷺ own period. The second period (of companions) may well be compared to the middle age of a man whose physical and intellectual powers begin to decline and he feels the downward journey of life. The third period (of the followers of the companions) very aptly marks the advent of the realities of old age and no effort on his part can succeed to retrieve the period of strength and youthfulness.

The prediction of the Holy Prophet ﷺ came true through all the periods. After the Khilafat-e-Rashida, elements of disintegration entered the collective life of the Muslims. With the martyrdom of Hazrat Usman ؓ (the third caliph) in 35 A.H., the collective social system of Muslims suffered a great set-back. Evil forces were not inactive even during the golden period of Hazrat Abu Bakr ؓ and Hazrat Umar ؓ but both the elderly caliphs possessed such high spiritual powers and such deep insight that they successfully foiled the mischievous efforts of the evil mongers.

Martyrdom of Hazrat Usman ؓ :

The incident of the martyrdom of Hazrat Usman ؓ was such a painful event which upset the central structure of the collective life of the Muslims and opened up the Pandora's box, letting loose all possible evils against the Muslims. There is no question of lavelling any blame against the pious and innocent person of Hazrat Usman ؓ who was a living model of great knowledge and forbearance. But, had he had the awe-inspiring personality of Hazrat Umar ؓ and his state policies were full of mighty wisdom like the policies of Hazrat Umar ؓ, mischief mongers like Abdullah Bin Saba and the ill-wishers of Egypt and Iraq would not have succeeded in their nefarious designs. The rebellion against the central government of Muslims could not be quelled because of the tolerance of Hazrat Usman ؓ and his ommission (as a matter of policy) in using effective force against the rebels. He gave his own life but did not allow the mischief to become widely spread. The decree of fate came to pass the third caliph of Islam was mercilessly slain. For two days his martyred body could not be attended to for burial and coffin. On the third day some courageous men made a bold attempt to get his dead body properly burried.

The Caliphate of Hazrat Ali ؓ :

The worst fears of Hazrat Usman ؓ came true. Despite his wish and his sincere effort to ward off dissersion among the Muslims, the collective system of state was scattered. Hazrat Ali ؓ was selected as the fourth caliph of Islam much against his desire. He put up the names of Hazrat Talha ؓ and Hazrat Zubair ؓ for the position of caliph and himself assured the people that he would personally support their selection and render him all possible help and support. But people insisted that he himself must shoulder the responsibilities of Khilafat. He was almost constrained to allow himself to be declared the Caliph of Muslims.

The high status of Hazrat Ali ؓ, his piety, his honesty, his sincerity and his godliness were above all doubt. Yet the machinations of the Hypocrites, and the ignorance of some newly converted Muslims made the internal struggle for power in Iraq and Syria reach a point of delicacy. To cope with this most unusual political situation, political wisdom of very high calibre was required along with great prudence and far sightedness which the pious character of Hazrat Ali ؓ and his purity of personal nature could not muster.

The first step he intended to take in the field of administration, was to remove Amir Mo'awiya from the governership of Syria when Amir Mo'awiya had built up great personal influence. Seasoned and well-versed in politics as they were, Hazrat Mughira bin Sho'ba ؓ and Hazrat Abdullah Bin Abbas ؓ advised Hazrat Ali ؓ not to remove Hazrat Amir Mo'awiya ؓ from his governership before he had pledged agreement with selection of caliphate of Hazrat Ali ؓ Unfortunately Hazrat Ali ؓ declined to accept the advice of elderly companions of the Holy Prophet ﷺ Such indeed was the decree of Fate which no one could alter or cancel. Hazrat Ali ؓ said to the two elderly companions; "Worldly prudence and political wisdom should make me agree with your opinion and I should not remove Amir Mo'awiya from the governorship of Syria. But I am in possession of certain facts which force me as an honest and God-fearing man to remove him. If he (Amir Mo'awiya) obeys my orders (as caliph), well and good. If he declines to obey, I shall use my sword against him. [1]

Hazrat Ibn-e-Abbas ؓ advised Hazrat Ali ؓ that, if he was intent upon removing all the officers belonging to Banu Omayyah, he may at least postpone the removal of Amir Mo'awiya ؓ till he had taken pledge to accept Hazrat Ali ؓ as the caliph. Unfortunately Hazrat Ali ؓ rejected even this proposal of Hazrat Ibn-e-Abbas ؓ. He terminated the services of not only Hazrat Amir Mo'awiya ؓ but of all the officials belonging to Banu Omayyah who were appointed at various places during the regime of Hazrat Usman ؓ. He sent letters of dismissal to all the Banu Omayyah governors and

---

[1] Tabri, V.5, P160

appointed fresh governors of his own choice at their places.

Usman Bin Hanif was appointed governor of Basra; Emarah bin Shahab was appointed governor of Koofa; Obaidullah bin Abbas was appointed governor of Ymen; Qais Bin Sa'd was appointed governor of Egypt and Sahl Bin Hanif was appointed governor of Syria. Unfortunately the political atmosphere of all these regions was so much charged against Hazrat Ali ؓ that the people refused to co-operate with his governors. Sahl Bin Hanif met a group of people at Tabook on his way to Syria. People asked him who he was. He said he was the Amir of Syria. The people told him bluntly:"If you have been appointed by Usman ؓ, you are welcome. If some one else has appointed you, you should go back". Sahl Bin Hanif said: "Are you not aware of the happenings, which have taken place so far?" They replied: "We all know." After this conversation, Sahl Bin Hanif returned to the Headquarters.

Similarly Emarah Bin Shahab (who was appointed as governor of Koofa) met Tolaiha bin Khowalid on the way at Zabala who advised him to go back because the people of Koofa will not accept any one in place of their present governor. If you refuse to go back, I shall behead you." Emarah was a man of weak nerves. He was frightened at the foregoing conversation and at once returned to Hazrat Ali ؓ.

Similar was the situation in Yamen. Obaidullah bin Abbas, the appointee of Hazrat Ali ؓ reached Yamen. By the time he reached Yamen, Ya'laa bin Omayyah collected all the revenues and came to Makkah with all the money.[1]

When Hazrat Ali ؓ came to know all these circumstances, he said to Hazrat Talhha ؓ and Hazrat Zubair ؓ: "What I had frightened you against had come to pass. The untoward events have to be taken serious notice of the mischief has to be coped with effectively. I shall display patience and forbearance to the extent I

---

[1] These were the finencers which were used against Hazrat Ali ؓ in the battle of Camel.

am able to. But, when the matters got out of control, I shall be left with no option but to use my sword because the best remedy of a disease is to stamp it."

The matter could have been peacefully handled and the above situation would have been controlled by Hazrat Ali ﷺ if he had not insisted on the removal of Amir Mo'awiya from the governorship of Syria. He did both the things together. He sent a letter of dismissal to Amir Mo'awiya and also demanded allegiance from him as the caliph of the Muslims. The worst fears of Hazrat Mughirah Bin Sho'ba ﷺ came true. Amir Mo'awiya had been ruling over the Syrians for the last twenty years or more and he was thoroughly acquainted with the habits, character, likes and dislikes of the Syrian people who were greatly impressed by his generosity and benevolence. This background was sufficient to arouse the Syrians against Hazrat Ali ﷺ, particularly when the movement for the revenge of the martyrdom of Hazrat Usman ﷺ had spread like blazing fire in the entire country.

Amir Mo'awiya ﷺ took another psychological step to arouse the anger of Syrians. He placed on the pulpit in the Central Mosque of Damascus the blood-stained shirt of Hazrat Usman ﷺ and three chopped off fingers of Hazrat Nai'la (Radhi-Allahu-Anha), the faithful wife of Hazrat Usman ﷺ. When the public gathered in the mosque and beheld this spectacle, all of the, young and old, began to weep profusely and they vowed openly never to owe allegiance to any caliph until the blood of Hazrat Usman ﷺ had been avenged. The messenger who visited Damascus with the message of Hazrat Ali ﷺ, saw the whole demonstration of the weeping public and narrated the entire incident to Hazrat Ali ﷺ on return. Hazrat Ali ﷺ, on hearing the whole incident, said loudly:

> "Oh Allah! You are a witness to my claim that I had no hand in the assassination of Hazrat Usman ﷺ."

What Hazrat Ali ﷺ said was above all doubt and suspicion. But, unfortunately his political steps taken much against the advice of Hazrat Abdullah Bin Abbas ﷺ and Hazrat Mughirah Bin Sho'ba upset his plans and charged the atmosphere positively against him. His appointment of Muhammad Bin Abi Bakr ؓ and Ashtar Nakh'i (who had been accused of participation in the murder plan of Hazrat Usman ؓ) made the political atmosphere totally against Hazrat Ali ؓ.

Another strange event of history needs to be mentioned. Hazrat Talha ؓ and Hazrat Zubair ؓ who had successfully persuaded Hazrat Ali ؓ to shoulder the burden of Khilafat, they surprisingly joined the party of Hazrat Ayesha (Radhi-Allahu-Anha) and began preparation against Hazrat Ali ؓ to avenge the innocent blood of Hazrat Usman ؓ. They must not have been ignorant of the fact that Hazrat Ali ؓ had absolutely no hand in the assassination of Hazrat Usman ؓ. The opposition of Hazrat Ali ؓ at Damascus and Makkah was making him agitated.

Another mistake was made by Hazrat Ali ؓ in quick succession of his erstwhile mistakes. As ill-advised by certain people, Hazrat Ali ؓ dismissed Qais bin Sa'ad (governor of Egypt) who was his supporter and well-wisher. In his place Muhammad Bin Abi Bakr was made the governor of Egypt. This change of governership caused a kind of ill-will in the hearts of Egyptians against Hazrat Ali ؓ and a majority of them began to support Amir Mo'awiya. In 36 A.H. after the Battle of Camel, Hazrat Ali ؓ changed the capital of Muslim State from Madina to Koofa because he thought Madina was being desecrated due to political unrest and commotion. This was certainly an act of piety on the part of Hazrat Ali ؓ but its effect was not wholesome. Hazrat Ali ؓ was totally deprived of the wise and good advice of many a companions who lived in Madina and who could not be moved to Koofa. On the other side the newly converted Muslims who had thronged Koofa came close to Hazrat Ali ؓ and he was influenced by their company.

All the above quoted actions of Hazrat Ali ؓ had no satisfactory explanation except that he considered every body pure, pious and selfless like himself. He thought that people would reject their personal and temporal interests and would render him unqualified obedience as the Caliph of Islam. This kind of thinking was a pointer to the virtues and perfections of Hazrat Ali ☪. But in the field of politics and administration such widespread optimism was harmful on many occasions.

Unfortunately Hazrat Ali ☪ did not possess the awe-inspiring and dominant personality of Hazrat Umar ☪ who always made it sure that his order were properly and fully implemented. When a general of the calibre of Khalid Bin Walid was removed from the control command, no body had the dare to question the action of the caliph. Similarly, the removal by Hazrat Umar ☪ of Hazrat Mughira Bin Sho'ba ☪ and Hazrat Sa'ad Bin Abi Waqqas ☪ from the posts of governor did not arouse any agitation or criticism. Unfortunately Hazrat Ali ☪ could not display that dominating attitude in the implementation of his state orders. He had all the means to quell any level of opposition to his orders. His order of removing Hazrat Amir Mo'awiya ☪ from the governorship of Syria was so much upset the public of Syria that opposition of Hazrat Ali ☪ assumed the tempo of a flood.

Opposition of Hazrat Ali ☪ :

The soaring opposition which was largely due to the fact that he could not avenge the murder of Hazrat Usman ☪ and had failed to catch the culprits. The causes of his failure in this particular case cannot be elaborated here. But the fact remains that success of any statesman or politician depends on his obedience by the people and on their carrying out his orders without let and hindrance. The people of Iraq who apparently obeyed and supported him were not in his favour from the core of their hearts. Once he said in a sermon addressed to his party people:

> "When I ask you to fight the Syrians in winter, you put excuse of hard and pinching season. When I ask you to fight during summer, you tell me it is too hot to fight as hot winds are blowing. People say: 'Ali does not know politics.' I agree that a man who is not obeyed, he does not know politics."

The Rise and Fall of Muslims

From the above paragraphs it can easily be inferred how complicated and difficult the circumstances had become. There were people belonging to Syria, Egypt and Hijaz who were openly opposed to Hazrat Ali ﷺ. The other people who ostensibly supported Hazrat Ali ﷺ, were lukewarm in his support and they never expressed any fervour or enthusiasm to carry out his order or policies. Since he had been chosen a caliph and his selection was absolutely justified, he had no alternative but to punish all those who flouted orders of the central government. There may be difference of opinion about the political wisdom of Hazrat Ali ﷺ but no one can even question his bravery and valour. The final outcome of this simmering situation was the battle of 'Jamal' and thereafter the battle of 'Siffin'. It was most unfortunate that the brave soldiers of Islam who had fought the infidels and unbelievers in the battle of 'Badr' and 'Honain' were now pitched against one another. Hard luck for Islam!

The Attitude of Amir Mo'awiya ﷺ :

Whatever happened and appeared on the screen of history, Hazrat Ali ﷺ alone cannot be held responsible for it. Amir Mo'awiya was a renowned thinker and a seasoned politician. There is no doubt that his services for Islam were glorious and many. He had conquered Tripoli and Syria. He had captured all the frontier lands around Syria and made it well protected and immune against any attack of the Romans. During the regime of Hazrat Usman ﷺ he had (with the permission of Hazrat Usman ﷺ) prepared an Armada and conquered the famous island of Cyprus in the Mediterranean Sea. This Armada was so powerful that it served as an effective deterrent against foreign attacks and the Muslim territories became safe and immune from any onslaught by the Romans.

Apart from his conquests, Amir Mo'awiya was always fully aware of any internal or external troubles and machinations and he curbed them with an iron hand. This was due to his political insight and his constant vigilance. Despite all these virtues and services, his attempts to foil the caliphate of Hazrat Ali ﷺ was unfortunate and unexpected of a person of his high stature.

If Amir Mo'awiya was keen upon wreaking the avenging of the murder of Hazrat Usman ؓ, he could have done it easily by strengthening the hands of Hazrat Ali ؓ in his Khilafat for he could easily pledge his support. The most unfortunate aspect of the situation is that despite bloodshed among Muslims and loss of many precious lives of the companions of the Holy Prophet ﷺ the innocent blood of Hazrat Usman ؓ could not be avenged. The house differences which appeared in the rank and file of the 'Mohajireen' (immigrants) and the 'Ansaar' (Helpers of Madina) at the sad desire of the Holy Prophet ﷺ, were resolved and completely supported the selection of Hazrat Abu Bakr ؓ and pledged his allegiance with him. If Amir Mo'awiya ؓ had followed this precedent and adopted a similar course of action, the Muslim Ummah could have been saved of the gigantic mischief and trouble and unrest among the rank and file of the Muslims. The insistence of Amir Mo'awiya for Khilafat against the selection of Hazrat Ali ؓ can hardly be called as service to Islam.

Event of Arbitration:

To resolve the serious differences between Amir Mo'awiya ؓ and Hazrat Ali ؓ, a proposal for arbitration was launched by Amir Mo'awiya ؓ. After the success of Hazrat Ali ؓ in the battle of "Laila-tul-Hareer", Amr Bin Al-Aas ؓ said to Amir Mo'awiyya: "I shall tell you a plan wherewith there will be dissension in the army of Hazrat Ali ؓ and we shall all benefit. On being asked, Hazrat Amr Bin Al-Aas ؓ elaborated his plan and said: "We shall raise copies of the Holy Quran on spear heads and invite the people of Iraq to agree to arbitration under the Quran." It was done and demonstrated. Hazrat Ali ؓ told his companions that this plan was a snare and we should not become its preys. But a greater part of the Iraqis had been convinced of the plan and they forced Hazrat Ali ؓ to accept the arbitration of the holy Quran. The war had been postponed and it was decided that one representative may be appointed each from the side of Hazrat Ali ؓ and Amir Mo'awiya ؓ. The decision taken by these two nominees may be accepted by both the political factions and strictly acted upon. The Advisors said among themselves: "Hazrat Ali ؓ may accept or reject this scheme, we shall be the real beneficiaries." [1] These very words betrayed the lack of sincerity on the part of the authors of the scheme. They actually wanted to grind their own axe. Knowing fully well the intentions behind this plan, Hazrat Ali ؓ rejected it. He knew that the proposal for arbitration after the great bloodshed of Muslims was not based on good intentions.

Since the Iraqis had differed with Hazrat Ali ؓ and there were serious differences among themselves, there appeared no alternative before Hazrat Ali ؓ but to accept the proposal for arbitration. Since the plan was not based on good intentions, its implementation produced dangerous results for the Muslims. Uptil then there were only two political parties among the Muslims but now a third party appeared under the name of "Khawarij". This was a new political sect which was opposed and enimical to both Hazrat Ali ؓ and Amir Mo'awiya ؓ.

The plan which the fertile brain of Amr Bin Al-Aas (the conqueror of Ajnedain) had invented became the cause of deep schism in the body politic of Islam and gave rise to innumerable troubles. The appearance of 'Khawarij' was one of its outcome. The elements of this sect were already there but they were latent and underground. After the so-called "Arbitratian" they gathered together at one centre and set up a permanent dangerous political front. The town of "Nehr-Wan" was the seat of their activities. Hazrat Ali ؓ foresaw the inherent dangers of those people. He fought with these rebellious outlaws and gave them a crushing defeat.

The organized activities of the "Khawarij" had been dissipated. But the remnant of the evil-mongers prepared a plot for the assassination of the three bulwarks of the current political field. They attempted murder of Hazrat Ali ؓ, Amir Mo'awiya ؓ and

---

1. Tibri, Vol.6, P26

Amr Bin Al-Aas ؓ. Amr Bin Al-Aas escaped the murder attempt unhurt. Amir Mo'awiya ؓ was wounded and recovered after proper treatment. Hazrat Ali ؓ was so grievously wounded in the murder attempt of the "Khawarij" that he lost his life. This shining sun of knowledge, piety and goodness who was the last brilliant star on the firmament of well-guided Khilafat, died in the month of Ramazan in 40 A.H.

Comments on the Rulership of Hazrat Ali ؓ :

His caliphate was not long enough. His way of rulership was strictly after the pattern of Khilafat-e-Rashida (the well guided Islamic polity). He was selected much against his own wish. He was unaminously selected by the "Mahajirin" (the Makkah immigrants) and the "Ansaar" (the Helpers of Madina), who had also selected Hazrat Abu Bakr ؓ and Hazrat Umar ؓ. The general attitude of Hazrat Ali ؓ was peace-loving and he never used methods of coercion and unlawful suppression against any body. The evil efforts of the Hypocrites had made the political circumstances so difficult and perplexed that Hazrat Ali ؓ could not resolve many entanglements. Yet his mode of government did not have the least sign of monarchy or autocracy. His personal life was as much full of piety, simple-living, selflessness and fear of God as were the lives of his illustrious predecessors. So much so that, lying on his death bed, he did not give any opinion for or against the selection of Hazrat Imam Hassan ؓ when such a question was posed to him. He left the entire matter to the good sense of the Muslims who were to make a selection. Not a single instance is available during his regime where he may have adopted the so-called "diplomatic" policy. His outer and inner self was one. Whatever he said was the voice of his heart. He did not get any benefit for his person or his kith and kin from his high office. Fear of God was always visible on him. His government was doubtlessly pattern of truely guided polity. There are two distinct things for the proper judgement of a historian. The personal character, conduct and behaviour of the Khalifa and the system which he adopted for the disposal of day-to-day affairs of the government. The second thing to be considered is: to what extent he had been successful in his aims and ideals. The first point affords no ground for adverse criticism. The second point was, unfortunately, against him as he did not succeed in running the affairs of the state in accordance with the democratic rules of Islam. There are very valid reasons for the aforesaid failure!

The Causes of the Failure of Hazrat Ali ؓ:

The cause for the failure of Hazrat Ali ؓ need to be probed into at depth. Before Islam, the Arabs were never an integrated political unity for centuries. The tribal system was in vogue and each tribe had its own likes and dislikes, aims and objects and an internecine underground war continued to be waged for the supremacy of each tribe.

Re-Appearance of Tribal Prejudices:

The family interests and the tribal supremacy were the dominant ideals of the pre-Islamic Arabs. Islam successfully replaced these feelings with higher ideals of human equality and international fraternity. The doctrine of 'Tauheed' rid their hearts of petty wordly considerations and made them get together at one national centre under the auspices of Islam. The erstwhile sworn enemies began to live peacefully as brothers. The Holy Prophet ﷺ warned the Muslims against the re-appearance of tribal prejudices in his last sermon when he said:

فان دماءكم واموالكم واعراضكم عليكم حرام كحرمة يومكم هذا

"Your life, blood, your properties and your honour is as unlawful for all of you as this day (of Pilgrimage)."

Then he continued to say:

وستلقون ربكم فسيسألكم عن اعمالكم الافلا

$$\text{ترجعوا بعدى ضلالا يضرب بعضكم رقاب بعض}$$

$$\text{(بخارى باب حجة الوداع)}$$

"Very soon you shall meet your Lord sustainer Who will question you about your deeds. Beware that you do not get astray after me and start killing one another."

Another narrative is more lucid where the Holy Prophet ﷺ said:

$$\text{الاكل شئ من امر الجاهلية تحت قدمى موضوع}$$

"Hearken! All the practices of pre-Islamic days (Jahiliyya) are beneath my feet."

It was a clear and emphatic declaration that all the distinctions due to pedigree, family honour, colour and shape, wealth and properties which are the basic causes of human strife and worldly quarrels were effectively done away with. In another narrative quoted by Tirmzi (a scholar of Traditions) the Holy Prophet ﷺ said:

$$\text{ان الله اذهب عنكم عصبية الجاهلية وفخرها بالاباء}$$
$$\text{انما هو مؤمن تقى وفاجر شقى الناس كلهم بنو آدم وآدم}$$
$$\text{خلق من تراب}$$

"Allah, the Exalted, has removed from you the prejudices of pre-Islamic (Jahiliyya) times when you boasted of your forefathers. Now (with the advent of Islam), there will be only two types of human beings – a pious and faithful, God-fearing Muslim – or an unfortunate rebellious unbeliever. All of you are the sons of Adam ﷺ who was created from clay."

The Holy Prophet made all possible efforts to root out the tribal prejudices from the Arabs and give them a consciousness of universal love and a human dignity for all. The process of "Mo-aa-Khaat" or Brotherhood between the emigrants of Makkah and the helpers of Madina was another step towards eradication of old prejudices. In the case of Salman Farsi ؓ, he ﷺ said:

سلمان منا اهل البيت

"Salman is a member of our own family."

Now Salman was a non-Arab whom Islam had raised to the status of a member of the Holy Prophet's own family. A non-Arab had become nearest of kin despite his having a different language, a different race and a different pedigree. This was to impress upon the Muslims that Arabs and Non-Arabs were close to each other as brothers if they were Muslims. This was indeed a great achievement and Allah, the Exalted, called it a great blessing when He said:

هُوَالَّذِىْ اَيَّـدَكَ بِنَصْرِه وَبِالْمُؤْمِنِيْنَ وَاَلَّفَ بَيْنَ قُلُوْبِهِمْ لَوْاَنْفَقْتَ مَافِى الْاَرْضِ جَمِيْعًا مَّاَلَّفْتَ بَيْنَ قُلُوْبِهِمْ وَ لٰكِنَّ اللهَ اَلَّفَ بَيْنَهُمْ اِنَّه عَزِيْزٌ حَكِيْمٌ

"It is He, (Allah, the Exalted) Who supported you (the Prophet) by his help and the help of faithful Muslims and He brought about mutual love in the hearts of the faithful Muslims. Had you spent the treasures of the Earth to achieve this, you would not have succeeded. But Allah (out of His mercy) brought about love in their hearts. Verily He is Powerful, Wise."

This was not a human act and no human effort could have achieved this change of hearts. Elsewhere in the Holy Quran, Allah, the Exalted, addressed His Prophet to impress this point:

وَاذْكُرُوانِعْمَةَاللهِ عَلَيْكُمْ اِذْ كُنْتُمْ اَعْدَآءً فَاَلَّفَ بَيْنَ قُلُوبِكُمْ فَاَصْبَحْتُمْ بِنِعْمَتِهِ اِخْوَانًا

"And remember the blessing of Allah (the Exalted) on you when you were enemies (of one another), He brought about love in your hearts so that you turned into (loving) brothers."

Differences in Spiritual Status:

After having studied the baneful effects of tribal prejudices and boasting for family superiorities during pre-Islamic days and the effective measures taken by Islam to curb those trends, we must realise that faith is the name of an internal spiritual condition which can vary and become strong or weak. Just as we watch now-a-days that all Muslims are not at one level of faith and moral strength, the same was the condition of the companions of the Holy Prophet ﷺ. All of them did not have the same and similar status of piety or moral rectitude. Personal capacities, inherent inclinations and varying traits of the human nature made them different from one another in acquisition of moral and spiritual bliss. The company of the Holy Prophet ﷺ was another big cause for difference of moral and spiritual perfections.

Example of Amir Mo'awiya ؓ:

The status of Amir Mo'awiya ؓ as a companion of the Holy Prophet ﷺ is above all discussion. However, the fact of the situation is that he, along with his father Abu Sufyan, embraced Islam after the conquest of Makkah by the Holy Prophet ﷺ. Unlike the first four caliphs of Islam, namely Hazrat Abu Bakr ؓ, Hazrat Umar ؓ, Hazrat Usman ؓ and Hazrat Ali ؓ, Amir Mo'awiya ؓ did not have equal time and occasion to remain in the company of the Holy Prophet ﷺ and to imbibe the spiritual wealth which the pre-conquest companions did imbibe. As a member of the most respected Qureshi family, Amir Mo'awiya ؓ had great qualities of political foresight, patience, forbearance, steadfastness and valour which, after his acceptance of Islam, he used in the service of Islam.

The family differences and rivalry between the great families of Banu Omayyah and Banu Hashim were ages long and Amir Mo'awiya ؓ was not above those feelings. Whatever he said and did against Hazrat Ali ؓ, this feeling of rivalry played its due part. Hazrat Ali ؓ may also be considered to have been swayed by his inherent feelings about Banu Omayyah, but the historical facts seem to deny any such accusation against him. He was a paragon of the teachings of Islam and the prejudices of the pre-Islamic times did not influence his conduct in the least.

There is no doubt that Amir Mo'awiya used his great qualities of bravery, endeavour, generosity and political wisdom for the advance of Islam and the results of his sincere efforts for Islam are now a part of history. Muslims can rightly boast of his conquests and other successes for Islam.

But, when Amir Mo'awiya ؓ began to use his great qualities of knowledge and action for the strength and uplift of the family of Omayyahs, the form and shape of government developed by him was no longer on the pattern of the polity developed by the Holy Prophet ﷺ and his well-guided caliphs. Attention is drawn to a prediction of the Holy Prophet ﷺ when he said:

> "O Muslims! After (my) prophethood; there will be Khilafat on the pattern of prophethood which will be followed by "Mulk-e-Aaz" i.e., government by force." (Masnad Imam Ahmad Bin Humble).

Effects / Influence of Non-Arab Muslims on the Islamic Polity:

The second important reason for the failure of Hazrat Ali ؓ was the influence of non-Arab Muslims, After the large conquests of Islam, many non-Arabic people embraced Islam. Due to unfortunate internecine struggle of the Arab Muslims for power and superiority, the non-Arab Muslims could not fully imbibe the great spiritual wealth of Islam. The pre-Islamic prejudices and inclinations among the new non-Arab converts to Islam were visible. The group of Hypocrites led by Abdullah Bin Saba worked for the destruction of Islam under the cloak of Islam. They were a very poweful single influence which slowly and stealthily poisoned the collective fabric of Muslims. Since the non-Arab converts had occasion to meet both true and sincere Muslims as well as the hypocrites of Islam, they were naturally influenced by both the parties. They did commit mistakes innocently and could not realise the real dangers to the strength of Islam and the Muslims.

Hazrat Umar ؓ had the foresight to see the future dangers to the body-politic of Islam. He, therefore, kept sending instructions to the government functionaries which kept them strictly bound to pristine Islam. On one occasion, he said: "I wish there was a wall of blazing fire between Arabs and non-Arabs." His wish clearly indicated that he wanted to save Islam and true Muslims from the baneful effects of the Non-Arab influences.

Asceticism and Solitude of the Elite Companions of the Holy Prophet ﷺ:

The third important reason for the failure of the Islamic polity was that the most pious and influential companions of the Holy Prophet ﷺ took to live in solitude and adopted asceticism after seeing the major events of strife between the companions themselves and the general atmosphere of evil-mongering and mischief. The political field was now left open for those who had political power in their hands but who lacked the moral and spiritual deterrents to defend righteousness against the forces of evil.

It is a well-known fact about Hazrat Abu Moosa Ash'ari ؓ that, when he saw the attitude of Amr Bin Al-Aas in the event of Arbitration, he was deeply hurt and this spiritual shock made him take to life of solitude in a village. Similarly, when Hazrat Ayesha (Radhi-Allahu-Anha) left Madina for Basra for the Battle of Jamal (camel), the people of Koofa were so much shocked that they cried in anger and wept incessantly so much so that – that particular day came to be recorded in history as "The Day of Weeping and Crying". Hazrat Mughirah Bin Sho'ba ؓ was among the elite of companions. He did not respond to the call of Hazrat Ayesha (Radhi-Allahu-Anha) and considered it safe and prudent to remain aloof in the strife between the companions of the Holy Prophet ﷺ. Hazrat Hafsah (Radhi-Allahu-Anha) intended to accompany Hazrat Ayesha (Radhi-Allahu-Anha) for the Battle of Jamal. But her brother, Hazrat Abdullah Bin Umar ؓ prevented her from participation and she declined to accompany Hazrat Ayesha (Radhi-Allahu-Anha).

All the exalted seers of Islam fully understood that the fountain of mischief had erupted in Islam and their hearts were wounded on this account. They wept and prayed and tried their utmost through sermons and speeches to avert the crisis of Islam. But these noble persons had no political power and no avenues of effective influence. The result was that pious and good people openly saw their in-effectiveness to save Islam and every thing untoward happened within their sight. As explained in the above paragraphs the decline of the Islamic polity had started during the reign of the third caliph. Yet it was rightly understood that it was still a period of good people and virtuous deeds. The elite of the companions were still living and the persons of reformation and moral improvement continued due to individual preaching and coaching. The individual life still feared to commit glaring sins and obeyed the injunctions of God. If a governor or a functionary of the Government committed an act of oppression, he made an effort to provide satisfactory excuse from the Quran and the Sunnah to justify his wrong action. Another very redeeming fact was that, men at authority always forgot their political differences if forces of infidelity challenged the Islamic institutions or territories and they all put up a concerted front against the enemies of Islam. Due to this situation the progress and conquests of Islamic forces continued. The proposition and preaching of Islam continued unabated.

REIGN OF BANU OMAYYAHS 41-60 AH

In 41 A.H., after the end of Khilafat-e-Rashida, the government of Banu Omayyah started with Amir Mo'awiya as its first Ruler. His reign lasted from 41 A.H. to 60 A.H. for twenty years. This period has many a story of the rise and fall of Islam in its fold. The government of Amir Mo'awiya was not a continuation of Khilafat-e-Rashida nor he himself could claim to be a Khalifa-e-Rashid. Despite all this, his moral character and his love for Islam were above board because he had benefited from the company of the Holy Prophet ﷺ and also had acted as a Scribe for the Divine 'Wahy' (revelation of the Holy Quran). Amir Mo'awiya continued his efforts for the uplift of Islam despite his mistakes.

Imam Tabri has stated that once Amir Mo'awiya was halting at a certain place in Syria when display of his pomp and glory was made before him in the form of studs, slave-girls, carriages and other articles of comfort and glory. He felt ashamed of all the worldly baubles and said to Ibn-e-Mas'adah (who was sitting near him): "Allah, the Exalted, may send His blessings on Abu Bakr ؓ who never wished to have any worldly things nor did the worldly thing ever approached him. This world wished to go before Umar ؓ but he never wished for it. Then came Usman who got something of this world and the world also benefited from him. Thereafter we find ourselves thoroughly drowned in the world and its delicacies."[1]

Apart from certain moral virtues, Amir Mo'awiya used his political wisdom, prudence and far-sightedness to strengthen the political power of the Muslims under very delicate and complicated circumstances.

A large part of North Africa had been conquered during the period of Khilafat-e-Rashida. Amir Mo'awiya made sizeable additions to the territories already conquered. The Berber tribes of

---

1. Tabri, Vol.6, P.186

Reign of Banu Omayyahs

North Africa rose in revolt against the Muslim government but Amir Mo'awiya curbed their rebellion and ensured the safety of the Muslims. Syrian and Egyptian borders were not safe from the attacks of Romans due to the Mediterranean Sea. Amir Mo'awiya raised cantonments at the borders to counterpoise the Roman forces and also built forts for effective defence of Muslim lands. He built an Armada and inflicted a crushing defeat on the Romans in the sea warfare in which he also conquered the islands of Cyprus, Rhodes and Arwad and erected cantonments there. He also attacked the islands of Sicily and Crete but could not conquer them. The political factors inside the country wanted to destroy the central organization of Islam by their revolutionary misdeeds. Amir Mo'awiya effectively crushed the anti-Islamic forces. Besides the conquests of enemy lands, Amir Mo'awiya also performed many a constructive works which were urgently required.

There is no denying the fact that there were many instances when the government of Amir Mo'awiya acted with coercion and dealt with an iron hand. But his oppression was like the cruel knife of a surgeon who removes one part of the body to save the rest of the organs from contagion and evil effects of disease, necessitating the operation. The process of punishment and suppression was unavoidable to ensure smooth running of the government. A dispassionate critic of circumstances necessitating the use of forces by Amir Mo'awiya will agree that the severity of the situations warranted and justified the use of force. The greatest need of the times was that the political power of Islam must be defended and it may be guarded against non-Muslim and Muslim miscreants. He had to bear and put up with some very unpleasant things which he did bear with patience and fortitude to save the future of Islam and the Muslim Ummah. The political policy of Amir Mo'awiya though charged with occasions of oppression and high-handedness, proved to be most successful under the circumstances then prevailing. The overall effect of this policy was that the march of Islam did not slow down and the number of converts went on increasing by leaps and bounds. Similarly the Muslim conquests are continued unabated. No body could have the impression that there was any measure of retardation in the spread of Islam or the pace of Islamic conquests had slowed down.

Hafiz Ibn-e-Temiyya ؓ, the famous dispassionate scholar of Islam, said in Part-II of his book "Minhaj-us-Sunnah": "When Khilafat became too weak to survive, it changed into monarchy or autocracy. Hazrat Mo'awiya ؓ kept it firmly standing by virtue of his knowledge and kind generosity. In the history of Islam no monarch was better than Amir Mo'awiya. He was doubtlessly the best among the monarchs of Islam. His conduct and character were certainly more pleasant and praiseworthy than all those who ruled as monarchs after him.

The Effects of Monarchy:

From purely Islamic view point the hard fact cannot be lost sight of that the mode of government adopted by Amir Mo'awiya ؓ gave a terrible shock to the spirit of collective system of rulership taught by Islam. The government was no longer a democracy. It was an open autocracy. The general interests of the Muslims and Islam which were erstwhile dependent on a democratic system, now became subservient to the whim and fancy of one individual who was the king or monarch of the Muslims. It was a fortune for the Muslims that Amir Mo'awiya was personally a true Muslim of many virtues. Due to his personal virtues and his generous conduct no body felt the difference in the change of government. But men of knowledge and insight felt the difference very painfully. But they could not express their feelings or opinion and the situation best demanded silence at the point. Any open condemnation of monarchy would have given rise to widespread commotion and troubles. But men whose hearts were lacerated did avail any suitable occasion for expression of truth. Once Hazrat Sa'ad Bin Abi Waqqas ؓ, the conqueror of Qadsia, happened to appear before the audience of Amir Mo'awiya. He greeted the Amir after the fashion of non-Arab Kings. At this Amir Mo'awiya ؓ laughed and remarked:

"Had you addressed me as Amir-ul-Mominin, you would not have lost any thing. The conqueror of

Reign of Banu Omayyahs

Qadsia replied with boldness: "The way you have obtained the authority of Khilafat, I would not have accepted it at all if it had been offered to me."

The greatest opponent of Banu Omayyah was the family of Banu Hashim. But it goes to the credit of Amir Mo'awiya that he used the best of his moral virtues like fortitude and softness in his dealings with Banu Hashim. After ascending the throne of monarchy, he never displayed any hardship or roughness in his dealings with the Banu Hashim. On the other hand, he was generous in sending them frequent gifts, granting good many stipends and making every effort to win their hearts. But features of monarchy were prominantly visible in the mode of Amir Mo'awiya's government. This assertion finds further support from an ordinary event narrated below.

The governor of Kufa, Zaid was born of a lewd woman whose name was Samiyyah. Since his father's name was not known due to illicit relations, Zaid was, under the age long practice of the Arabs, called Zaid Bin Abihe i.e., Zaid, the son of his (unknown) father. This was an ugly mark on his reputation. Amir Mo'awiya wanted to utilize the capabilities of Zaid but his origin (as a bastard) constantly proved to be a hindrance. Side-tracking the famous order of the Holy Prophet that correct ancestry is proved only by lawful marriage and the adulterer deserves to be killed with stones", Amir Mo'awiya got it publicly proclaimed that Zaid should in future be called Zaid Bin Abi Sufyan and not Zaid Bin Abihe. Allama Blazri wrote in "Futuh-ul-Buldaan" that once Hazrat Ayesha (Radhi-Allahu-Anha) wrote a letter to Zaid in which she addressed him as Zaid Bin Abi Sufyan. This gave Zaid so much joy that he went about showing that letter to all and sundry.

Bai'at (Pledge of Loyalty) for Yazid:

Amir Mo'awiya took another important step towards cementing the monarchical mode of government. In his life-time he obtained pledge for Yazid, his son, to succeed him as the caliph. This single step, apparently an ordinary event, was so much important that it confirmed the mode of government chosen by Amir

Mo'awiya in place of Islamic democracy which was the essence of Khilafat-e-Rashida. He could have avoided this step as it was an outrage against the Islamic mode of government and appointment of a Khalifa. Although 'Khilafat' was non-existent but Banu Omayyah did not give it up to reap the advantage of religious bias attached with this term. Amir Mo'awiya could have avoided the occurrence of unpleasant events in the future if he had acted according to the precedents of Hazrat Abu Bakr ؓ and Hazrat Umar ؓ who made a selection or a nomination from among the elite of the companions of the Holy Prophet ﷺ who were still available. With the nomination of Yazid as the successor of Amir Mo'awiya, the monarchical way of government was confirmed.

Comments on the Regime of Banu Omayyah:

Amir Mo'awiya obtained the government by coercion. Similarly he obtained the Bai'at (pledge) of Muslims for his son by coercion. People who did not like Yazid, even they had to extend their hands for the pledge under duress. The most baneful effects of monarchy or autocracy are that freedom of thought and opinion is taken away from the masses. Under the Banu Omayyah governments, these malicious elements were apparent and visible.

After Amir Mo'awiya ؓ, the regime of Yazid was so much cursed that the grandson of the Holy Prophet ﷺ, Hazrat Imam Hussain ؓ had to lay down his precious life to avoid the rule of despotism but the despots continued. The elite of companions, Hazrat Abdullah Bin Zubair ؓ laid down his life for the return of Islamic polity. But he also failed. Now the rule in force was "Might is Right". Whosoever had the power to capture power, he became the ruler irrespective of his moral and spiritual degeneration. The basis and the criteria laid down by Islam were totally ignored and violated. With one or two exceptions, the entire linkage of the Banu Omayyah caliphs from Amir Mo'awiya ؓ to Marwan, the common factors were coercion, usurpation and oppression. Hisham Bin Abdul Malik was comparatively a better man. He gave orders to stop vilification of Hazrat Ali ؓ from the pulpits in the mosques. Yet his prejudice against Banu Hashim was alive in his heart and he could not hear the praises of any one from among the family of Hazrat Ali ﷺ.

The respect of the family of Hazrat Ali ﷺ was deeply imbedded in the hearts of the general public. Once Imam Zain-ul-Abideen (the son of Hazrat Imam Hussain ﷺ) was circumambulating the Holy Ka'aba. When he advanced towards the Hajr-e-Aswad (the sacred black stone), people all around receded to make room for the son of Hazrat Imam to kiss the black stone. But, when Hisam Bin Abdul Malik wished to kiss the sacred black stone, no body left his position to make room for him. On seeing this contrast in the attitude of the people, a Syrian pilgrim pointed towards Hazrat Imam Zain-ul-Abideen and enquired as to who he was. Hisham was well acquainted with the person of Imam Zain-ul-Abideen but he posed ignorance purposely. The famous poet of Arabia, Frazdaq was present on the occasion. He could not bear the affront displayed by Hisham about Imam Zain-ul-Abideen. He read out an extempore eulogy in praise of the Ahle-Bait (family of the Holy Prophet ﷺ). This eulogy is present and written in almost all good works of Arabic literature. It is a pretty long eulogy but we are quoting here below some selected verses.[1]

1

هذا سليل حسين و ابن فاطـــمه   بنت الرسول من اخابت به الظلم

He (Imam Zail-ul-Abideen) is the dear son of Hussain ﷺ who was the son of Fatima (Radhi-Allahu-Anha). Who was Fatima? She was the dearest daughter of the Messenger of Allah ﷺ through whom the darkness of the age was dispelled.

اذاراته قريش قال قائلـــهم   الى مكارم هذا اينتهى الكرم

When people from the Quraish see them, they speak out: "Virtues of conduct and character have reached their height of glory through them."

هذاالذي خير عباد الله كلهـــم   هذا التقى النقى الطاهر العلم

He (Imam Zain-ul-Abideen) is the son of the best of human beings; he is pure of origin, pious in conduct and a leader of the virtuous people.

يكاد يمسكه عرفان راحــة   ركن الحطيم اذا ماجاء يستلم

While circumambulating the House of Allah he raises his hand to kiss the 'Rukne Hateem", the "Rukne Hateem" also recognizes him and stretches forward to catch hold of his hand palm.
(Remaining on next page)

How strange it is that the caliphs of Banu Omayyah bore illwill towards the family of the Holy Prophet ﷺ and at the same time displayed generosity and liberal attitude towards Christian poets like 'Akhtal' who visited their court without let or hindrance,

كالشمس ينجاب من اشراقها القتم   يبين نور الضحى من نور غرته

The light of his forehead shines like brilliant mid-day sun and which dispels the dark dust around him.

طابت عناصره والخيم والشيم   مشتقة من رسول الله نبعة

His deaf was leavened with the prophetic substance. On this account the elements collected in his creation are pure and sacred and so are his conduct and demeanour.

جدد انبياء الله قد ختموا   هو ابن فاطمة ان كنت جاهله

He is the dear son of Fatima (Radhi-Allahu-Anha). If you (O Hisham!) do not know him, enjoy your ignorance of him. With his grand father, the prophethood came to an end.

العرب تعرف من انكرت والعجم   وليس قولك من هذا بضائره

If you ask (wickedly) who he is? Your query can in no way harm him. This whole of Arabia and the whole world besides Arabia know him except you.

كفروقرهم منجى ومعتصم   من معشر حبهم دين وبغضهم

He belongs to the noble family whose love is the core and spirit of true faith. To bear illwill towards him is apostasy because his nearness is the guarantee for salvation and shelter.

اوقيل من خير اهل الارض قيل هم   ان عداهم التقى كانوا المنتهم

If men of piety are counted, he will certainly be their leader. If it is asked, "Who is the best living soul on Earth?" The reply will be: "He is Zain-ul-Abideen."

سيان ذالك ان اثروا وان عدموا   لا يقبض العدم بسماحة اكفهم

Lack of wealth does not stand in his generosity. His munificence and gifts for humanity continue under thick and thin.

والدين من بيت هذا ناله الامم   من يعرف الله يعرف اوليته ذا

He who knows Allah, the Exalted, he equally knows the distinction and great status of Imam Zain-ul-Abideen, because nations of the world have obtained the wealth of Truth (and Islam) from their sacred house.

لولا التشهد كانت لا ده نعم   ماقال لا قط الا في تشهده

Due to excessive generosity he has never uttered the word 'No' except in the prayer when 'There is no deity but Allah' has to be said. His 'No' would have changed into 'Yes' but for the Divine formula.   (Shazrat-uz-Zahab. Vol.1, P.144)

Reign of Banu Omayyahs

who chatted with the caliphs and even committed unIslamic acts which were tolerated by the caliphs of Banu Omayyah. Soon after the death of Amir Mo'waiya ؓ, the destructive effects of monarchy had become visible. The actual aim of these caliphs was to maintain the high position and dignity of their family and to give preference to personal gains and interests to collective or national interests.

Oppression of Government Functionaries:

It is common experience that when the Rulers are selfish and oppressive, their underlings recklessly indulge in corruption and looting of the public. The government functionaries under the Banu Omayyah Rulers had totally ignored the true spirit of Islam for right and straightforward government. Unfair and oppressive acts were the order of the day. What governor Ziad and his son Obaidullah did in Madina and Iraq is a most harrowing tale. Hajjaj Bin Yusuf, as said by historian Masoodi, killed no less than 125000 innocent persons. Yet Abdul Malik Bin Marwan who was a wise and conscious Ruler connived at the misdeeds of Hajjaj. As a matter of fact he looked upon the oppressive acts of Hajjaj to be useful for the consolidation of his despotic rule.

Prejudices of Banu Omayyah:

Prejudice of all types was the keynote of the collective character of Banu Omayyah. Apart from tribal prejudices, they also looked down upon those non-Arab converts who had embraced Islam and were living side by side with the Arabs. At times uncalled for tyrannies were perpetrated upon them. It is narrated about Hajjaj that he treated the 'Mawalis (non-Arab converts to Islam) very roughly. Just to avoid any chance of their picking up the correct tone and accent of the Arabic language due to their close neighbourly association with the Arabic he scattered them widely to live in the outskirts of the cities so that in the rural areas they had no such chance of free association and contact with the Arabs. The outcome of this inhuman and uncalled for oppression was that the non-Arab Muslims were forced to hatch conspiracies to undo the Muslim government of the Arabs. The opposition of the non-Arab Muslims gained momentum and a harmful movement came into existence under the name of "Shau' Biyat" which, on development, was responsible for the destruction and death of many an important Muslims.

Mal-Administration of National Treasury:

During the periods of the early well-guided Caliphs the 'Baitul Maal' or the National Treasury was looked upon as a sacred Trust wherefrom every penny was carefully spent and the rulers took only for their bare minimum requirements. The caliphs of Banu Omayyah treated it as their personal property and spent extravagantly without let or hindrance. They lived like non-Arab monarchs and spent lavishly on their personal needs and for display of pomp and glory. The officers were paid big salaries, which encouraged them to live like aristocrats. People who supported Banu Omayyah or indulged in propaganda in their favour, they were also freely given large moneys. The stipends of persons were stopped who lived with personal dignity and who were not inclined to sing praises of Banu Omayyah. Yazid, the son of Amir Mo'awiya was so much deprived of good conscience that he abruptly stopped the stipends of the families attached to the Holy House of Allah and the Holy Shrine of the Prophet and even of the deserving Ansars.

When the National Treasury was depleted due to the extravagant expenses of the ruling class, the caliphs resorted to inhuman pressures and coercion for realising taxes and revenues. The care for lawful and unlawful taxes was not observed. The non-Muslims who had embraced Islam were not liable for the 'Jizya' tax yet they were forced to pay this tax. The result of this high-handedness was that in Africa and Khorasan the new converts began to dislike Islam.

Dissension and Disunity:

The Banu Omayyah were well known for their political shrewdness and effective ruling power. They could have spent their capabilities for the re-establishment of Islamic polity. But their goal of personal interest and tribal glory made them indifferent to Islamic values. Every effort on their part was diverted towards consolidating

Reign of Banu Omayyahs

the Omayyah's rule and, with that aim, seeds of dissension were sown in other tribes so that different tribes came to fighting like the old days of Jahiliyya. The Egyptian and Yeminite tribes settled in Arabia were envious of each other. The force of Islam had united them on one platform. But the Banu Omayyahs rekindled the fire of tribal prejudices with the result that in the inter-tribal skirmishes many noble Tabi'een (followers of the companions) were killed.

The events of the Omayyah reign leave no doubt that their mode of government was secular, despotic, selfish and autocratic. The spirit of collective benefits target by Islam had totally disappeared. Our negative criticism based on facts should not hold us from narrating the bright side of the picture.

Soundness of Religious Tenets:

It is creditable on the part of Banu Omayyah that, despite lapses in character and action, the members of this ruling dynasty were rigid in their belief and tenets of Islam. The timely and brave action in annihilating the ideological enemies of Islam must win for the Banu Omayyahs the rightly earned praise of all well-wishers of Islam.

Services of Abdul Malik Bin Marwan:

In connection with service to the ideology of Islam, the name of Abdul Malik Bin Marwan stands at the top. He ruled for 21 years from 65 A.H. to 86 A.H. This whole period is full of troubles, mischief and rebellions.

Extirpation of the Kharijites:

After their defeat in the battle of Nahrwan, the Kharijites re-assembled their force in Persia and Iraq. They so vehemently preached their false dogmas and ideology that many a seasoned Muslims began to agree with them. They had become a powerful force against pristine Islam and Abdul Malik Bin Marwan crushed them with determined efforts till they lost their vital force.

Mischief of Mukhtar:

Mukhtar Bin Obaid Saqfi was a political mischief monger. His evil was even greater than that of the Kharijites. He had political tact and daring to get support of different effective parties to topple the well-established government. Mukhtar was a free-lancer with very lewd ideas and his success would have created an awful situation of unrest and religious turmoil for the Muslim world.

Tawwabeen:

The people who had betrayed Imam Hussain ؏ and left him alone to face the bloody encounter at Karbala, they now designed to topple the government of Banu Omayyah and thereby make atonement for the murder of Imam Hussain ؏. They called themselves "Tawwabeen" or the Repenters.

Agitation in Iraq:

By their nature the Iraqis were mischief-minded. They made Abdul Rehman bin Ash'ath their tool and started large-scale agitation to topple the government of Abdul Malik Bin Marwan. He sent a big army under the command of Hijaj who inflicted a crushing defeat on them.

After coping effectively with internal agitations, Abdul Malik began the process of punishing the rebellions people of North Africa, Sicily and Crete. The Romans were so heavily punished that the possession of Muslims was not only restored but made more effective. Abdul Malik's rule is creditable in re-establishing the political centre of genuine Islam by eliminating the forces which were attacking the ideology of Islam.

Abdul Malik is called the founder of Banu Omayyah government. He not only consolidated the Omayyah government on solid grounds, but also did a lot to re-establish the glory of the centre of Islam by eliminating prople with false ideologies. For this reason, historians are inclined to hold the status of Abdul Malik equal to that of Amir Mo'awiya ؏.

Reign of Banu Omayyahs

Historian Masoodi[1] has written an event which is narrated below: In 66 A.H. Abdul Malik was commanding the Syrian army and was going to Koofa to deal with Mukhtar Saqfi. On the way he learnt that Abdullah Bin Ziad had been slain, and his army had suffered a defeat. He also received the news that commander of his army who had reached Madina to fight Abdullah Bin Zubair, had been killed. Immediately after these two bad news, he was informed that army of Abdullah Bin Zubair had entered Palestine and his brother Mos'ib Bin Zubair had also joined him. He also got the news that the Roman Emperor had left for the conquest of Syria with a large army and his troops were stationed at Maseera. An informer also told him that the agitators of Iraq had created trouble and were terrorising and looting the people of the town, so much so that some convicts had broken the iron bars of the jail and had run away. He also was told that a group of the Bedouins had entered the towns of Hims and Bal'bak and were plundering properties of the population.

Any one else would have lost his senses after hearing a series of bad news quoted above. But Abdul Malik remained calm and composed without any signs of worry over his face. The whole night he kept laughing loudly which was an indication of his undaunted courage, his value and his political ability to deal with any odd situation. Abdul Malik lost no time to effectively cope with the miscreants to save the centre of Islam and its activities. Abdul Malik successfully quelled the rebellions against his regime. Then he turned to the foreign invaders and, inflicting a crushing defeat on the Romans and the Burbers, he made the center of Islam so powerful that Islam continued its activities for preaching and teaching.

Besides providing political support to Islam, Abdul Malik had the credit of constructing many buildings of importance. He was himself a man of knowledge and perfections. He made special arrangements for the teaching of the Holy Quran and built up centres of Quranic studies at all important places. The official language of

---

1. Murrawag-uz-Zahab, Vol.2, P.113

government offices was Persian and Roman. Abdul Malik got the government files translated into Arabic. This step increased the importance of Arabic language. He also built new towns and made them populated.

Walid Bin Abdul Malik:

After Abdul Malik, his son Walid ascended the throne of Khilafat. He was not a scholar like his father, but he was acquainted with the rules of State craft. His religious life was also better than many of his family people. The internal rebellions and commotion had been effectively curbed by his father and circumstances were peaceful and encouraging for Walid.

Fortunately he had around him a group of capable and sincere commanders who became responsible for very important conquests and added new flowers of glory to Islam. Muhammad Bin Qasim, Moosa Bin Nusair and Qutaiba Bin Muslim. Qutaiba Bin Muslim conquered Khorasan, Khwarism and Chinese Turkistan. Muhammad Bin Qasim conquered Sind. Moosa Bin Nusair reached the land of Andalusia (Spain) where he hoisted the flag of Islam. By the efforts of this group of sincere and brave commanders, the Muslims conquered the lands between China and Spain

Apart from conquests, Walid also had deep interest in construction works and buildings. He got many fine and beautiful mosques built. He re-organized the Army on a sound footing. He made centres of Islamic studies and Quranic Schools where teaching of the Holy Quran was done and plans were prepared for the preaching of Islam. Besides effective teaching, the institutions also produced good preachers of Islam. Walid also did away with the curse of begging in his country.

Repeated Attacks on Constantinople:

The conquest of Spain by the Muslims had added a new chapter of glory to the Muslim history. This was also a pointer towards their political wisdom and statesmanship. Similarly the repeated attacks of the Muslim armies on Constantinople (which was

Reign of Banu Omayyahs

the capital of the Roman Empire) was another enterprise of national level. But it proved a failure. It was an indication of the dwindling spirit of Islam without which miracles could not be anticipated.

Constantinople was the gate of Eastern Europe. The Muslim Rulers were fully aware of its importance. First of all an attack on Constantinople was made in 663 A.D. when, (in the regime of Hazrat Usman ؓ), Amir Mo'awiya led an army against the Romans. He marched through Asia Minor and reached the shores of Basphorous. At that time Basar Bin Artat defeated the Roman Armeda in front of the Phoenix mountain. The Roman forces were under the command of Constantinnople-II. In this Sea Warfare no less than twenty thousand Roman soldiers lost their lives. The losses of the Muslim Army was also not insignificant. The expedition did not finalise and the Muslims had to return without conquering Constantinople.

The second expedition against Romans was undertaken in 680 A.D. Hazrat Mo'awiya ؓ made large scale preparation for the attack. Under the command of Fuzailah Bin Obaid-al-Amin, a big fleet was stationed at the ports of Egypt and Syria. During its operation it went on conquering the areas from Anatolia to Kalsidon. The next year in 681 A.D. an army was sent for the conquest of Constantinople under the command of Auf-al-Azdi. Yazid Bin Mo'awiya also joined this army. Veteran companions like Hazrat Abdullah Bin Abbas ؓ, Abdullah Bin Umar ؓ, Abdullah bin Zubair ؓ and Hazrat Ayub Ansari ؓ took part in this expedition. Apart from land army, a sea fleet was also sent under the command of Basar bin Artat. This fleet crossed the Danial Pass and reached very close to the capital of the Roman Empire. Virtually the Muslim forces had reached the very shadow of Constantinople. The Roman Emperor of the Eastern Europe knew full well the preparation made by the Muslims. He had, therefore, prepared very well to fight the Muslims. A new weapon called "Greek Fire" was also brought in the field by the Romans who had planned to torpedo the Muslim Weaponry.

For many days Muslim Army and Navel forces held the siege of Constantinople and attacked the fort many times. Hazrat Abu Ayub Ansari ؓ and Abdul Aziz Zararah were martyred in this skirmish. But Constantinople remained invincible. The Muslim forces left the suburbs of Constantinople and re-camped 80 miles from the city. For many years this became the practice that the Muslim Armies laid siege to Constantinople in summer and receded to distant camps in winter. The result of the repeated futile attacks was that the Muslims suffered tangible losses in men and material. At long last the Muslim Forces came back home in 689 A.D. The estimated loss of Muslims man force was thirty thousand. The repeated defeats lowered the morale of Muslims and raised the morale of the Romans. At long last Amir Mo'awiya ؓ signed an agreement with the Romans which lasted for forty years.

The repeated failure of the Muslims in this years-long-siege of Constantinople undermined their morale and, with this passage of time, they could not regain their original moral force. So much so that it had become an obsession with the Muslim Army Generals. When Moosa Bin Nusair steered from his successful conquest of Spain, he made up his mind to turn his attention to the East and wished to reach Damascus after conquering Constantinople. The intended advantage of the planned march was to vanquish the Christian governmental force and the Christian ideology or religion. But the central government did not allow him to undertake this expedition. The obvious result was that the conquests of Islamic forces could not extend beyond south of France.

Period of Sulaiman Bin Abdul Malik:

After the death of Walid, his real brother Sulaiman Bin Abdul Malik ascended the throne of Khilafat in 96 A.H. corresponding to 715 A.D. The government of Banu Omayyah was safe and immune against internal dissension and rebellions till then. Political conquests had raised the morale and consolidated the courage of rulers. Well organized and fully trained military force was available. There was no dearth of weapons and army equipment. On the other side, the Roman government had become weak and, in

Reign of Banu Omayyahs

the twenty years short period as many as six Qaisers (Kings) had come to power and were dethroned. Bulgarian and Salovians had trampled the Northern provinces of the Roman Empire and reached the precincts of the Roman capital. On the other side, the Arabs had crossed the Asia Minor and extended their conquests to the waters of Basforus. Within the Roman Empire itself dissensions and rebellions had become the order of the day.

Making a realistic estimate of the circumstances, Sulaiman Bin Abdul Malik planned another attack on Constantinople. He mustered in large numbers the units of land and sea forces. He equipped all the forces with suitable arms and ammunitions and despatched them to the front under the command of his brother Muslimah Bin Abdul Malik. Sulaiman himself stayed at Wabiq. He gave instructions to Muslims either to conquer Constantinople or wait for his further instructions.

In the beginning of 98 A.H. corresponding to September, 716 A.D. the commander Muslimah ransacked the plateau of Anatolia and conquered several Bazantine forts and cities. Then he turned to Aamooriah, the capital city of Anatolia. The Roman governor of Aamooriah was Leo who was very brave, sensible, and clever. He made peace with Muslimah. Thereafter he dethroned the Qaisar and captured the seat of the Central Roman government. Muslimah displayed great courage and bravely marched upon Constantinople at the head of a large army. The Historians have written that on this occassion, as many as 8 million Muslim troops had gathered and camped under the walls of Constantinople. Sulaiman continued to sit at Wabiq and kept reinforcing the Muslim troops under his control for the conquest of Constantinople.

Muslimah spread his forces along the coast of the sea of Marmora and laid the siege of Constantinople. The Manjaneeqs and the canons fired ceaselessly for many days. But this time also Muslims suffered a setback and did not succeed. In this siege the Muslims suffered very heavy losses in men and material. The extreme cold climate was beyond bearing of the Arabs and thousands died with cold. Many thousands fell and were incapacitated. The reinforcement also finished.

During this siege Sulaiman Bin Abdul Malik died and Hazrat Umar Bin Abdul Aziz became the caliph. He at once sent directions to Muslimah to end the seige of Constantinople and return with his armies. The Greeks caught the opportunity and attacked the Muslim Sea forces stationed at Adrianople. Many sea ships were drowned and only a few ships managed to reach the Syrian ports.

The failure during the regime of Sulaiman Bin Abdul Malik was so colossal and discouraging that the Muslims could not think of any further attempt to conquer the Roman capital till 1452 A.D. After full 800 years the Turks captured Constantinople. Had the Muslims been successful in capturing Constantinople, the map of Europe would have changed dramatically and, like Egypt, Syria and Iraq, the bulk of the population in Europe would have been Muslim.

يريدالمرء ان يعطى مناه   ويابى الله الامايشاء

"Man wants that his desires should be fulfilled, but Allah, the Exalted, does what He Himself wishes to do."

Causes of Muslims' Failure:

Historians have apparently counted the following causes for the failure of Muslims: (1) The Arabs did not have full experience of Naval Warfare. (2) Muslimah Bin Abdul Malik was mistaken in his reliance on the Roman governor Leo and in making him his confident (3) The inclement weather of Europe was unbearable for the Arabs. (4) The Romans were superior to the Muslims in weaponry, men and material.

From the secular view point, the causes have been enumerated above. But the real causes are moral and spiritual. The Muslim Aristocracy and the ruling class who were shaping the affairs of the nation were not true to their faith. High handedness, oppression, injustice and terrorism at the state level were felt both by Muslims and non-Muslims. The Christian ruler of Constantinople sent a versified letter in the Arabic language to the Abbasi Caliph in which he said:

"O people of Baghdad, there is ruin and perdition for you. You get ready to leave because your government is weak and unstable. You return to the land of Hijaz and vacate the cities of Rome for the honourable Romans. We became dominant over you when your powerful groups committed injustice on your weaker groups and you began to indulge in all sorts of immoral activities. Your judges began to sell their verdicts as cheaply as the son of Jacob (Prophet Joseph) was sold for a few coins."

The Abbaside Caliph got his reply prepared by the famous scholar and man of literature, Qaffal Maroozi. In his reply the Abbaside Caliph frankly and candidly admitted the truth of the situation. He wrote:-

"You say that you (Christians) came to dominate us because our Judges did injustice and sold their decisions for nominal gains. We admit that this is correct. At the same time this very fact establishes the truth of our religion. We became tyrannical and, as a punishment, tyrants have came to dominate us."

The causes of the Muslims' downfall were correctly pointed out by a Christian monarch two hundred years after Sulaiman Bin Abdul Malik. The basic cause had been our deviation from the moral values taught by Islam. The same principle holds good to the entire history of the Muslim's rule. When Babar was a drunkard and a free-lancer, indulging in all kinds of lewd and frivolous activities, he could not conquer India. But when he repented from immoral activities and gave up drinking, he became successful.

Sulaiman Bin Abdul Malik who was a scholarly being and had quite a few moral virtues, was no less a despot than other caliphs of Banu Omayyah. His acts of injustice and tyranny were many and despicable. Under his orders two great generals of Islam, Qutaiba Bin Muslim and Muhammad Bin Qasim were put to death despite their memorable services to the cause of Islam. The only cause for their unjustified murder was that Sulaiman suspected that

Qutaiba and Muhammad Bin Qasim were in favour of Walid's son for the high office of Caliph in preference to Sulaiman. Even Moosa bin Nusair who had conquered Spain was not spared by Sulaiman who got his son Abdul Aziz murdered for no valid reason.

There is also no gainsaying the fact that during the autocratic rule of Banu Omayyah, some of the governors and government of the functionaries rebelled against the central government and declared their independence. This was not uncommon and unexpected. The law of nature is active and it spares no body. What we sow, we must reap.

Hazrat Umar Bin Abdul Aziz:

After Sulaiman Bin Abdul Malik, Hazrat Umar Bin Abdul Aziz became the caliph. Unlike his predecessors he followed the footsteps of the Khulfa-i-Rashideen (Hazrat Abu Bakr ؓ, Hazrat Umar ؓ, Hazrat Usman ؓ and Hazrat Ali ؓ.) He had realised that self-purification and self accountability were the basic requirements of a truely Muslim ruler. Conquest of territories was not the real aim of ruling. The real aim is that the Word of Truth should prevail throughout the world, and no satanic power should stand in its way or prevent its dissemination. On this account he sent orders to Muslima Bin Abdul Malik to give up siege of Constantinople and return home immediately.) Umar Bin Abdul Aziz ؓ concentrated his attention and efforts at moral reformation of his governors and government functionaries.[1]

He began the process of reformation from his own house. He got all his family members gathered around him and said to them:

> *"I think that half or two third of the lands occupied by the Muslim peoples is in your possession. You should return the lands to their rightful owners."*

Banu Marwan were not the type of people who could hear and act upon such a piece of moral advice. They said:

---
1 Tabri. Vol.8. P.130

"Our heads may be removed but the properties in our possession can not be restored to their rightful owners. We do not prepare to make or declare our forefathers as non-Muslims so do we prepare to make our children poor and penniless."

Hazrat Umar Bin Abdul Aziz was well determined to undo the cause of despotism and betrayal and he told the people bravely and bluntly: "By Allah! If you do not restore the usurped lands to their rightful owners, I shall debase and dishonour you." To implement his scheme for restoration of justice and fair play to all the classes of his people, he addressed the House of Banu Omayyah as under:

"The caliphs of Banu Omayyah gave us such estates and properties for which we had no genuine claim nor we deserved them on merit. Hereby I restore and return all those estates and properties to their original, rightful owners. I start the process by returning my personal and my family's properties to their rightful owners."

After the above speech, Hazrat Umar Bin Abdul Aziz returned his estates to their original owners. He kept nothing with him or his family members and even the smallest item was returned. Some elderly persons tried to persuade him to desist from such drastic and immediate action. They asked him: "What will happen to your children after you?" He replied: "Allah shall look after them. I entrust my affairs to Allah." His wife was the daughter of Abdul Malik. She had received a most precious ruby from her father. Hazrat Umar Bin Abdul Aziz asked his wife to deposit the ruby in the "Bait-ul-Maal, failing which she may sever her relations with him.

After restoring his personal and his family's estates and properties to their rightful owners, Hazrat Umar Bin Abdul Aziz wrote firm orders to the governors and government functionaries that "they must return and restore to the rightful owners all the estates and properties usurped by Banu Omayyah and should never indulge in such unlawful practice in future otherwise severe disciplinary action would be taken against them." The result of this circular was that all the estates, properties and wealth obtained under duress and by oppression or high handedness was restored to the genuine owners.[1] The government functionaries had imposed all sorts of unlawful taxes, custom duties and dues to extract moneys from the public who were crawling helplessly under heavy taxes. Hazrat Umar Bin Abdul Aziz passed immediate orders for stopping such taxation. In this connection he wrote the following letter to Abdul Hamid, governor of Koofa:

> *"The people of Koofa have to bear unbearable difficulties and tribulations due to the oppressive attitude of unjust and heartless functionaries of the government. The basis of the religion of Islam is justice, fairplay and equity. Do not extort revenue from barren lands at the rate of arable lands and do not get the barren taxes from the arable lands. Get full assessment of the value of the barren land before charging any tax on it. You should help to make the barren lands cultivable and taxes may be imposed only after there have become fertile and fit to yield produce."*

The revenue may be realised gently and leniently, keeping in mind the convenience of the tillers of the soil. You should not realise any tax from the mint-masters. No gifts may be accepted on the New Year Day. Price for the Holy Quran, House Tax and monetary fee for marriage sermon must not be taken. It may also be widely publicised that whosoever embraces Islam, he will not be liable to any tax on account of his previous state of being a non-Muslim."[2]

He was not satisfied merely by the issuance of his circular orders. If any governor or government officer was suspected of disobedience of his orders or of maltreatment of the people, he was

---

1. Tabqat-e-Ibn-e-Saad, Vol.5, P.252
2. Tabri, Vol.8, P.139

taken to task and effective punishment was meted out to him. Yazid Bin Malik was a famous aristocrat of Arabia. He could not clear his position regarding realisation of taxes and revenues. He was arrested and put in prison wherefrom he was not released despite many intercessions and recommendations.[1]

The reformatory measures taken by Hazrat Umar Bin Abdul Aziz ؓ are unique in Islamic history as well as in the history of mankind. He had correctly diagnosed the malady of the Muslim Ummah and that was autocratic rule in which there was no idea of accountability of the ruling class as well as the corrupt bureaucracy. He paid almost no attention to conquest of new lands. He considered moral and spiritual reformation of rulers and the ruled as of paramount importance.

The caliphs of Banu Omayyah did not follow the conduct of the first four caliphs of the Holy Prophet ﷺ for which they put forward the excuse that, if the rulers had deviated from the straightforward path of Islam, even the people who were under their rule were also not sincerely following the teachings of Islam. Abdul Malik bin Marwan had once expressed this view openly but Hazrat Umar Bin Abdul Aziz ؓ held quite an opposite view. He used to say:

> "The parable of a king is like a market place. In the market place things displayed for sale are precisely those which are in demand. If the king or the ruler is himself good and virtuous, the people under his care will also be good and virtuous. If he is not good, his people also cannot be good."

Once Imam Auzai ؓ had, in his course of his counsel to the Abbasi Caliph Mansoor, said: "The Rulers are of four kinds. One is such that he controls his own self and enjoins on his governors and functionaries to control their evil self. Such a kind is indeed a

---

1. Ibn-al-Aseer Al-Jazri, Vol.5, P.19

warrior in the way of Allah. His reward for one prayer will be equal to 70,000 prayers of ordinary people. The blessings of God will always attend on him. The second type of Ruler is such that he himself takes away the public moneys without any right and also allows his underlings to snatch wealth unlawfully from the common people. Such a Ruler is the worst type of human being. He will be severely punished for his own high handedness as well as the high handedness of his underlings and government officials. The third kind of Ruler is such who himself fears God and avoids corruption at personal level. But he fails to check his officials from indulging in corruption. Such a king is most unfortunate and un-blessed because he is selling his Hereafter for the worldly gains of others. The fourth type of Ruler is such that he himself is careless in his matters of human rights but he enjoins to his officials not to indulge in corruption. This is bad wisdom.

According to the classification of Rulers made by Imam Auzai ؓ Hazrat Umar Bin Abdul Aziz doubtlessly belonged to the first category of rulers. He himself lived a life of piety and righteousness and forced his governors and government officials to live according to the Laws of Shariat. That is precisely the reason why the period of his Caliphate is considered to be Khilafat-e-Rashida on the pattern of the Holy Prophet's ﷺ rule and is called as such. His character and conduct, his love for justice and fairplay and his active introduction of Islamic rules and equity in all circumstances and on all occasions of his state dealings with the public made him a beloved Ruler. All and sundry, his friends and opponents were all unanimous in calling him a Just and God-fearing Ruler. Historian Masoodi said that: when the Qaiser of Rome learnt about the death of Hazrat Umar Bin Abdul Aziz ؓ, he was greatly distressed and expressed his deep grief. He freely and lovingly mentioned his virtues and perfections and wept for him. So much so that he said: "If some body had the spiritual power to raise the dead to life after Hazrat Eisa ؑ, he guessed that only Umar Bin Abdul Aziz could do it." Then he (the Qaiser) said: "I do not like a monk who renounces the world and takes to prayerful life in solitude in a church. I rather looked with wonder at that monk (Umar Bin Abdul

Aziz) who had the world under his feet, yet he lived like a monk and an ascetic."[1]

Hazrat Umar Bin Abdul Aziz wished that the system of government for the Muslim Ummah may be purged of all dirt and defects and may be reintroduced in its original purity and effectiveness. Unfortunately his period of rule was too short to allow the fulfilment of his high wishes.

Yazid Bin Abdul Malik:

Yazid Bin Abdul Malik succeeded Hazrat Umar but he could not maintain the spirit and tempo of the rule of Hazrat Umar Bin Abdul Aziz. After some time, he removed all the governors and officials who were appointed by Hazrat Umar bin Abdul Aziz ؓ and appointed men of his own liking and choice. He bluntly said:

> "The policies of Umar Bin Abcul Aziz are not workable. His policies have reduced the revenue of the state. As such you should follow the old practice and do not care for the property or poverty of the masses."

Yazid Bin Abdul Malik was an extremely corrupt and easy-going ruler who indulged in free sexual intercourse. Two of his beloved slave girls – Salamah and Habenah were always on his nerves. So much so that, when Habena died in an accident, Yazid kept her dead body in his palace for three days and kept kissing and caressing her dead body. His grief over her death was so great that he cried and wept at times.[2] Some historians have opined that the death of Yazid himself was largely due to the death of his beloved. Hazrat Umar Bin Abdul Aziz had brought about reformation in many social fields and people had heaved a sigh of relief and were happy to receive justice and fairplay. Unfortunately the advent of a

---

1. Murrawaj-uz-Zahb, Vol.7, P.120-121
2. Ibn-e-Aseer, Vol.5, P.45

corrupt-minded and debauch ruler soon after Hazrat Umer Bin Abdul Aziz upset the positive measures which were liked by people. The poison of corruption and moral degeneration began to return with the coming of Yazid Bin Abdul Malik.

Hisham Bin Abdul Malik:

After ruling in his corrupt way, Yazid Bin Abdul Malik died after four years and one month and, according to his will, his brother Hisham came to the throne. Hisham was a wise, sensible and statesman-like ruler. His status was as good as that of Amir Mo'awiya and Abdul Malik Bin Marwan. His financial morality was great and he was extremely careful in day-to-day expenses. His care and cautious attitude some times earned him the label of being miserly. His attitude regarding governors and government officials was almost at par with the attitude of Hazrat Umar bin Abdul Aziz

The historians have opined that the system of taxation and revenue was ideal during the period of Hisham Bin Abdul Malik and it was better than during the regime of any of his predecessors. The administrative genius of Hisham was praiseworthy. He curbed with an iron hand any rebellions which took place in different parts of his large empire. The Khawarij raised their head again and were effectively dealt with. In Sind conquered by Muhammad Bin Qasim, there was local trouble by powerful miscreants which was effectively curbed by Junaid, a well trusted general of Khalifa Hisham Bin Abdul Malik.

Apart from quelling the rebellions, Hisham also had some conquests in Asia Minor. In Spain there were some administrative troubles which were rectified by Hisham and normal circumstances returned. The Berber tribes of North Africa again created trouble and they were effectively dealt with by Hisham who successfully restored peace in the area. Several attacks were also made on the French territory. Hisham by his nature was not a happy go lucky person and he liked and acted upon the teachings of Islam. He was also interested in providing goal and effective chances for the teachings of Islam and for preaching and dissemination of Islamic values. He respected and encouraged the activities of the scholars of Islam.

Hisham had no mental reservation regarding the teachings of Islam. If any one tried to propagate distorted version of Islam, he was severely punished. The mischief of the Holy Quran being called a "Creation" was first of all raised during the reign of Hisham who got the sponsor of this mischief (Ja'd Bin Darham) arrested and sent him to Khalid Bin Abdullah Al-Qasir for being put to death. Khalid, the governor of Iraq, was lukewarm in obeying the orders of the Caliph. Hisham once again wrote to Khalid emphatically that Ja'd must be put to death. This time he obeyed and on the day of Eid-ul-Azha which was a day of rejoicing, Khalid beheaded Ja'd immediately after Eid Prayers.[1]

Similarly Ghilan Bin Yunes was another religious miscreant who propagated the tenets of "Qadria" sect and Hazrat Umar Bin Abdul Aziz called him to repent which he did. During the period of Hisham he again indulged in mischief and Hisham got his hands and feet chopped off and made him ineffective.

Hisham may well be considered as the last caliph of Banu Omayyah dynasty. He well guarded the political stability of the centre of Islam. His period of ruling was fifteen years. After him till Marwan, the second, all the caliphs who came to rule, were either incapable or, if they were good and God-fearing, they lacked political wisdom and administrative genius and were not equal to the task in facing the repeated rebellions and dissension in the large empire

Caliphs of Banu Omayyah after Hisham Bin Abdul Malik

Walid:

After Hisham, Yazid Bin Abdul Malik's son "Walid" ascended the throne. He was a thoroughly spoiled man who had no

---
1. Ibn-e-Aseer, Vol.5, P.97

good in him. His only concern was to eat, drink and be merry. He was also a cruel and heartless tyrant. Hisham knew him so well and tried his best to put some one else on the throne. But circumstances did not permit him. Walid took a revenge from Hisham on account of this opposition. He got many an innocent men killed for his enmity for Hisham and also maltreated the sons and other close relatives of Hisham. The difference between the tribes of "Muzir" and "Nizaar" were again revived and asserted dangerous trends. Walid was killed as a result of these differences.

Yazid Bin Walid:

After a year of the death of Walid, his son Yazid came upon the throne. Personally he was a religious type and was fond of worship. But he lacked statesmanship. On this ground he was known as "Yazid-un-Naqis" i.e., imperfect Yazid. Soon after his coming into power, a pandora's box opened. There was opposition and rebellion all around. The "Muzarri" tribes of Arabia were his strong opponents. He created trouble. In "Hims" and "Palestine" also, rebellious elements became active. Half-hearted measures were taken to cope with the trouble spots but no effective action could be taken to curb the rebellions completely. During the regime of Marwan, the second, these troubles which were minor at first, assumed big volume and appeared like a volcanic, which swept away the splendors and glory of the Omayyah.

The Historian Tabri has stated that Marwan, the second, was an elderly person and was also experienced in statecraft. He had qualities of wisdom and foresight. Unfortunately he got the Empire at rather a very late stage when here was unrest and rebellion almost everywhere in the Empire. In the Omayyah own family serious differences and enmities cropped up. In Syria many political parties were at loggers heads. In Khorasan the Abbasis had built up their centre of political activity. The Khawarij once again raised their head and began to muster strength in Yemen. They saw a good opportunity for the propagation of their views and left Yemen for Makkah and Madina. Marwan sent a big army to counter these activities. The army went deep into Yemen and Hijaz and killed thousands of these men to restore peace.

The hero and the Commander-in-Charge of the Abbaside Movement was Abu Muslim Khorasani. He found that the Banu Omayyah's large force was engaged in bloody warfare against the "Khawarij". It was a good opportunity to strike at the Omayyah. Abu Muslim organized an army of one hundred thousand and successfully ran over Khorasan. Having conquered Khorasan, he handed over the administration of the conquered areas to his trusted men and sent a large and well-equipped army to conquer Iraq-e-Ajam at the head of 'Qahtaba', a second general and commander. The control of the Omayyah had diminished and was almost finished on the centre of the Empire. As soon as, Khorasan's forces captured 'Raiy', 'Isphahan', 'Nehawand' and other central points without much resistance. Between 'Mausil' and 'Arhal', Marwan himself had camped on the bank of 'Zaab-e-Aala' with a very heavy force. Both the Abbaside armies and the Omayyah armies fought a pitched battle in which Marwan received a crushing defeat and ran towards Syria where he hoped to receive help and reinforcement. The people of Syria belied his hopes and gave him no support. The reaction of his defeat was that his government's functionaries and helpers were mercilessly killed, wherever they were found.

Seeing all the big changes, the people of Egypt and Hims themselves killed their governors who were appointed by the Omayyah Caliph. The people of Madina did not kill their governor but turned him out of the city. The land of God, despite its extensive expanse, was squeezed for the Banu Omayyah. The Nizari tribes who were well trusted by the Banu Omayyah, also turned out against them. Disappointed and discomfited, Marwan reached Egypt via Damascus and Palestine. The Abbaside army chased him closely. Here Marwan again fought in desperation. This encounter was like a wounded fowl trying to regain his wings to fly. But he failed and was killed on the battlefield. He being the last ruler of Omayyah, their rule came to end in 132 A.H.

A cursory glance at the history of the Omayyah reveals that causes for the rise of this dynasty kept up despite dwindling of the real spirit of Islam. The Omayyah period of rule was an anti-thesis of the period of the Companions of the Holy Prophet ﷺ both in ideology and action. Short of their comparison with the Muslims of the golden era of Islam, the Omayyah were a great nation when compared with the other nations of the times. The spirit of Islam had not died in that period although it was feeble and inactive. They did fight for worldly gains and prosperity. But they were not altogether oblivious in carrying the message of Islam to other peoples of the world. But for the collective unity of the Omayyah, they could not have grasped astounding success in their conquests in China, India, Africa and Spain.

Their collective unity was not due to tribal or family coherence. It was entirely due to the uniting force of Islam which had knit together the Muslims of Africa and China into one healthy texture.

The greatest characteristic of the Banu Omayyah caliphs was that they well guarded and kept alive the pure Arab civilization in their epoch of the history. People of many civilizations like the Persians, Turks, Tartars, Indians, and Chinese were converted to Islam and were living side by side with the Arabs. But it was the Arab civilization of the Rulers which influenced the civilizations of the converted communities. The Arabs were not influenced by them. That was the cause of the spread of the social system of Islam along with the Muslim conquests. Whereever the Muslims went as conquerors, mosques sprung up in large numbers and the atmosphere resounded with the noise of Truth. People of the conquered territories were anointed with the colour of Islamic civilization and culture. Arabic language which is the language of the Holy Quran, got a free hand to develop. In all the conquered lands under the Banu Omayyah, scholars and institutions were largely set up for the teaching of the Holy Quran and the Traditions of the Holy Prophet of Islam ﷺ.

PERIOD OF THE RULE OF BANU ABBAS

The crushing military force of the Khorasani shattered the mansion of the Banu Omayyah's government into pieces. On this dilapidated building the high palace of the Khilafat of Banu Abbas was erected. The splendour and glory of the Abbasides high mansion had, perforce, to be given the blood of the Banu Omayyah in its foundation.

Harrowing Tales of Tyranny:

On the bank of the Zaab canal, thousands of Omayyah and Khorasani warriors were killed. In Iraq, Khorasan and the other places of warfare, countless men were slain and human blood was profusely spilt. Marwan (the last Caliph of Omayyah) was slain at 'Boseerah' in Egypt. Before his murder, the first caliph of Banu Abbas, Abul Abbas Saffah, had taken Bai'at (pledge) for his caliphate in Koofa in the month of Rabi-ul-Awwal, 132 A.H. yet the spirit of revenge of the Abbasides was not quenched and countless dignitories of Banu Omayyah were put to death with no apparent fault. Dawood Bin Ali, an uncle of Saffah (the first Abbaside Caliph), killed every one who had sympathy for the defeated Omayyah in Makkah and Madina. According to Ibn-e-Aseer Al-Jazi (historian), Suleman Bin Ali (Abbaside's governor of Basrah) got all the well-dressed Omayyahs of Basrah put to sword. After death, their dead bodies were desecrated by dragging them (with strings in their feet) in the high way of Basra where the corpses of the nobles of Omayyahs became the food of dogs.

Abdullah Bin Ali was so vindictive that he was not satisfied with the massacre of living Omayyahs. He got the dead bodies of the prominent caliphs like Amir Mo'awiya ؓ, Abdul Malik Bin Marwan, and Hisham Bin Abdul Malik disinterred from the graves. The dead body of Hisham was complete except his nose. He got these dead bodies beaten with whips. Ibn-e-Asir has mentioned events of the brazen-faced tyranny of Banu Abbas perpetrated on the Banu Omayyahs which it appears only shameless to mention and which are, by and large a slur on the face of decency. The Abbasides had lost their mental equilibrium in their zeal of revenge. An event quoted below would explain it. Once Sulaiman Bin Hisham Bin Abdul Malik was sitting with Saffah who was respectfully talking to him. Suddenly a poet, Sadeef by name appeared before Saffah and read out the following verses:

"O Saffah ! These people (Banu Omayyahs) whom you are seeing in front of you, should not beguile you. There are hiding ills in their ribs and their hearts are not pure. You learn to use your sword and whip till not a single person of the Omayyah is left on the face of the Earth."

After hearing the above verses, Saffah silently went into his palace. After that Sulaiman was caught and slain. Besides the Banu Omayyah, people who were suspected of supporting the progeny of Ali ☬, they were also similarly maltreated. That is how the Era of the Abbaside caliphate which is called the golden period of Islamic history, started. Unfortunately our historians do not feel ashamed of the untold acts of tyranny and oppression perpetrated by the Banu Abbas.

Contrast in Speech and Action of Saffah:

At the time of pledge for Khilafat, Abul Abbas Saffah had delivered a speech in the Jamia Mosque of Koofa in which he had said very proudly:

> "Allah has strengthened His religion through us and we have been made its protectors and fort. We are defending the faith and fighting for it. Allah has made us steadfast in piety and purification. He has favoured us with Kinship of the Holy Prophet ﷺ and thus made us the most deserving family for Khilafat."

There he recited some of the verses from the Holy Quran in which mention has been made of the rights of Kinship. Thereafter Saffah reviled and condemned Banu Omayyahs and the people of Syria. In sugar quoted language he tried to prove that the Banu

Omayyahs were the usurpers and they never deserved the offices of Khilafat.

It is indeed strange and paradoxical that the people of Koofa who had betrayed and martyred Hazrat Imam Hussain, Saffah addressed them as amicable friends. He said:

> "O people of Koofa! I swear that you are the centre of our love and affection. You are the people whom vicissitudes and oppressions could not deviate from the right path. You are the most honoured and blessed people in my estimate. From today I am adding 100 Dirhams in the stipend of each one of you." At the end of his speech, he said in self-praise: "I am a great spiller of blood and can make any bloodshed lawful for me. I am also a hard avenger."

At that time Saffah was in fever and could not prolong his speech. After him, his uncle Dawood Bin Ali came to the pulpit. He delivered a very long speech in which he pointed out time and again that Khilafat was their ancestral right which they had inherited from the Holy Prophet ﷺ. God be thanked that the usurpers of our right have been ruined and our right of Khilafat has been restored to us. He was so daring and brazen-faced that he bluntly said: "Listen carefully, O people, after the Holy Prophet of Islam ﷺ no body was justified in sitting on the seat of Khilafat except Hazrat Ali ؓ and Amir-ul-Momineen Abdullah Bin Muhammad, i.e., Abul Abbas Saffah."

The contrast in words and deeds is thought provoking. The above quoted speeches of Saffah and Dawood may be studied against their deeds. There can be no worse example of cleverness, churning, falsehood and lame excuses than the one which Saffah and Dawood had created on the minds. They claimed to be the foremost successors of the Holy Prophet ﷺ. So much so that they bypassed the mention of Hazrat Abu Bakr ؓ, Hazrat Umar ؓ and Hazrat Usman ؓ who were the greatest heroes of Islam and the true caliphs of the Holy Prophet ﷺ.

It is a matter of concern and sorrow for the Muslims to find in history that only 125 years after the sad demise of the Holy Prophet ﷺ, the then living generation of Muslims established a government which was based on acute spirit of vengeance, rancour and hatred for the Arabs, and selfishness par excellence. Every act forbidden and disapproved by Islam was done to build up and stabilise that government. There is an Arabic proverb that Banu Omayyahs were 'the First Diggers of buried bodies' and the Banu Abbas were the 'Second Diggers of burried bodies'. Perhaps the first group of the digger of graves were less cursed.

People who are blessed in nature they always take lessons and reform themselves from past experiences. But Banu Abbas took no lesson from events of history. The fall of Banu Omayyah was largely due to their exceeding repression and tyranny and also due to their nomination of successors within the life period of the working caliph. The Banu Abbas also committed the same blunders and they never cared to change their attitude and conduct.

Fatal Effects of Nominating Successors:

The Banu Abbas made it their practice to nominate their sons or nephews or both kins as their successors to the caliphate till the period of Mutawakkil Billah. The psychological effect of this ill-conceived practice was that the ruling family became divided among themselves and enimical action against one another became order of the day. Cases of poisoning, quarrels and skirmishes among members of the ruling families spoiled the peaceful atmosphere of the people and the subjects were largely upset to see the rulers fighting among themselves. There were instances where the ruling father and his own sons became at daggers drawn due to the wrong practice of nomination to the caliphate.

The author of "Shazraat-uz-Zahb" stated about Mutawakkil Billah that "he revived the practices of the Holy Prophet ﷺ and killed altercations." Now this reviver of the Sunnah created troubles for himself by nominating his three sons, Muntasir, Mo'taz, and Mo'ayyid as his successors to the caliphate. As an after thought he decided to limit his nomination to Mo'taz because he loved Sabihah, (mother of Mo'taz) most dearly. He tried to prevail upon Muntasir to return and forego his nomination in favour of Mo'taz. This proposal infuriated Muntasir so much that he seemed prepared even to kill his own father. At long last Mutawakkil Billah was killed by his son along with his minister Fateh Bin Khaqan. After assasinating his father, Muntasir pressed his two brothers to surrender their nomination in his favour which both the princes had to obey for fear of their lives.

Transfer of Authority to Turkish Slaves:

After the murder of Mutawakkil, the de-facto authority of Khilafat came into the hands of Turkish slaves who gave the throne of Khilafat to an Abbasi of their choice and, when displeased, snatched the throne at their sweet will. Not only that; they went to the extent of killing the caliphs after tormenting them in various ways. Most of the Banu Abbas caliphs after Mutawakkil were the victims of the Turkish slaves. Even Mutawakkil was killed by these slaves at the instance of his son Muntasir.

Likewise, these Turkish slaves kept the Caliph Musta-een Billah as a captive for some days and then beheaded him in 252 A.H. In 255 A.H., they killed the Caliph Mu'taz Billah by drowning him in boiling water. In 256 A.H., they killed Moh'tadi after mercilessly beating and slapping him. In 296 A.H., they strangulated Caliph Ibn-ul-Mo'taz to death. They killed Muqtadir Billah in a most merciless and wild manner. First of all they chopped off his head; then they put his head on a spear for demonstration and made his body stark naked. Caliph Qahir Billah was mercilessly killed by these slaves by choking his eyes with a red-hot piece of rod. Caliph Mustakfi Billah was killed in 324 A.H. by first dragging him with a string tied to his feet and then choking his eyes with a red hot piece of iron rod. Muttaqi Billah was also treated with similar ruthlessness. Caliph Mustarshid Billah was attacked suddenly by seventeen miscreants who attacked him with sharp knives and cut his body into pieces. His nose and ears were cut off and burnt in fire. Rashid Billah was kept in prisons along with his son for many days till they died. The end of the last Abbaside Caliph, Mus'ta'sim Billah was pathetic. With the conspiracy of his minister, Ibn-e-Alqami, the Tartars arrested the Caliph, put him in a bag and then trampled him to death. With the death of Mus'ta'sim Billah caliphate of Banu Abbas came to a tragic end.

Two Phases of the Abbaside Caliphate:

Historically the period of the Banu Abbasides caliphate can be divided into two dintinct phases. The first phase which is known in history as the golden era began in 132 A.H. and ended with the caliphate of Mo'tasim Billah in 227 A.H. The second phase began after the caliphate of Mo'tasim and ended with murder of Mus'ta'sim Billah in Baghdad in 656 A.H.

Period of Decline and Deterioration:

The last phase of the caliphate of the Abbasides was an era of decline and deterioration. The central authority of the caliphs had practically come to end. The interference in governmental business by slaves, eunuchs and women had increased beyond all proportions. Inside the Empire, there was trouble and turmoil. In various provinces there was complete anarchy and local rule. During the caliphate of Raazi Billah, from 322 A.H. to 329 A.H. the caliphate was only in name. There was open self rule and local government in various provinces. In Basra Ibn-e-Ro'iq established his stable government and so did Breedi in Khuzistan, Imad-ud-Daula Bin Bawaih in Persia, Abn Ali Bin Ilyas in Kirman, Ruk-nud-Daulah Bin Bawaih in Isphahan and Jabal, Banu Hamdan in Mausil, Diar-e-Bakr and Muzir, Akhyad in Egypt and Syria, Qaim Aalvi in Africa and Maghrib, Abdul Rehman Bin Mohammad Al-Amwi in Spain, Nasr Bin Ahmed Bin Saman in Khorasan and Ma-wra-un-Nehr, Dailam in Tabrit and Jurjan, Abu Tahir Al-Qareeti in Bahrain and Yaman – set up their own governments in defiance of the Central Khilafat. The real picture was that authority of Khilafat was confined to Baghdad and its suburbs. Even in Baghdad, the caliph was not entirely free to act according to his own free will. The independent governments had to maintain some sort of relation with the Court of

Khalifa for their own prestige because, without obtaining a certificate of authority from the caliph, no body could rule in his area of jurisdiction. The reality of the situation was that the caliph feared those independent rulers more than they feared the caliph. Approval of the caliph was very easy to obtain for any administration through the good offices of slaves or maidens.

The interference of non-Arab slaves in administration had started from the period of Caliph Mansoor. If the matter was kept limited to the appointment of slaves to governmental posts or they had been properly trained on purely Islamic lines, the empire would not have been ruined through their interference. It would have gained stability through their acts of service. Like the Abbaside caliphs, Sultan Alaud-Din Khilji and Feroze Shah had fifty thousand slaves who were running both civil and military departments. However, these slaves were properly educated and trained, and they became a source of strength and stability for the empire rather than a cause of weakness and ruin.

Shams Siraj Affif said:

"Feroze Shah took services from his slaves in accordance with their aptitudes and capacities. Persons who were fit for political duties, they were given jobs of administrative nature. Persons who were fit for educational and knowledgeable duties, they were given admission in schools and colleges and were taught different arts and Islamic Sciences. Some of these were sent to Makkah Moazzama so that they exclusively dedicated themselves to seclusion and prayers." [1]

The policy of the Abbaside Caliphs was opposite to the policy of Feroze Shah. They did not care for any training or education of their slaves nor did they make any efforts to keep a watch on their activities because of their ill-placed and extravagant

---

1. Tareekh-e-Feerozshahi, P.268, 273

trust in their slaves. The result of this miscalculated policy was that the non-Arab slaves came to occupy most important positions of the government. They had no sufficient knowledge of Islam and their inner selves were still used to habits and behaviour of pagan cults. The second devastating branch of this erroneous policy was in the royal palaces and mansions, slave girls of every non-Arab region and country were let in and they began to rule the hearts and spirits of the princes of the Abbasides. With the passage of time the indoor and out-door evil influences went on increasing till they became formidable.

The pinnacle of the rising slave influence was that, in the second phase of the Abbasides rule, their caliphate was only nominal and the de-facto ruling authority vested in the slaves. The caliphate was left only in name and the epithets of the caliphs were used as symbols of royal pomp and glory without de-facto influence.

Corruption at Ministerial Level:

Caliphate was left in name. The office of a Minister also became a commercial commodity. High amounts of bribery were offered to obtain an office of Minister. The appointment orders for a Ministerial post were issued from the Central Secretariat of Khilafat for a candidate who offered the maximum amount of gratification. Merit was not the criterion. Historian Ibn-e-Tiq-Taqa stated that, in the 4th century A.H. Ibn-e-Maqlah obtained the office of a Minister after payment of 5,00,000 Dinars (gold coin) to Raazi Billah, the then Abbaside Caliph.[1] Similarly Ibn-e-Jubair purchased the office of Minister from Caliph Qa'im Bi-Amr-illah for an amount of 30,000 Dinars.

A very shameful instance of high corruption has been quoted in the "Kitabul Fakhri" at page 197 wherein it is stated that, for vacant post of Care Taker of Public Affairs, Minister Khaqani (Working under the Caliph Muqtadir Billah) appointed ninteen

---

1. Kitabul Fakhri. P.207

candidates after taking illegal gratification from each one of them. They all left for Koofa where the post existed. Perchance all of them got together on a place on the way to Koofa. They were astonished at the treatment they had met at the hands of Khaqani. However, after discussion, they decided that the candidate, who received the letter of appointment last of all, should join the post. All the rest returned to Baghdad where the Minister gave them alternate jobs.[1] A contemporary poet wrote the following verses in condemnation of Minister Khaqani:

> "He is such a Minister who is never tired of writing letters of appointment. He appoints a man and, after an hour, terminates his service. Persons who are quick in giving him illegal gratification, they become his close associates. But the persons who try to get jobs by recommendation, they are not allowed to approach him. When persons willing to bribe him come to his audience, the richest among them is successful in getting an appointment from Minister Khaqani."

The above-quoted events are sufficient to prove that the Abbaside Caliphate was tottering and it could hardly be called even a Muslim state

Division of Khilafat into Pieces:

The Islamic Caliphate had original conception of a Central Executive body for the entire world of Islam. Its division into pieces had started as early as the 3rd century A.H. In the North-West Africa the Fatimides had declared their own Khilafat and Imamate. They were also looking towards Egypt for annexation. On the other hand, Abdul Rehman Nasir, the Amir of Andalusia (Spain) declared his caliphate in 300 A.H. when he ascended the throne. Thus the institution of caliphate had been divided into three parts. During the

---

[1] Kitabul Fakhri, P.214

period 322 A.H. to 329 A.H. when Raazi Billah was the caliph, countries and provinces contiguous with Baghdad began to declare independence and establish their own autonomous governments. Ali Bin Bawaih had held possession of Persia. On Ray, Asphahan and Jabal, his brother Hassan Bin Bawaih held the sway. Banu Hamdan held the reins of government over Mausil, Bakr, Rabiah and Muzair. Egypt and Syria were held by Mohammad Bin Tafij. Eventually Egypt and Syria came under the rule of Banu Fatimah. Khorasan and the Eastern areas were under Nasr Bin Ahmed As-samaani. The central caliphate had been squeezed to the the city of Baghdad and its precincts. Even in Baghdad the authority of the Abbaside Caliph was only in name. The real and de-facto authority vested in Minister Ibn-e-Raa'iq who was supposed to be under Caliph Raazi Billah. He was originally the governor of the city of Wasit. Later, he was made Commander-in-Chief of the Army and got the epithet of Amir-ul-Umaraa. It is said that at a later stage, the caliph had directed that the Friday Khutba may be read out in the name Ibn-e-Raa'iq which was admission of his de-facto authority. [1]

Severe Repression of Hanbalites:

Due to evil conduct and frivolous life of the caliphs, their Ministers and functionaries and the princes of the royal families and aristocrats there were widespread sins and moral crimes in Baghdad. The careful and indifferent government had no intention to improve the atmosphere of moral corruption and increasing crimes. The conscientious scholars of Islam and the good-natured reformers came out to bring about moral reform and condemn the sinful lives of the wayward public. The forces of evil were so arrogant and hot-headed that they stood in the way of moral reformers. The followers and pupils of Imam Ahmed Bin Hanbal took up seriously the mission of preaching and prohibition. They adopted solid and practical ways to undo evil. They would spill the containers of wine or "Nabeez" wherever they found it. Similarly they would stop by force any singing girls found entertaining the people in public places. This was intolerable for the spoiled aristocracy and they

---

1. Encyclopaedia, Fareed Waijdi, Vol.11, P.123

could bear no hindrance in their luxurious ways and habits. The police offices of Baghdad promulgated orders that no two Hanbalites should get together anywhere in Baghdad. The Caliph, Raazi Billah, wrote a threatening proclamation in which he addressed the Hanbalites thus: "If you people do not give up your condemnable tenets and crooked conduct, I shall deal with you effectively and will not be reluctant to beat you, to slender you openly and even to kill you. The swords will be in your necks and fire in your houses and places of residence."

End of Abbaside Caliphate of Baghdad:

During the caliphate of Raazi Billah his rule was confined to Baghdad and its near suburbs. He died in 329 A.H. After his death, as many as sixteen caliphs came upon the throne. But the decay which had started in the fabric of the caliphate went on increasing. In between, if a caliph had personal goodness and virtues, he could not bring about any palpable improvement in the body-politic of the Caliphate which had become rotten. No caliph of this last, dying period, had any de-facto authority. At long last in the year 654 A.H. the so-called Caliphate came to its logical end. The last Caliph, Mo'tasim Billah was mercilessly killed by the Tartars through the conspiracy of his Minister, Alqami.

We have narrated above the conditions of the golden period of the Abbaside Caliphate. This period had nothing to offer of which the Muslims could be proud in the real sense of the word. Maulana Shibli Nomani, the famous writer of historical events of the Abbaside period and a great scholar, has said about Mamoon-ur-Rashid, the most illustrious and scholarly caliph of this dynasty, that his ideology was neither purely Islamic nor was it purely un-Islamic. His ideas about life were hotch potch, unidentified and confused.

Development of Knowledge and Arts under Abbasides and Its Effect on the Decline of Muslims:

The greatest achievement of the Abbaside period of caliphate is that the Muslims codified the various branches of Islamic Sciences and translated from other languages into Arabic a great number of books about philosophy and wisdom. They also critically studied the scholarly works of other nations and made valuable comments thereon. They analysed the subject matter of many important works and pointed out the defects and shortcomings of many authors. During the Abbaside period, the Muslims took keen interest in the dissemination of knowledge and established schools, colleges and universities as also many publication centres. The scholars were given munificent stipends to enable them to work on scholarly projects with peace and composure of mind.

Apart from scholarly works, there was also great development in industry, arts, architectures, engineering and literature including poetry. Instances have been given by historians of the popular trends for acquisition of knowledge and advancement of poetical genius. Even women and slave girls had good taste of poetry and literature. Extempore versification and anecdotes were common features of the polished society.

The development of arts and literature made the society cultured and intelligent. But the basic tenets of Islam and spirit behind them appear to have suffered due to popularisation and wide dissemination of Greek philosophy and mythology. The Muslims were mentally confused by inter-mixing of the simple Islamic ideology and the labyrinth of Greek mythology and philosophy.

Mamoon-ur-Rashid once wrote to the Christian monarch of Constantinople to send him some of the Greek books on philosophy and other sciences. The king was reluctant at first. But the Bishop of Constantinople advised him to send the books without any hesitation because their study will make the Muslims confused about their own beliefs and tenets. Having agreed with the Bishop, the king sent all the required books on Greek philosophy and Arts and Literature to Khalifa Mamoon-ur-Rashid. Time revealed that the best expectations of the Bishop of Constantinople came to be true.

The influence of the Greek philosophy and literature made the Muslim scholars confused and they began to reflect on the Islamic doctrines of faith from rational new angles and from philosophical view points as taught by the Greek writers. This mode of thinking was opposed to the original thought process of the Muslims who were basically impressed by the line of reasoning taught by the Holy Quran. They had built up firm and stable convictions on matters physical and meta-physical so that no intellectual power or influence could deviate the Muslims from the correctness of their convictions.

Quranic Principles of Education:

It is a general principle of the Holy Quran that, at first it builds up a peculiar thought process for a particular thing. Then it makes the thought a certainty by evidence and parable. The certainty assumes the shape of urge and willingness to act. Good deeds are then built up on good ideas. Such deeds are necessary for a wholesome and healthy civilisation and culture.

We may, for instance, take up the basic tenet of monotheism. The Holy Quran awakens the inner depth of a man and creates faith and firm belief in the existence of God and His unity. It avoids philosophical entanglements and simply appeals to the heart which readily responds. It is like a child who, as a child, is ready to obey his parents. But, on attaining majority, his sentiments of love and obedience assume a secondary position and his approach also becomes rational.

The nature's way is to appeal to the heart and not to intellect. That is why the Holy Quran does not tell the pagans and infidels that they have no intellect. It says:

$$لَهُمْ قُلُوْبٌ لاَّ يَفْقَهُوْنَ بِهَا$$

"They have hearts but they do not understand"

Or it says:

$$خَتَمَ اللهُ عَلَى قُلُوْبِهِمْ$$

"Allah has sealed their faculty of heart."

The Quranic approach made the Muslims of old firm in belief and ready for action as induced by the Holy Quran. They had full and complete faith in the Creator, His Attributes and His immanence and omnipotence.

Line of Reasoning Adopted by Philosophy:

With the approval of philosophical ideas of Greek in the Abbaside period of Muslim history, they had to change their thought process under the philosophical doctrines and formulae. Greeks called God as the First Cause or the Infinite Cause. They also firmly believed in the formula:

الواحد لا يصدر عنه الا الواحد

"From One only one can be derived."

Perforce they had to believe in "The Ten Intellects". With the above ideas in the mind, the Islamic concept of One God cannot be retained in its original form.

The Holy Quran says that God has the Attribute of intention and will. What He deems fit, He does without let or hindrance. Whatever He does not wish to appear, it can never appear. But the Greek philosophy looks upon God as the Foremost Perfect Cause which leaves no room for the Divine Attributes of will and intention. Whatever appears in existence, it appears automatically. Since cause and effect take place simultaneously, there is no gap of time between the two. As such, the philosophers have to believe that the First Intellect is as ancient as God Himself. This trend of thought cannot support the edifice of religious thought in Islam or even any other religion which believes in God as Creator and Deity.

Likewise the various Attributes of God became subject of speculation for the philosophies. They argued about unity or otherwise of Essence and Attributes; the reality of the Attributes. If knowledge cannot exist without the known, how can God be conceived as knower of all when nothing had come into existence. Similarly the philosophers speculated if man was the creator of his own actions or not, is man free to act or his power to act is controlled? Three possibilities have been brought out by the philosophers towards solution of the above ticklish questions which have assumed the existence of three regular sects. This sort of thinking affected the concept of punishment and reward.

The philosophical thoughts upset the original Quranic thinking of the Muslims. Another discussion started about the Holy Quran whether it was a creation of God or not. If it was not a creation, how is it that it is not ancient like God Himself. How "Wahy" or revelation takes place. What is the reality of Divine Speech? Is the beholding of God possible or not? Is the punishment in Hell lasting and eternal or for specific time?

All such questions were put to the hard test of intellect. The result of this philosophical approach to the understanding of religious beliefs was that the best brains of the Muslims became perplexed, confused and restless. The intellectual anarchy gave rise to so many schools of thought. During the period of Banu Omayyah the Muslim Ummah were yet immune against the catastrophe if intellectual anarchy and the poisoning of their basic beliefs and doctrines of faith despite their many failings in the field of action and conduct. But the fatal influence of the Greek philosophers and thinkers made the Muslims a willing prey to ideological attacks which made them lose their basic thought structure of pristine Islam. Jalal-ud-Din Suyuti, a renowned scholar of Islam, wrote a regular book in refutation of Greek philosophy and tried to prove and establish that the study of Greek philosophy and logic was unlawful due to these evil effects on the basic beliefs and tenets. Jalal-ud-Din also claimed that his contemporary scholars were totally in agreement with him. [1]

Rationalism or Dogmatic Theology:

With the inter-action of religion and philosophy a new branch of knowledge came into existence under the name of

---

1 Sharh Fiqhul Akbar, P.3

"Dogmatic Theology". This took away the authenticity of Divine "Wahy" or revelation and made the entire fabric of Islamic beliefs and doctrines subject to confirmation by the inductive logic. Faith given by Islam changed into doubt and perplexion which took away from the Muslim hearts the real fervour and spirit of Islam. The scholars of Islam declared the study of "Dogmatic Theology" as unlawful.

Imam Shafi'i declared that the persons indulging in studies of Dogmatic Theology may be punished by whips and shoes and they may be openly dishonoured to tell the people that they had given up the Holy Quran and the study of Sunnah (Traditions) and had gone astray.[1] The state patronage of the Abbaside caliphs made the situation most critical. The very foundations of Islamic belief and dogma appeared to be tottering. Imam Shafi'i compared the lovers of "Dogmatic Theology" to an idiot who is trying to measure the depths of an ocean with a metre rod.

It was fortunate for the Muslims that scholars like Imam Ghazali, Ibn-e-Rushd (Arerroes) and Imam Raazi through their scholarly efforts and the well guided rulers like Mutawakkil Billah Abbasi and Sultan Sanjar through their state efforts effectively fought against this heresy and saved the fabric of Islamic belief and dogma from incalculable harm.

The apostatic trends which developed among the Muslims were largely due to the following two factors: (i) the false and morbid system of government founded by the Banu Omayyah and (ii) the patronage and propagation of rational branches of knowledge and dogmatic theology by the Banu Abbasides.

A Doubt and Its Satisfaction:

The detailed examination of the philosophy and Dogmatic Theology or Rationalism which had obtained firm foothold during the Abbaside Caliphate is likely to arouse in thinking minds an

---

1   Sharh Fiqhul Akbar, P.3

erroneous doubt that Islam discourages the advancement of knowledge and any secular advancement. Nothing is against the spirit of Islam if it is within the framework of Islamic dogma and ideology. If the Islamic spirit and intuition is active and alive, no branch of knowledge can harm a Muslim student. The philosophical schools which spread apostasy and doubts among the Muslims, the self-same atmosphere also gave birth to scholars like Imam Ghazzali, Imam Raazi, Ibn-e-Rushd and Ibn-e-Taimiyyah. They harnessed philosophy into the service of Islam and never accepted philosophy as the criterion for the religious dogmas and ideology.

Most of the translation work was done by non-Muslims and the Iranian Muslims (whose conviction of Islam was not yet mature) to convert the Greek works of philosophy, art and literature into Arabic language. The translators were over-awed by the grandeur of Greek knowledge with the result that Greek philosophy, art and literature came to occupy a position of authenticity above the basic Islamic sources of religious knowledge -- the Holy Quran and the Sunnah (Traditions of the Holy Prophet ﷺ.)

Another basic point needs to be kept in mind. The secular branches of knowledge are of two kinds. The one branch deals with the created things in the universe, their properties, their usefulness and harmfulness and the methods of their proper use.

The second branch of secular knowledge is intended to discuss the metaphysical realities of life. Islam does not forbid the acquisition of such knowledge. But it does demand and expect that a true Muslim will keep the rationalistic trends subservient to the Islamic dogma and ideology. A Muslim student should be so thoroughly versed in the basic knowledge of Quran and Sunnah that no secular knowledge can change his conviction about the truth of Islamic ideology. Rather he may be able to refute the basic dogma and ideology of Islam and to convince the opposing scholars of thought of the flimziness of their conviction. Any secular knowledge which can be useful even for the worldly life may be acquired by Muslim students.

CRUSADES AGAINST ISLAM

The rise of Islam has always been pinching the hearts of the European powers who have left no stone un-turned in disintegrating the political power of the Muslims. During the first phase of the Banu Abbas Caliphate, the Romans attacked the Muslim territories repeatedly but were always repulsed.

In the 5th century A.H. the fall and increasing weakness of the Abbaside Caliphate, and the division of the Muslim empire into pieces encouraged the European states to make inroads into the Muslim territories and to conquer as many lands as possible. In 478 A.H. the Spanish Christians conquered the Muslim town of Tolado and the adjoining towns. In 484 A.H. they turned towards the Sicily island and took it from the Muslims. In 491 A.H. they mustered courage to attack Syria which was a stronghold of the Muslims.[1] They conquered Antakia.

One political reason for this unexpected attack has been given by Ibn-e-Asad that Alwi forces in Egypt did not like the rising power of Saljuqis whom they feared would attack Egypt. They therefore, in self-defence asked the European forces to attack Syria.

After the fall of Antakia, the Muslim forces gathered together under the leadership of Qawam-ud-Daula Karbuqa and camped at Marj-e-Wabiq to meet the Christian forces. The Muslim army included Arab and Turkish soldiers. They attacked Antakia and were about to conquer it. But the Christian strategy got the upper hand and Muslim forces were defeated.

The Victorious Christian forces turned towards Ma'raj-un-Noman where the local population fought the enemy very bravely but were defeated. The Victorious Christian forces entered the Muslim town and the massacre of the local Muslims continued for three days. Historian Ibn-e-Aseer Jazri states that in this massacre

---

[1] Ibn-e-Aseer Aljazri, Vol.10, P.94

more than one hundred thousand Muslims were killed and countless men and women were arrested.[1]

After repeated successes, the crusades made up their mind to conquer Bait-ul-Muqaddas (Jerusalem). They laid seige of the town in 492 A.H. which continued for 40 days till the Christian forces entered Jerusalem on 27th of Sha'ban. As usual they began to kill the Muslims who had taken refuge in the Bait-ul-Muqaddas (which was a sencuary). In this massacre in the House of 70,000 Muslims schools and ascetics were assassinated.[2] All golden lamps and other costly decorations of the Muslims were looted by the ruthless Christian force. The looty from other parts of the town was beyond calculation. The Christians set up three states Antakia, Roha and Bait-ul-Muqaddas.

The same year the Christians turned towards Egypt where the commander of the Muslims armies Afzal began to make preparations for defence on a large scale. But the Christians launched a sudden attack, which resulted in a defeat for the Muslims and a great loss of life. This attack was followed by skirmishes but the greatest attack made by the Christians was in 542 A.H. Sultan Noor-ud-Din Zangi took the challenge of this crusade and defeated them in the battle in 542 A.H. seizing Roha that was s strong hold of the crusade.

The defeat in the hands of Sultan Noor-ud-Din Zangi upset the crusaders who approached the Pope of Rome to induce the European States to help them. The Pope made an appeal to all the Christian states of Europe to come forward for the defence of the Christian faith and their sacred Churches. Armies of Italy, France, Germany, Austria and England gathered to reinforce the crusading Army. King Louis VII and Konrad, the king of Germany accompanied the re-inforcements of crusaders. The entire European forces came to the help of crusades except Portugal and Spain. The attack of the united crusading armies on the Muslims was impending.

---
1. Ibn-e-Aseer Aljazri, Vol.10, P.96
2. Ibid, Vol.10, P.98

Crushing Defeat of Crusades:

The tottering Abbasides caliphate was helpless. But Allah, the Exalted gave the Saljuqis the will and power to defend Islam. In 489 A.H. the first crusade of European forces left for attack on the Muslim lands. After pillaging in Hungry and Romania, they reached Asia Minor where Sultan Qulaij Arsalan Saljuqi fought a pitched battle against crusaders and inflicted a crushing defeat on them.

Sultan Noor-ud-Din Zangi:

Unfortunately, the Saljuqis forces became weak due to their inner difference and the government displayed signs of decay. At that time Allah, the Great, selected Sultan Noor-ud-Din Zangi and, after him, Sultan Salah-ud-Din Ayyubi for the annihilation of the crusaders. When the combined forces of Europe advanced towards Asia Minor to Conquer Syria, Sultan Noor-ud-Din Zangi dealt a crushing blow at the Christian forces and conquered Roha, which was their stronghold.

Sultan Salah-ud-Din Ayyubi:

Sultan Noor-ud-Din Zangi died in 569 A.H. Sultan Salah-ud-Din Ayyubi mustered power and conquered Aleppo, Roha, Syria, and Mousil. Inner dissentions in Egypt and Syria were rectified by Sultan Salah-ud-Din Ayyubi who devoted all his energies to fight the crusaders. In 574 A.H. regular JEHAD (Holy War) was started with the crusaders which continued for 14 long years. The crusaders were turned out of all the Muslim territories one by one till the Sultan conquered Hittin, Acca, Tibris, Asqalan and suburbs in 5583 A.H. Last great conquest of Sultan Salah-ud-Din Ayyubi was the fall of the Bait-ul-Muqaddas to Muslim hands.

The loss of Bait-ul-Muqaddas upset the Christian powers of Europe and another crusade was propagated by the Pope Aryanis III. In this crusade King Phillip Augusts of France and King Richard the Lion-hearted of England led the crusading armies. King Fredrick of Austria had joined with his armies. All the united forces reached Palestine by sea routes. They did not have courage to fight sultan Salah-ud-Din Ayyubi and offered to make peace in Sha'ban 588

A.H. which was accepted by the Sultan after consultation with his commanders. An Affidavit was signed to ensure that there would be no fighting during the coming 3 years and 6 months. Sultan Salah-ud-Din Ayyubi came to Damascus in 589 A.H. after this peace when he died at the age of 57 years.[1]

A few days before his last illness, Sultan Salah-ud-Din Ayyubi called his son Afzal and his brother Malik Aadil and said to them: "We are immune from the crusaders march and there is no danger of their attacks on our cities." He expressed his intention to capture Rome so that the Christians could not advance on Muslim lands by land routes. But death overtook him too soon to act upon his plans.

Death of Sultan Salah-ud-Din Ayyubi and After:

With the advice of his Chiefs, the Sultan had divided his Empire among his three sons during his lifetime. Egypt was given to Imad-ud-Din Usman, Damascus (Syria) to Noor-ud-Din alias Malik Afzal, and Iraq again to Ghayas-ud-Din Abul Fath Ghazi alias Malik Zahir. The remaining sons were given lesser estates.

---

1. The personalities of Sultan Salah-ud-Din Ayyubi and Sultan Noor-ud-Din Zangi were unique in the annals of Islam. They were raised, as it were, by the Mighty Hand of Providence, to fight the anti-Islam forces. Before the rise of Sultan Salah-ud-Din Ayyubi to power Egypt was under the hold of Fatimides who were extremists in their faith of Ismailit Shia'ism. In Jamia Azhar (which was the oldest University of Islamic Sciences) Ismailiat (Shia'ism) was regularly taught and the call to prayers had to include the Shi`a expression of "Hayya Ala Khair-ul-Amal". Sultan Salah-ud-Din Ayyubi abolished all these orders of the Fatimides and restored the Muslims dogma and ways of worship which the majority of Muslims in Egypt were used to observe for centuries. He also much hospitals and dispensaries for public health, gave impetus to agriculture of the country and re-introduced the four schools of Muslim jurisprudence in the schools and universities. The people became prosperous and lived happily in peaceful atmosphere.

Sultan Noor-ud-Din Zangi was also a lover of Islam. He got no salary from the public funds and lived on the income from his ancestral properties and estates.

Imad-ud-Din, ruler of Egypt was idle in his administration despite his other virtues. He died in 595 A.H. He was succeeded by Mansoor son of Malik Aziz when he was only 8 years old. Malik Aadil brother of Salah-ud-Din Ayyubi saw this and with the help of his armies occupied the government.

The European nations got the news that Sultan Salah-ud-Din Ayyubi had died and his government had been divided. At the instance of the Roman Pope, Crusaders began to prepare for another onslauglet on Muslim lands. The king of France and England could not join this crusade. But Henry, King of Austria led an army but his forces could not go beyond the island of Sicily.

In 599 A.H. the crusaders left for attacks on Muslim lands. A person from the court of Qaiser advised them to conquer Constantinnople first because that conquest would make the capture of Jerusalem easy. They entered Constantinnople and made it into pieces. This prevented them from advancing towards the Muslims. The Church dignitories admonished them on this stratigical blunder.[1]

After capture of Constantinnople it was easier for the crusaders to go to Syria. In 600 A.H. they left for Bait-ul-Muqaddas at the head of a larger army and camped at Acca. They plundered the surrounding areas, which were occupied by Muslims. Malik Aadil, brother of Sultan Salah-ud-Din Ayyubi, was in Damascus. He collected armies for Syria and Egypt and advanced to meet the crusaders. He camped near Acca but did not attack the Christians. In 601 A.H., a peace was made between crusaders and Malik Aadil.

In 613 A.H. the crusaders again attacked and, due to heavy forces, captured most parts of Syria. In 615 A.H., they advanced towards Egypt, and captured Damyat. Meanwhile Malik Aadil died. His son Kamil ascended the throne and turned the crusaders out of Damyat.

In 635 A.H. Malik Kamil died and Malik Saifuddin Abu Bakr alias Malik Aadil Asghar ascendid the throne. He lost his

---
1. Ibn-e-Aseer Aljazri, Vol.12, P.73, 74

valuable time in playful habits and, due to sharp differences with his brother Malik Salih Najmuddin, he was killed in 637 A.H.

Malik Salih came to the throne. Emperor Louis IX attacked Damyat. Malik Salih kept defending despite his illness and he soon died. His wife, Shajrat ul Dur was a wiser woman. She kept his death secret and she kept signing all the state orders. Her son, Toran Shah was in Kurdistan. She called him to fight the crusaders. Toran Shah fought so well that he was able to capture King Louis IX but was himself killed soon after. Now the authority was in the hands of Shajarat ul Dur (wife of Malik Salih). She set King Louis IX from after getting very sumptuous funds in ransom.

The role of the Caliphs of Banu Abbas (in Baghdad) end of Banu Fatimid (in Egypt) was lamentable. The entire Muslim World was under constant pressure of crusaders but the so-called caliphs did nothing to defend Muslims or Islam. The Abbasi Caliph Faiz Be Nastrullah (556 A.H.) had to send annual huge money to the crusaders to save Egypt from their attacks. At that critical time, Sultan Noor-ud-Din Zangi, Sultan Salah-ud-Din Ayyubi, Malik Aadil, Malik Kamil and their families kept the crusaders away and saved Islam and Muslim lands from total domination of crusaders. That was most creditable.

Saljuqis:

Like the Kurdistan soldiers, the Saljuqis also had positive role in defending Islam and Muslims against crusaders. Their headquarter was in Qonia. Sultan Alp Arsalan was the most prominent among the Saljuqis who fought the Romans successfully and had many achievements. In 463 A.H. the Roman King Armanos marched at the head of the two hundred thousand force to capture the Muslim towns. When he reached Kurdistan, Alp Arsalan was informed of his advance in Azerbaijan.

Alp Arsalan had a small force of only fifteen thousand. He could not get any reinforcement from Aleppo. He, therefore, sent a message of peace to the Roman King, which he refused. This infuriated Sultan Alp Arsalan. The Imam and Scholar of the Royal Army, Abu Basr Muhammad Bin Abdul Malik told the Sultan to leave for the battlefield after Friday prayers so that all the praying Muslims would beseach Allah, the Great for his victory over the enemies of Islam. Alp Arsalan agreed with the Imam. On Friday, he led the Juma prayers himself after which he prayed to Allah most fervently for a victory against the crusaders. He himself was weeping and all the public in the mosque was weeping and praying for success. Alp Arsalan put on white dress and equipped himself with sword and spear. He rode on a horse and attacked the enemy so courageously that the enemy forces were forced to retreat and they took to heels. Many crusaders were killed and the King of Rome was arrested. He talked to Sultan Alp Arsalan and agreed to give a very great sum of money for his release. After some basic conditions, he was let free

In this battle, innumerable wealth was taken by Muslims as looty. It included horses of finest brand, the most efficient and modern weapons and other military equipment. The Romans had lost courage and the Muslims gained in strength and resources. The Romans did not think of any attack on Azerbijan or Armenia after this defeat.

Alp Arsalan was also a lover of knowledge and buildings. His minister Nizam ud Din Malik laid foundation of a Madrasa-e-Nizamia in Baghdad. In 465 A.H. he left at the head of a large force to conquer China. After he had crossed the river Jehoon his death approach. Historians have rightly praised Sultan Alp Arsalan as a defender of Islam. His conduct, character, faith and love for Islam was all praiseworthy. His rule was very much near the just rule of "Khulafa-e-Rashideen". Allama Ibne Aseer Aljazri wrote in his praise "The world was obedient to the Sultan and he was rightly called the Sultan of the World".[1]

Banu Hamdan:

In 320 A.H. the government of Banu Hamdan was established in Aleppo. The founder of this dynasty was Saif Ud Daula Abul Hassan Ali Bin Abi Haija. According to a historian Ibne

---

1. Ibn-e-Aseer Aljazri, Vol.10, P.22-26

Khalqan, he fought a holy war with the Romans forty times. The dust, which covers his face badly in these forty battles, Saif ud Daula kept collecting it. He left a will that with the collected dust a brick may be prepared and placed in his lateral.

Abu Tayyab Mutanabbi was the court poet of Saif ud Daula. He has given the accounts of his master's courage and fighting in a large of his parigyries in which he has also mentioned how a large number was killed and how the Christian priests were arrested from the battlefields. Extraordinary love for holy war was a great mark of character of Saif ud Daula.

The Attacks by Tartars and Defence of Muslim Leaders:

Like the crusaders, the Tartars began to attack the Muslim lands from the middle of the seventh century AD, so much so that in 656 A.H. the Khilafat of the Abbasides in Baghdad breathed its last at their hands. After the fall of Baghdad, they gained in courage and conquered Damascus and the suburbs and Syria. They now planned to conquer Egypt.

In 648 A.H. after the end of the Ayyubi dynasty, the Mamaleek Bahria had set up their government. Its first ruler was Muiz Jashenger. He was assassinated after which his son Malik Mansoor Noor ud Din, a boy of twelve, ascended the throne. Saif ud Din Mahmood Qatoozi was his guardian and teacher. He called all the prominent scholars and statesmen of the country and discussed the situation arising from the successful inroads of the Tartars who could attack Egypt any time. As a result of discussion, Malik Mansoor was deposed and Saif ud Din Mahmood Qatoozi got into power. His title was Malik Muzaffar.

The worst fears came true. Halaku Khan was intent upon taking Egypt. He wrote to Malik Muzaffar to hand over the country to him or be prepared for similar fate as that of Baghdad. The Egyptian army was brave and had already defeated the crusaders. They were ready to fight Halaku Khan. In the month of Shaw'al, 685 A.H. a pitched battle was fought at Ainul Jaloot a suburb of Palestine in which commander of Tartar forces Katbagha was killed, his son was arrested and the Egyptian had a glorious victory. Under the order of Malik Muzaffar. Saifuddin, Ruknuddin Babris chased the defeated Tartars and turned them out of the border of Syria.

Malik Zahir Babris:

Malik Muzaffar Saif ud Din had promised that, if Babris turned the Tartars out of Syria, he would make him governor of Aleppo. But he went back on his promise. This infuriated Babris who, with the co-operation of some other senior officers, beheaded Malik Muzaffar and got hold of the throne in 658 A.H. At the advice of his minister Zain ud Din, he took for himself a title of Malik Zahir in preference to Malik Qahir.[1]

Malik Zahir Rukn ud din Babris had a special status in the Islamic history. He was a great statesman, a ruler of high moral character, a brave soldier and commander, a follower of Shriat laws, just and tender hearted. He set right all the unjust laws and abolished all the unfair taxes of provision rulers.

Annihilation of the Batinia Sect:

During the Fatimid rule, the Batnia sect had grown very strong. Attack of Halaku Khan had weakened them but they were annihilated during the reign of Malik Zahir by repeated attacks.

Repeated Successes against Tartars:

After setting against all the internal affairs of his kingdom, Sultan Rukn ud Din Babris turned to kill the menace of Tartars. After their defeat at Ain ul Jaloot, the Tartars again attacked the Syrian lands. Malik Zahir sent his commander Ameer Qalaoon to meet them. They were given a fatal blow and Syrian land became free from their attacks.

In 675 A.H. Abaqa Khan, a son of Halaku Khan attacked Iraq when Malik Zahir himself met the Tartars at the head of an army and after a bloody battle, defeated the enemy who left number of dead soldiers, and was totally routed.

---

1. Husnal Mohazira Fi Akbar-I-Misr-o-Qahira, Vol.2, P.36

The crusaders were also active like the Tartars and had occupied some areas of Syria after the death of Sultan Salah-ud-Din Ayyubi. Malik Zahir fought with the crusaders during 663 A.H. and 664 AD and turned them out of Syria. He then came to Egypt and prepared to inflict a crushing blow on the crusades. In 666 A.H. he attacked the crusaders in Palestine and went on defeating them from Antakia to Marquis. He then turned to Baghdad and turned the Tartars out of this old capital of the Abbaside caliphate. He also captured Qaisaria, which was under the possession of crusaders and turned them out in 675 A.H.

Malik Zahir Babris was rightly praised by the second Abbasi Caliph who said in his sermon "when the Tartars had entered our homes and brought havoc in our lands, Sultan Rukn ud Din Babris, despite his small kingdom, defended the Muslim Unimah and dealt crushing blows on this armies of infidels." [1]

Allama Jalal ud Din Sayyuti also praised him: "Malik Zahir despite his very small kingdom, came to defend the Muslims and the faith of Islam and God helped him to rid the Muslims of all the troubles and misfortunes which they were getting from infidels." [2]

The personal character of Sultan Babris was so high that historian present him to say that, despite his being a slave, he exalted in high character and great moral values all the Abbaside Caliphs. Allama Jalal ud Din Sayyuti quoted Ibn-e-Kaseer who wrote: "On 9 Rajab, 660 A.H., Rukn ud Din Babris appeared before Qazi Tajuddin in a civil suit about the ownership of a water well. The court got up in respect but Sultan asked them to sit down and he himself appeared as a party in dispute and personally argued his case before the Court and won his case on merits". In 667 A.H. he performed Haj pilgrimage and, with his own hands washed the Holy Ka'aba with rose water. Then he visited the holy tomb of the Holy Prophet ﷺ in Madina. He saw the gathering of his pilgrims very

---

1. Husnal-Mohazira, Vol.2, P.48
2. Ibid, Vol.2, 67

close to the tomb, which was a mark of dis-respect. He at once got a surrounding fence built around the holy tomb, which kept the pilgrims at a distance.

In the Justice Department in his state, he appointed a separate Qazi for each school of jurisprudence. He was very generous in alms giving and, during the month of Ramzan, he had public kitchens to feed the poor and needy people at 'Sehri' and 'Aftari'. He had set aside big estates whose income was spent on the burial ceremonies and requirements of the poor and indigent people.[1] After the conquer of Qaisaria, Malik Zahir was staying in Damascus where he fell ill and died in 676 A.H.

Conversion of Tartars to Islam:

The troubles from the Tartars continued even after the death of Malik Zahir. In 680 A.H., Halaku Khan's two sons, Abaqa Khan and Mango Temur attacked Syria at the head of eighty thousand soldiers. Malik Mansoor Saif ud Din of Egypt met the Tartar forces near Himus. On 14th of Rajab there was pitched battle in which Mango Temur was killed and Abaqa Khan fled away for his life to Hamadan. There his brother, Neko Dar Oghlan poisoned him to death and captured his throne. He then, accepted Islam and was named Ahmad Khan. A peace was signed with the Egyptians because both monarchs were now brothers-in-Islam.

At the acceptance of Islam by King Ahmad Khan, the Tartars began to accept Islam in large number so much so that the grandson, of Qublai Khan, Ananda Sultan who was ruler of Jokhta, embraced Islam along with his army of fifteen hundred thousand soldiers. It was a great achievement of the ideology of Islam that the Tartars who were deadly enemies of Muslims for the last fifty years, they now became the defenders of Islam. Iqbal rightly said:

> "It is manifest from the story of Tartar onslaught against Muslims that, at long last, Islam got its defenders from among the worshipers of idols."

---

1. Husnal Mohazira, Vol.2, P.66

Hero of the Abbasid Caliphates:

In order to decide as to which of the Abbaside Caliph may be declared the hero of the dynasty, we have to judge the active role of all the caliphs under the tracking of Islam and the services rendered by them to the cause of Islam.

Ordinary historians are opting to declare Mamoon Rashid as the hero of Banu Abbas. But dispassionate judgement picks up Abu Jafar Mansoor as the right hero. He was hard and secular in averaging and punishing like Saffah. He treated the Alvis as harshly as Saffah had treated the Banu Omayyads. But his mental structure was Islamic and he had the consciousness of work for the betterment of Islam and Muslims.

Conduct of Mansoor as Well Wisher of Islam and Muslims:

As a brave general and soldier Mansoor curbed the rising trouble of the Romans in Tripoli and Syria. He also put an end to internal trouble, which had increased due to encouragement of Kharasanis. He carefully guarded the conduct of the Muslims and did not allow them to indulge in frivolous activity, music or dancing or drinking.[1] Once he heard a noise in a corner of the royal palace. He at once put on his shoes and reached the spot where he saw a slave playing as the Tambourine and slave girls sitting round and laughing. All the assembly dispersed. Mansoor ordered that the Tambourine may be struck at the head of the slave which was done, resulting in the breaking of the instrument. Mansoor turned out the slave and sold him away as an undesirable person.

Mansoor did not drink wine and did not allow anybody to indulge in drinking. Once Christian physician Bakhtishoo was his guest. He was served as royal friend vith the orders of Mansoor but there was no wine. The physician said he could not eat the lunch without wine. The royal servants told him that royal orders forbade this service of wine to anybody. The physician refused to take food without wine, which was brought to the notice of Caliph Mansoor

---
1. Tabri, Vol.9. P.294

who did not care for the untoward demand of the Physician. He went without food. At night dinner was served without wine. The Physician demanded wine again but was given water from the river Tigris which he took with the remarks:

> "After taking the water of the Tigris river there is no need left of any wine".[1]

He was very considerate of the state treasury and unlike the ordinary caliphs of Banu Abbas; he did not spend on improper occasions and carefully avoided squandering of national wealth. To state poets he gave away meager rewards. Once a Qari Hasheem by name, recited before him the Quranic verse: "Do not spend recklessly because reckless spendthrifts are the brothers of the Satan who is ungrateful to God". On hearing this, Mansoor prayed to God: "Save me and protect my children from spending lavishly". He regarded the state wealth as a trust of the Muslims.

Mansoor was forbearing in his conduct and did not react with anger on hearing his own criticism. If the criticisms was just and correct he at once agreed to it. Once a Qazi who was a class-fellow of Mansoor came from Africa to the Court of Mansoor who asked him: "You are coming from a long distance. What difference of administration in normal conditions of the people have you noted in comparison with the Omayyad reigns?" The Qazi replied: "O commander of the faithful, I have noted corruption and injustice all along the way and the nearer I became to this Headquarters of Khilafat, the worse has been the condition of the administration". On hearing this, Mansoor downed his head out of shame and then said wishfully: "What can I do to correct the corrupt people?" The Qazi replied: "Have you not heard what Hazrat Umar Bin Abdul Aziz said? He said that the public is under the rulers. If the ruler is good, the public will also be good. If the ruler is not good, the people can never be good." [2]

The prudence, far-sightedness and political wisdom of

---

1   Tabri, Vol.9, P.309
2   Ibid, Vol.9, P.319

Mansoor can be judged from his will, which he gave in writing to his son, Mehdi a few days before his death. Ibne Jareer Tabri and Ibne Aseer Al Jazri have copied the complete wording of Mansoor's will in their respective history books. He said: "O my son! I have leveled and provided everything for you. Now I am giving you a few counsels as my death bed will, although I fear that you may not act on any one of them". Then he got a box, which contained many registers. This was locked and no one could open it except a respectable person authorized to do so. Mansoor opened the box, took out the register and handed them over to Mehdi, saying: "Keep them well guarded. These contain the precious knowledge of your forefathers. If a difficult situation arises read to its solution in the first register. If you can not find in it, turn to the second, then to the third, fourth and so on till the seventh. If no reply is forthcoming from the seven main registers, turn to the small register which I believe will have answer to your problem".

Thereafter Mansoor gave special instructions to Mehdi and exhorted him to abide by them strictly. These instructions were:

1. Keep a special watch for the protection of Baghdad City.

2. I have collected in the state treasury so much wealth that it would suffice for you for ten years even if no taxes are received by you. You spend this money on the salaries of your army and on the stipends of the deserving persons and the protection of the borders of your state.

3. Be good, kind and generous to your kith and kins because they are source of honour and respect for you.

4. Beware that you abide by rules of piety, inner cleanliness, justice and fair play in all matters. A king lacking these qualities is not a king at all.

5. Never seek advice of women. Never take a decision without prolonged and deep consideration.

Mansoor had real fear that his points of will shall not be acted upon. That is why after each point he said,

ومااظنك تفعل

(i.e., I guess you will not act upon it).

Mehdi ascended the throne in 158 A.H. He performed very good and constructive works. His greatest achievement was that he annihilated the movement of apostasy, which had widely spread among the Muslims. For this, he had a permanent department of government, which was headed by Amir Umar Al-Kalwazi. This department was contently in search of the Apostates who were arrested and punished effectively. Bashaar Bin Bardaas was an apostate poet in the regime of Mehdi. Mehdi once came to Basra with Hamdweya who had the duty to look for and capture the apostates. Bashaar fell into his hands and was ordered to be punished most severely.

The administration and punitive policy of Mehdi did not solve the problem of apostasy. This was not effective because the causes from which apostasy arouses was not taken into notice were for effective remedy. The influence of eunauchs minor boys and gamblers had increased in the Royal Palaces. Non-Arab persons with evil ideas were fast increasing in the Royal court and poets like Bashaar and Abu Nawas were propagating the evil ideas of drinking and debauching by their poetry. In the schools and religious institutions education of philosophy and rationalism was gaining ground instead of the Quranic sciences and traditions. There was abundance of all kinds of means for the satisfaction of youthful urges of wine and women. Free lancers had the upper hand and moral degeneration was increased. Some pious and thoughtful elders of the country were in constant anxiety to see things gaining from bad to worse.

Re-establishment of Abbaside Rule (Caliphate) in Egypt:

Between 14th of Safar, 656 A.H. to Rajab, 659 A.H. there was no Caliphate in Egypt due to this anarchy and widespread ruin created by the Tartars.

Abul Qasim Ahmad, son of Zahir Bi-Amirullah, uncle of caliph Mus'ta'sim and a brother of Mus'tansar was confined to prison when Mus'ta'sim was assassinated. He managed to attain his release and came to Iraq in the company of some people. Then he proceeded to Egypt when Sultan Rukn ud Din Babris welcomed him along with Qazi Taj ud Din and some ministers and scholars.

On a Saturday, 13th of Rajab, a grand meeting was called in the state Hall when Sultan Babris, Qazi Taj ud Din and scholars, ministers and senior officers came to attend. The antecedents of Abul Qasim were scrutinized and it was agreed by all the dignitories that Abul Qasim was correct in his claim that he was a member of Royal family of Abbasides. He was accepted as the de jure caliph and Shaikhul Islam. Izzuddin Bin Abdus Salam, Qazi Tajuddin and Sultan Babris – all of them entered with "Bai'at" (pledge) at his hands which signified their recognition of his caliphates. In 17th Rajab, Abul Qasim came to the Jame Mosque to read the Friday sermon. In his sermon he praised the Banu Abbas and prayed for Sultan Ruknud Din Babris. He came down the pulpit and led the Friday prayers. It was an impressive show.

On 4th of Sha'ban, a large meeting place was arranged in Cairo in which all the dignitories of the state participated. The caliph wrapped a black turban round the head of the Sultan and made him wear a black robe and granted him the title of "Ameer ul Momineen".[1] All the state affairs of the Muslim Empire were entrusted to Sultan Rukn ud Din Babris who had been granted the title of Ameer ul Momineen by the new caliph Abul Qasim who had taken the title of Mustansir Billah which was previously enjoyed by his brother.

The spirit of caliphate was not achieved by all the formal acts taken to appoint Abul Qasim as caliph. Babris himself was true Muslim and capable ruler who paid due respect to the office of the caliphate during his lifetime. But the caliph who was not Ameer ul

---

1. Husnal Mohazira, Vol.2, P.44,45

Momineen did not inspire this respect from other Muslim rulers as a caliph who was supposed to be a symbol of central authority of the Islamic World.

Only a few years after the death of Sultan Babris, the third Abbaside Caliph of Egypt, Mustakfi Billah (701 A.H. – 740 A.H.) was imprisoned in the Tower by Sultan of Egypt, Muhammad Bin Qalaoon in 736 A.H. In 737 A.H., he was turned out of Cairo with all his family and went to a place called Qaus. He also forbade mentioning about Mustakfi Billah (the caliph) in the Friday sermon. Mustakfi Billah died in 740 A.H.

Mustakfi Billah had, at his deathbed, wished that his son Ahmad might be appointed as Caliph. But the ruler of Egypt did not care for his will and appointed Ibrahim Bin Muhammad (a grandson of Hakim Bi Amrillah) as caliph and gave him title of Wasiq Billah. But even this caliphate was only in name and the name of Wasiq was not mentioned in the Friday sermons.

After Muhammad Bin Qaloon his son Saif ud Din Abu Bakr came to the throne of Egypt. He held a great audience in 731 A.H. and after consulting the Chief Justice, removed Wasiq Billah from caliphate and appointed Ahmad Bin Mustakfi in his place.

The Abbaside Caliph of Egypt was caliph only in name and he was always at the mercy of the Sultan of Egypt. With this background some sad and shameful events took place. In 763 A.H. the 7th Caliph, Mutawakkil Ala-Allah was deposed by the Egyptian Sultan and imprisoned in Qous due to some misunderstanding event. In his place Zakaria Bin Wasiq was made caliph with the title of Mo'tasim. There was no gathering and no "Bai'at" which were considered to be the formal necessity. After only 15 days, Mutawakkil was recalled from Qous and appointed as caliph.

The 8th caliph, "Musta'een Billah" was more daring and courageous. He arranged to get the Sultan of Egypt, Nasir Zain ud Din Bin Barqouq killed and himself assumed the powers of Sultan. But a senior chief, Shaikh Mahmoodi had acquired great political power. He deposed Musta'een from both the authorities of caliph and Sultan and imprisoned him in a fort. Thereafter he took all the powers and became Sultan of Egypt.

After Musta'een some caliphs tried to capture power but they could not succeed. In 923 A.H. Sultan Saleem I conquered Egypt and he did away with the office of caliphates. He assumed the role of caliph and with his advent, the office of caliphate went to Al-e-Usman and Banu Abbas lost it forever.

The history of caliphates of the Abbasides at Baghdad and Egypt makes it clear that this institution had become lifeless and the central role of defending Islam and Muslim lands was and could not be performed by the caliphs. God, in His eternal mercy and intention to keep ·Islam strong and in practice, got the noble task of defending the true faith by small Muslim states who were friendly under the caliphates.

The Aghliba whose hero was Ziada-tullah Aghlabi conquered the island of Cyprus in the Mediterranean Sea. The Saljuqis defeated the crusaders of Asia Minor and set up a Muslim state. This warrior of the family of Sultan Salah-ud-Din Ayyubi recaptured Bait-ul-Muqaddas and Syria from the usurping crusaders. The Ghaznawi and Ghouri warriors of Islam conquered India. After the fall of caliphate of Egypt, the Mumaleek e Bahria annihilated the turmoil of the Tartars and guarded the Western gates of the culture of Islam for about two centuries and a half.

AAL-E-USMAN (THE CHILDREN OF USMAN)

As has been stated above, Sultan Salim I conquered Egypt in 923 A.H. and transferred both the institution of Caliphate and Sultanate from Abbasides to the family of Usman. The foundations of this government of Aal-e-Usman were laid down in 699 A.H. when to Usman Khan I, the elder son of Al Tughral, a Turkish chief, laid the foundation of Usmani state in Qonia which was the capital of the Saljuqi's kingdom whose last Ruler, Ala-ud-Din II was killed. To begin with it was a small kingdom which was surrounded by 13 small states of Asia Minor.

Character of Usman Khan I:

Usman Khan I was a very brave, courageous and pious Muslim. He was a staunch lover of Islam. After coming into power, he called upon all the Roman rulers of Asia Minor to accept Islam or else pay him Jizya tax, failing which, get ready for a war. Some of them embraced Islam while some others agreed to pay Jizya. But a large number of Roman rulers got ready for war. Usman Khan sent a large army under the command of his son Oor Khan to wage war with Romans who had already received great help from the Tartars. But, despite all their combined forces, they were repeated defeated. But these victories were not of much happiness for Usman Khan. His real aim was to acquire the Byzantine Empire against which he was fighting for the last ten or twelve years. He conquered some important forts of the Byzantine Empires and extended his war activity to the shores of the Black Sea. He conquered the city of Yeni and made it his capital.

In 717 A.H. he laid siege to the city of Barusa which was an important stronghold of the Byzantine in Asia Minor. This siege continued for ten years. At long last, in 727 A.H. the besieged forces similarly left this fort at night times with the explicit order of the Roman Emperor. The Turkish army extended this fort. But Usman Khan heard this news on his deathbed. Oor Khan took the glad tidings to his dying father who praised him for his bravery and appointed him his successor. He gave him good commands to fear

Aal-e-Usman (The Children of Usman)

God under all circumstances, keep his character free from hypocrisy, do every thing for the pleasure of God, have mercy on the public, have justice between the weak and the strong, take guidance always from the Holy Quran and the Sunnah of the Holy Prophet ﷺ, always try hard for the proceeding of Islam, and never act against the injunctions of the Shariat Law. According to his will, he was buried in Barusa, and a glorious tomb was erected over his grave.

The Usmani empire continued for 643 years from 692 A.H. to 1342 A.H. when its last ruler, Sultan Abdul Majid II was deposed. There were 37 Rulers during their long centuries. From 886 A.H. to 918 A.H. as many as eight rulers were called "Sultan", the last of them was Sultan Ba-Yazid-II. Then Sultan Salim declared himself to be a "Caliph" after which all the Usmani rulers went by this title of "Caliph".

Continuous Conquests and Entering of Islam into Europe:

The great plan of Usman Khan to conquer the Byzantine Empire continued and his successes proved true to his endeavour. His son Oor Khan came to authority and, after setting against his internal affairs, he diverted his full attention to the conquest of Europe. He seized opportunity and captured Geli Poli which was an important fort on the Daniel coast. Before capturing, there was a big earthquake in which transport of Geli Poli fort was totally destroyed. Oor Khan got the rampart re-build by his son Suleman Pasha and placed a strong detachment of Turkish army in it. Then he captured a few other places in the Thrace area and got them populated by Arabs and Turks.

According to Mr. Aziz, the author of "Daulat-e-Usmania", this conquest of Geli Poli was the opening of the new chapter in the Usmani conquests. In 755 A.H. comprising to 1354 AD, they entered Europe as conquerors for the first time, and laid foundations of a Muslim state in the Christian Europe. This Muslim state was extended to the gates of Vienna to another two hundred years. True faith of Islam was carried to the cities of Europe. Eastern Europe was illuminated with the light of Islam and knowledge. What the Arab warriors had done for Western Europe, the Turk warriors did for the Eastern Europe.¹ The Byzantine government was so much over-awed by the Turkish inroads that Qaiser Cantakozin thought of friendly relations with the Usmani Rulers. He offered the hand of his daughter, Theodora for marriage with Oor Khan which was accepted by him. He allowed his new queen to continue to abide by her Christian faith.

Oor Khan was brave and courageous ruler and a dedicated Muslim who also did lot for the common welfare of his people. He built more than four thousand mosques, Madrassas, Khanqahs, (monastries) bridges, public kitchens, baths and inns. He died in 670 A.H. at the age of 82.

Sultan Murad I:

Suleman Pasha, the elder son of Oor Khan, had died in his lifetime by a fatal fall from horseback. As such the younger son of Oor Khan, Sultan Murad, the first, ascended the throne. He continued the mission of his father. The Chief of Angora, Alla-ud-din, had risen against the central power at the instigation of anti-Islam forces. He then turned his attention to the Balkan Peninsula, captured Aurana and made it his capital.

At that time the Christian powers of Europe were at loggerheads with the Byzantine rulers. But the Pope appealed to them to unite against the forces of Islam. They agreed and decided to fight against the Usmani forces. Sultan Murad-I was at the most besieging the city of Beeja in Asia Minor. He at once left for Europe on getting the news of Christian intentions. But, before he reached the battlefield, his brave General, Lala Shaheen had reached the bank of Murtaza River where the Christian army was having drinking, boating and enjoying a picnic. Lala Shaheen attacked them suddenly at night and killed them in large number. The survivors ran away for their lives.

In 780 A.H. the King of Serbia tried his fate with that of the ruler of Bulgaria and advanced to defeat Sultan Murad. But very soon they realized their weakness and agreed to pay a big amount of

---

1. Daulate Usmania, Vol.1, P.36, 37

money annually as homage. The king of Bulgaria also gave his sister in marriage to Sultan Murad.

In 791 A.H. the allies consisting of Serbia, Bosnia, Bulgaria, Albania, Walachia, Hungary and Poland, brought a united army of two hundred thousand strong men to turn the Turks out of Europe. At that time Sultan Murad was in Baroosa. He had grown very old but he at once left for the fight with enemies. In the Kasuda Desert a pitched battle was fought but the Europeans combined force was routed.

King Lazaar of Serbia was captured. He was brought before Sultan Murad who got him killed.

After this big battle, Thrace, Maqdoos and western Bulgaria were annexed to the Usmani Empires and Serbia, and Seena began to pay homage to Usmani Sultan. The battles of Kasoda had not yet finished when a wretched Serb Christian attacked Sultan Murad by treachery and surprise. He inflicted injuries with a dagger. The Sultan could not survive the fatal wounds and breathed his last. The war also ended.

Sultan Ba-Yazid Yaldram:

The elder son of Sultan Murad, Ba-Yazid had displayed guts and extraordinary valour in the battle of Kasoda. As such he was given the title of "Yaldram" (Lightening). In the battlefield he was unanimously nominated as the successor of his father.

The first thing which Sultan Ba-Yazid did after coming to power, was that he got his younger brother, Yaqoob Pasha killed mainly on his guess that he would claim relationship because he had also fought very bravely in the battle of Kasoda. This was a big slur on the fair name of Usmani rulers.

Apart from the heinous crime of murdering his brother, Sultan Yaldram performed acts of heroic splendour for Islam and the Turkish nation. He put the son of the murdered king of Serbia on the throne and apart from the usual annual large sum of money being paid to him by Serbia, he also made it incumbent on the king of Serbia to keep in readiness for him a detachment of five thousand soldiers. He readily agreed to this condition. He was so much overawed by the Turkish Sultan that he offered the hand of his sister, Princess Despina in marriage to which Sultan Yaldram agreed.

After connecting his political relations with Serbia, Sultan Yaldram turned his attention to Constantinnople. He forced the Roman Qaiser to enter into a renewal agreement with him whereafter he was to hand over the fort of Philadelphia to Sultan Ba-Yazid Yaldram. The Qaiser had no option but to agree. The Greek Commanders of the Philadelphia fort refused to hand over the fort to Sultan Ba-Yazid Yaldram despite Qaiser's orders. Sultan called upon the Qaiser of Rome to send his own army to capture Philadelphia from the Greek commander's control and then hand it over to the Sultan. Qaiser obeyed. He also asked the Qaiser to set aside one part of the city of Constantinnople for the habitation of Muslims who will have the right to build a central mosque in that part and have their own Qazi (Judge) to decide the disputes of the Muslims. The fields in the suburbs of Constantinnople growing vegetable and vine were to deposit one tenth of the income in Sultan's Treasury. All these demands were accepted by Qaiser and henceforth, the Usmani Turks gave the name of Istanbul to Constantinnople.[1]

Ba-Yazid was able to achieve some outstanding successes without fighting the Romans. Now he got opportunity of displaying his bravery in the battlefield. He turned to Walachia and made it his territory. Meanwhile the king of Hungary, Sajasmand collected a big army to fight Ba-Yazid. The forces of Bosnia also came to help of Hungarian forces. There was a pitched battle and the king of Hungary was routed and ran away for his life.

In 795 A.H. Ba-Yazid sent his elder son, Suleman Pasha to Bulgaria the western part of which had already been occupied by the Usmani Turks during the reign of Sultan Murad. The King of Bulgaria fought with courage to save the eastern part from Turkish occupation. But after three weeks defence Bulgarian capital fell to the Turks. The whole country became part of Usmani Empire and

---

1. Daulate Usmania, Vol. I. P.57

Aal-e-Usman (The Children of Usman)

the Royal family of Bulgaria was no more in power. The Lord Bishop was exiled. The people, who embraced Islam in Bulgaria, were allowed to retain their lands. The remaining land was distributed among Turks and military estates.

Crusaders Alliance:

After the capture of Bulgaria by the Usmani Turks, the way to Hungary was open. The King of Hungary, Sajasmand felt the imminent danger and he called upon all the European monarchs through the good office of the Pope to unite against the Turks. The church of Rome and Greek had united to the call against the Turks. Franc and England had also made up their differences and now both eastern and western Europe made one formidable alliance. They planned to turn out the Turks from Hungary in the first instance, and then advance towards Constantinnople, and after crossing the Daniel Pass to fight on their way to Jerusalem and Syria. With this big plan in mind the Christian forces gathered at Bowa in Hungary. They were hundred thousand times stronger. They advanced towards the Usmani Empire. But the ruler of Serbia was loyal to the Turks. The crusaders ran-sacked the Serbian territory and kept advancing after capturing many forts. The forces of Sajasmand advanced towards Nankopollis and laid siege to it. The Turk governor Yu-Alan-Buk refused to surrender the fort. Ba-Yazid hastened with his selected army and reached Nankopollis after fifteen days of siege. He attacked the besieging crusaders with the swiftness of lightening and on 23rd Zekad, 798 A.H. there was a pitched battle in which the allied army of Europe was badly routed. The battlefield was all red with blood. Ten thousand soldiers were arrested. The king of Hungary fled for his life. The Serbian forces helped Ba-Yazid in this encounter.

The news of this big victory over the combined forces of Europe acclaimed in the Islamic countries with great joy. The Abbasides caliph of Egypt Muta-Wakkil Ala-Allah also expressed his great pleasure and sent to Ba-Yazid a formal "Farman" authorizing him to administer the captured territories. Ba-Yazid sent his commanders to deal effectively with Austria, Walachia and Hungary who had joined the Christian alliance. Some extra territories of these kingdoms were conquered by Turks. Ba-Yazid himself turned towards Greece and occupied Sicily, Fossais, Dorais and Locrais without much difficulty. Two of the Turkish commanders Yaqoob and Afrinos crossed the Corunth dry plate and occupied the whole of Moria on the south. Thirty thousand Greek nationals of Moria were transferred to Asia Minor under order of Ba-Yazid, and Turks were allowed to build habitations in their place. Thus a Turkish colony was established in Moria.

The Battle of Angora:

There was a sudden revolution in the World of Islam. Sultan Ba-Yazid Yaldram had a big battle with Temur, which proved a misfortune for Islam and Muslims. According to a historian, Maulana Akbar Shah Khan Najeeb Abadi, the events took the following shape:

> "In 800 A.H. when Temur attacked India, the Tughlaq Empire was tottering but there was no danger for Islam or the Islamic splendour. The Christians had determined to do away with the Muslim rule in Spain which had Granada as its capital. But the battle of Kasoda and the swift victories of Ba-Yazid had over-awed the Christian monarchs of Europe. The result was that Muslim Spain survived for another 150 years. Temur attacked India from the east and reached as far as Hardwar. He shed rivers of blood in Delhi, Multan and foot of Kashmir Mountains. But he went from India, leaving his conquered territories to the courageous local Muslims."

Temur was in Hardwaar when he got the news that Sultan Ba-Yazid Yaldram was conquering land after land in Europe. At the same time, he also got a letter from the Qaiser of Rome informing him that his rebel Commanders Sultan Ahmad and Qara Yousuf Turkman were leading respectable lives under the protection of Sultan Ba-Yazid Yaldram.

Aal-e-Usman (The Children of Usman)

The Qaiser of Rome went on to inform Temur that Ba-Yazid had been disrespectful to him in protecting his rebels he ransacked the ancient kingdom of Europe which Haroon ur Rashid and Mutasim Billah, the Abbaside Caliph allowed to flourish. He also wrote that Ba-Yazid had collected his armies in Daghistan and was planning to capture Azerbaijan. He visited Temur to turn his march to Europe and save the old Christian kingdoms and his own frontiers.

Temur was expected like Hazrat Ameer Moawia ؓ to turn down the request of the Qaiser who wrote letter to him: "If the army of Hazrat Ali ؓ has to march to meet your armies, the commander to fight you under the banner of Ali will be Moaawiya ؓ". But Temur could not conquer his weakness of rivalry against Ba-Yazid. He could not bear the insult of his rebel commander Sultan Ahmad and Qra Yousuf-Turkman having gone under protection of Ba-Yazid. He left India at once, marched towards Europe to deal with Ba-Yazid. He killed all the one hundred thousand prisoners of war captured from India instead of releasing them on the way. He reached Samarqand via India and Afghanistan. He prepared to fight Ba-Yazid and reached the eastern border of Usmani Empire. Ba-Yazid had laid a siege to Constantinnople when Temur wrote to him to let his rebel commanders be brought in his audience. Ba-Yazid refused.

In 803 A.H. Temur entered the territories of Ba-Yazid from the side of Armenia. He laid siege to his fort of Sewas where Al Tughral. the elder son of Ba-Yazid was the governor. He resisted and fought the Temuri forces but was killed. The fort of Sewas fell. Temur captured 4000 Turkish soldiers and buried them alive. This inhuman act of barbarism had no parallel in history – not even under the Tartars.

Ba-Yazid got the bad news and left at the head of a Turkish army of 120 thousand strong. Meanwhile Temur had left Sewas and reached Angora. The army under Temur was seven times the army of Ba-Yazid. Ba-Yazid fought with valour and tact too, unfortunately, some of his Tartar units joined the army of Temur. Ba-Yazid got a crushing defeat in the Battle of Angora. He was arrested alongwith his son, Moosa. After eight months' imprisonment under Temur he was killed.

Temur was not content with mere defeat of Ba-Yazid. He released all the Turkish Chiefs whose lands were annexed by the Usmani Sultans and gave them back all the territories, which they once had. Thus the entire suzerity of the Usmani empire was brought to a misfortunnate end.

Effects of Battle of Angora on Islam:

With the fall and decline of the Usmani empire, the advance of Islam in Europe got a terrible setback. Maulana Akbar Shah Khan Najib Abadi wrote: "With the capture and defeat of Ba-Yazid the forces of Islam in Europe got a terrible setback. If Temur had been defeated and captured, the Temur dynasty or the Islamic forces in Asia would have lost nothing. The only blame which can be put on Ba-Yazid was that he was imprudent and displayed un-necessary valour. The Battle of Angora saved the European Christians from domination of Islam and Muslims. If this Battle of Angora was not fought, the entire land from Japan to England would have been vanquished by the Islamic forces.

The Revival of the Usmani Empire:

The Usmani Empire had received most grievous wounds at the hands of Temur Lane. The effect of the Usmani defeat in the Battle of Angora was that the European part of the Usmani territories began to show symptoms of unrest and rebellion against the central powers. But Allah, the Great had planned yet to have more services of Islam from the Usmani Turks. In a period of ten or eleven years after the Battle of Angora the Usmani Turks succeeded in regaining their past glory and power.

Sultan Ba-Yazid Yaldram had five sons. The eldest, Arl Tughral had died in the Battle of Sewas. The remaining four set up their individual kingdoms in different provinces. Muhammad, the youngest of them, was the wisest of all and dominated his elder brothers. In 816 A.H. he emerged as the sole Ruler of the Usmani empire. As Sultan (supreme ruler) he ruled for eight years from 816

A.H. to 824 A.H. During this period of eight years he infused fresh spirit into the almost dying body of Usmani empire. He did not conquer any more lands, but his prudence succeeded in returning the original pump and glory of the Usmani empire which had existed before the Battle of Angora. As an individual, Muhammad was a just, kind, merciful and cool-headed monarch. He died in 824 A.H.

Sultan Murad II:

After the death of Sultan Muhammad I, his eldest son, Murad-II came into power. The revival of the Usmani empire had already started with the efforts of Sultan Muhammad I. But Sultan Murad-II was destined to do much more on his behalf. Sultan Murad-II subdued and reconciled with some of the Asia Minor Chiefs who had tendencies of rebellion. Then he turned towards Europe. The King of Hungary was over-awed by Sultan Murad-II and he readily handed over all the territories fromnorth of River Danube to the Sultan. Salonika, an important town of the Byzantine empire had thrice fallen under the control of Turks and then slipped away. It was then under occupation of the Greeks. Sultan Murad-II conquered it. He also rendered the state of Serbia and made it loyal to the Turks. He also laid siege to Constantinnople but could not conquer it.

Sultan Murad-II had a desire to live in peace and calm for the rest of his life. He abdicated in favour of his son, Muhammad. The emperor thought that young and inexperienced Muhammad would be an easy prey than them. They joined hands collectively to strike unanimously at the central power of the Turks. Hungary, Germany, Poland, Bosnia and Walachia brought their armies at the battlefield of Kasoda where Sultan Murad-II met them effectively and they were defeated. They retreated in despair and went to their respective countries.

The European powers were proud of commander Honiaday who was at the head of Hungarian force. He had defeated the Turks many times and the allied powers were putting their trust in his valour. But in the battle of Warna he got a bad defeat at the hands of the Usmani Turks and their dreams were shattered. Many Christian rulers and chiefs were killed in this battle. Sultan Murad-II died on 15th Moharram 855 A.H.

Sultan Muhammad Fateh:

After Sultan Murad-II, his son Sultan Muhammad came to power. His forefathers had already paved the way for the capture of Constantinnople. He started to prepare for his great enterprise. He constructed a fort at a distance of about six miles from Constantinnople. Then he prepared for the Constantinnople siege. A Hungarian technician built up big cannons for the siege. These huge cannons were so heavy that they were driven by a team of bullocks. After complete preparations, Sultan Muhammad himself left for Constantinnople from Aderna at the head of ninety thousand well trained soldiers. On the other hand he dispatched warships to lay siege of Constantinnople from the seaside.

20th Jamadi-ul-Awwal, 857 A.H. was fixed for the siege of Constantinnople. The entire army kept praying for success the whole night proceeding the siege. Immediately after dawn, the Muslim forces said their prayers and then advanced to the rampart of the fort to lay the siege. The Roman forces fought with valour and courage so much so that the Qaiser, Constantinnople was killed on the battlefield. The battle raged till mid day when the Roman armies stood like a steel wall against the Muslim Turkish armies. On the Muslim side Sultan Muhammad behaved like true hero and Martial. He fought with courage and continued shelling at the rampart which caused many holes. The Romans fought with utmost bravery. Sultan Muhammad advanced towards the rampart with a detachment of his loyal troops. The holes widened and a part of the rampart was broken to let in the invading armies. A detachment of Muslim army entered the fort. It was followed by another detachment. The process of entry continued till Sultan Muhammad captured the fort of Constantinnople in 857 A.H. corresponding to 1453 AD Thus a prophecy of Holy Prophet ﷺ was fulfilled by the 7th Ruler of the Usmania Turks. At after-noon prayer's time Sultan Muhammad entered the fort with his ministers and senior army officers. At the gate of the famous Aba Sophia Church the call to prayer was loudly delivered and the Zohar (after-noon) prayer was offered in the Church after which this old church was changed into a Jame Mosque.

This great victory sent a wave of enjoyment throughout the Muslim World. Congratulations and greetings came to Sultan Muhammad from scholars, poets, kings and monarchs of the world of Islam. The words: " Balda-tun-Tayyibah",- a part of the Quranic verse, indicate the date of capture of the Constantinnople fort. The epithet of "Fateh" (Conquerer) was given to Sultan Muhammad who made Constantinnople his capital. This old city which had been the capital of the Roman empire for a thousand years now became the capital of an Islamic state. After three days of the victory, the grave/tomb of Hazrat Abu Ayyub Ansari ؓ (great companion of the Holy Prophet ﷺ) was discovered. Sultan Muhammad got a big mosque constructed near the tomb of Hazrat Abu Ayyub Ansari ؓ. This mosque came to be the regular follow for the crowning ceremony of the Usmani Sultans. It is an interesting historical fact that the age of Sultan Muhammad at the time of his conquest of Constantinnople was only 26 years.

More Conquests by Sultan Muhammad:

The world historians have acknowledged the conquest of Constantinnople as a major event of world history. The Eastern part of the Roman Empire was now totally finished. Sultan Muhammad Fateh continued his process of conquests. In 883 A.H. he conquered a number of forts in Albania. Then he advanced upon Hungary and conquered quite a few islands of the Mediterranean Sea in 884 A.H. He also attacked the Rhodes island but could not conquer it. On the 14th Rabi-ul-Awwal, 886 A.H. Sultan Muhammad Fateh breathed his last.

His reign not only famous for great conquests but was also conspicuous for his welfare projects and administration measures. He was succeeded by his son, Ba-Yazid Sani. His reign was not conspicuous for only more conquests. But he was able to hold effective control of what his elders had conquered and annexed to the Usmani Empire. In 918 A.H. he abdicated in favour of his son, Salim and took to life of solitude. He died in a journey.

Sultan Salim I:

After the death of his father, Sultan Salim-I advanced towards Iran where Shah Ismail Safwi had planned to undo the victories of the Usmani Turks. In 920 A.H. Sultan Salim I defeated Shah Ismail Safwi at Chaldiran and conquered Tabriz, Hamdan, Azer Baijan and Qafqaz. Then he turned towards Arabian lands and conquered the township of Bakr. He trampled the kingdom of the Zul Qadria which had been set up around the towns of Mur'ash and Bastan. He reached Syria wherefrom he planned to meet the Ruler of Egypt, Ghouri at the battlefield. At Marj Wabiq, a suburb of Aleppo, Sultan Salim met the army of ruler of Egypt and inflicted a crushing defeat on him. Ghouri fell from his horse and died on the battlefield. He was succeeded by Sultan Tooman Bay. He turned to resist the Sultan Salim's force but was defeated. He was captured and put on gallows. Then Egypt was annexed with the Ottoman Empire.

Transfer of Caliphate:

On 24th Rajab, 924 A.H. Sultan Salim reached Constantinnople. He took along with him Mutawakkil Ala-Allah, the last Abbaside Caliph. On entering the grand mosque of Aba Sophia, the Abbaside caliph handed over to Sultan Salim the authority of the caliph along with all the auspicious symbols of caliphate like the sword, the hammer, and the holy cloth sheet attributed to the Holy Prophet of Islam ﷺ. From that day the institute of Caliphate was formally transferred from the Banu Abbas to the Ottomans, and Sultan Salim came to be recognized as a caliph of the world of Islam.[1] Salim was still in Egypt when a son of the Sharif of Makkah (Ruler of Makkah) came to him and handed over the keys of the Holy Place to him on behalf of his father. After this ceremonious handing of the keys of the Holy Place, the Ottoman Turks proudly called themselves the Servants of the Holy Places of

---

1. Conflict of East & West in Turkey. P.25

Aal-e-Usman (The Children of Usman)

Islam (Khadim-ul-Haramain-e-Sharifain). An interesting episode requires to be mentioned at this stage. Once, in the Friday sermon, the Khatib uttered the words:

> "The owner of the Holy Places of Islam" for Sultan Salim. On this the Sultan immediately stood up and said: "Suffice it for me to claim with pride that I am the servant of the Holy Places of Islam".[1]

After formal occupation of Egypt, Syria and Hedjaz, the area of the Ottoman Empire doubled, and its power became so formidable that European rulers of Hungary, Spain and Italy sent their Ambassadors to Sultan Salim along with precious gifts and expressed keen desire to establish friendly relations. The Sultan accepted the gifts and displayed the Islamic spirit of tolerance.

Sultan Salim was an extremely intelligent and proudest person who rightly considered that the real purpose of "KHILAFAT" was to defend the frontiers of the Muslim countries and to provide a powerful center for the world of Islam. With these genuine aims in view he got the Institute of Khilafat transferred from Banu Abbas (who had no defacto power) to the Ottoman dynasty. The defacto rulers of Egypt, Syria and Hedjaz were the Mamaleek and the Institute of Khilafat was living like a weakling under their political control. As against this nominal authority of Banu Abbas, the Ottoman dynasty was rendering real service to Islam and the Muslim World during the past one-century and a half. The big powers of Europe were trembling with fear of the Ottoman. As such the genuine claim to Khilafat was of the Ottoman which Sultan Salim timely acquired from the Banu Abbas who had no political power at the moment.

Service to the Holy Places of Islam:

Sultan Salim adopted for himself and his successors the epithet of "Servant of the Harmain Sharifain" which embellished the name of the Ottoman family for four centuries. Sultan Salim had

---
1. Al Islam Walhizaratal Arabia, Vol.2, P.491

only three years to serve the cause of the Holy Places of Islam. But, even during this brief period, he had rendered real, true services to the Holy Places of Islam as is quoted by Mufti Dahlan who wrote at page 180 of his book "Conquests of Islam":

> "The stipend of Sharif-e-Makkah which he annually received from the Mamaleek rulers was increased by 500 Dinars (Gold Coins). He also set up an office in which names of the attachment of the "Harmain Sharif" were entered and they were all paid a stipend of one hundred Dinars each. He also appointed a body of reciters of the Holy Quran. Their number was 30. They were all paid at the rate of 12 Dinar each. Sultan Salim continued this practice of sending grain to the poor rustics of Hidjaz every year. Every year fourteen thousand monds of grains were sent to Hidjaz for free distribution among the poor and the indigent. Out of this ten thousand monds were fixed for the indigents of Makkah Mukarrama and four thousand for the residents of Madina Munawwara." Mufti Dahlan went on to write: "After Sultan Salim, the Ottoman rulers continued to increase the annual grant of the grains for the Harmain so that the amount of grain was almost double for both Makkah and Madina. Sultan Salim got the Maqam-e-Hanfi re-built for the Harm-e-Kab'a. He also sent Ameer Muslah to Madina for welfare services".

Shaikh Qutbi, a famous scholar of Makkah, described the people of Hedjaz as prosperous and contented during the Ottoman rule.

Respect and Regard for the Shariat Law:

Sultan Salim was a person of hot temper and self-conceited yet he had high respect for the Shariat Law and, whenever his attention was drawn to the injustice or prohibition of Shariat, he at once bowed his head in obedience. He had prohibited trade with the

Aal-e-Usman (The Children of Usman)

Iranian merchants but the merchants in his kingdom continued to have touch with Iranians imperceptibly. On knowing this he passed orders for the murder of such merchants. Shaikh ul Islam Mufti Jamali intervened and called upon the Sultan to withdraw his order as it was against the Shariat Law. Sultan Salim at once withdrew his order. In another case, Shaikh ul Islam again pointed out the mistake of Sultan Salim that Christians could not be converted to Islam perforce because Allah, the Great, had clearly laid down the rule of guidance that:

لَا اِكْرَاهَ فِى الدِّيْنِ

"There is no coercion in the matter of religion."

On hearing this, Sultan at once changed his view and cancelled his order for forcible conversion of any non-Muslim to Islam).

Sea-Power of the Ottoman Turks:

Sultan Salim had a strong military force of Turks under him. He considered it necessary that the naval force of the Ottoman Turks should also be at par with their military forces. So that they could maintain effective control over the Mediterranean Sea and ward off any danger of crusader's attack on the Ottoman territories. He built up a big army comprising of 150 big and small ships of modern construction. In addition he had 100 more ships which were kept in reserve for any eventuality and emergency. He, perhaps, had an idea of attacking the Rhodes island but death did not allow him to conduct all these expeditions. He died on 9th of Shawaal 926 A.H.

Suleman the Great:

Sultan Salim was succeeded by his great son, Suleman whose period of reign was from 926 A.H. to 975 A.H. Then 48 years of the Ottoman rule were the most glorious period of the dynasty. He conquered and annexed Yemen, Ethiopia, Iraq, Tripoli, Barqa, Tunis, Algiers, the great Sahara and Sudan to the Ottoman Empire. With his extensive conquests, many Asiatic and Arab countries became part of the Ottoman Empire. He also conquered the Balkan states of Rome, Hungary, Serbia, Bulgaria, Bosnia and Albania and made them part of the Ottoman Empire. The Ottoman occupation of the Balkan states continued till 1829 AD The famous fort of Belgrade in Hungary and the Rhodes island which were the active centres of the crusaders were conquered by Suleman. The islands of Croats and Cyprus had already been captured by the Ottomans. With the conquest of the Rhodes island, control of the Ottoman Turks on the Mediterranean became complete and effective. Now was the time when the Ottoman empire had come to be recognized a the biggest world power. Its boundaries extended from Podolia and Bova to Egypt on one hand and from uphrates to Gibraltar on the other side. The vast empire of Suleman, the Great was inhibited by persons of different races and colours, numbering no less than 500 millions.

Justice and Good Administration:

Apart from being a great general and a conqueror, Suleman, the great, was also a just ruler and a wise administrator. His father, Sultan Salim had forced 600 Egyptians to get settled in Constantinnople. Suleman allowed their repatriation to their homeland. Similarly Salim had confiscated the merchandise of some traders for violating the royal order and trading with Iran. Suleman cancelled the unjust order of his father and also compensated the losses of some merchants by cash payment. He removed from service all such government functionaries who had been found guilty of corruption and dis-loyalty. With his administrative measure, there was complete peace and harmony in all the lands in his empire. He had repeatedly issued circular orders to his governors that there should be no injustice done to any class of his subjects and the rich and the poor may be treated equally in the eyes of law. He earned the title of "Suleman the Law Abider".

Military Preparations and Equipment:

The era of Ottoman supremacy had seen the European nations entering the period of Renaissance. New inventions in weaponry and warfare were in the office. But the Ottoman forces under Suleman, the great was already ahead of the European armies in the equipment and weaponry. In the field of artillery, forts constructions and defence matter, the Ottoman had clear supremacy over their rivals in Europe. Cripsy wrote:

> "Suleman was so keen and watchful of the physical and moral well being of his forces that the European rivals stood no comparison with him. They were all indolent and care-free."[1]

Works of Public Welfare:

Suleman, the great, was not indifferent to works of public welfare. He got a canal constructed in Constantinnople. He got repaired the old canals of Makkah Mukarma. He had dispensaries and bridges made in all big cities. After the conquest of Baghdad he got the shrines of Imam Abu Hanifa and Shaikh Abdul Qadir Jilani built. He also spent some days near the Karbala and other sacred places. He doubled the amount of stipends and grain which Ottoman rulers were already giving to the residents of Makkah and Madina. The period of Suleman the great was indeed a golden era in the history of Islam as well as in the history of mankind. He died on 30th Safar 974 A.H. at the age of 74.

Two Distinct Periods of Ottoman Rule:

Like the Abbaside caliphate the Ottoman power had two distinct periods of rise and fall. The period of supremacy lasted from Usman Khan, the first (700 A.H.) to the death of Suleman, the great till 974 A.H. This period covered 274 years after which the fall of Ottoman started.

Comparison of Banu Abbas with the Ottomans:

Knowledge and the services made great progress during the Abbaside rule due to their great patronage as compared with the Ottoman rule.

But the Abbasides stand no comparison with the Ottoman when conquests were wide-spread and astonishing, covering three

---

1. Vol.1, P.324

continents of Asia, Africa and Europe. Banu Abbas had no time for conquest due to their internal rivalries and rebellions. The conquest of Constantinnople which was an old dream of the Muslim rulers was fulfilled only during the Ottoman rule. The Ottomans reached the wall of Vienna in Europe. The Ottoman rule was also immense against the religious and dogmatic evils and aposapostatic trends which were born due to the interaction of greek philosophy with the teachings of Islam. The Ottoman Sultans were rigid followers of Imam Abu Hanifa. They were race of strong build and simple, rustic habits. The evil and negative qualities of prosperous nations were not quickly born in them. The Sultans personally commanded their armies in the battlefields. They considered JEHAD (Holy War) in defence of Islam as the greatest virtue.

The Ottomans were true Muslims like the Arabs of old. They had burning desire to see Islam flourish and reach the distant corners of the world. They spared no pains in the preaching of Islam. At one stage Sultan Salim had issued royal orders that all non-Muslims in his reach must embrace Islam. This order was cancelled at the timely intervention of Shaikh ul Islam who called it un-Islamic and against the injunctions of the Holy Quran. The Muslims and non-Muslims, the Turks and non-Turks and, as a matter of fact, people of all creeds, colours and races were treated with equality and justice. So much so that some Europeans of the Balkan states liked to leave their homelands and settled in the countries held by the Ottomans.

There was another psychological contrast between the two dynasties. The Banu Abbas liked to have a dignified title like "Muqtadir Billah" or "Mustasim Billah" to justify their claim of successors to the "Khilafat-e-Rashida". They took pride in being called "Zill-Allah" (The shadow of Allah) and "Ameer ul Momineen". As against the attitude of Banu Abbas, the Ottoman Sultan called themselves "The servants of the Harmain Sharifain" (the Sacred House of Allah and the Sacred Shrine of Holy Prophetﷺ). They were proud of being the "Servants of Islam". Even today when Turkish respect and love for "Harmain Sharifain"

Aal-e-Usman (The Children of Usman)

is mentioned before the elderly Arabs (who had seen those days), their eyes are filled with tears.

It is true that the Ottoman Turks have made no contributions to the advancement of knowledge and unification of the Islamic people. But they had worked hard for the maintenance of the culture of Islam and preaching and spread of the true religion of God. The Ottoman had no kinship with the Quresh or the family of the Holy Prophet ﷺ and, on this account some sections refused to accept their claim to the "Caliphate". This denial was not justified.

Fall of Ottoman Power:

The laws of the nature are always operative in our individual and collective lives. Nations rise and fall under distinct laws of nature. If they heed and improve their moral conditions, they are saved from sudden fall and catastrophe. If they are oblivious and carefree, the process of deterioration continues in their body and they are ultimately faced with complete ruin.

Causes of Deterioration:

The reign of Suleman, the great, was the pinnacle of glory for the Ottoman power. After him, the process of deterioration began. The great Turkish lady writer, Khalida Adeeb Khanum has analyzed

---

Maulana Shibli Naumani (a great scholar of Indo-Pak Sub-continent) recognized the validity of "Khilafat" for the Ottoman Turks and wrote the following verses to Sultan Abdul Hameed, the last Ottoman ruler and "Khalifa":

1. "Due to you, we feel that the grandeur of Badar and Hunain, the dignity and splendor of the "Harmain" is only due to you.
2. Who else except yourself is the supporter and defender of the love of the Holy Prophet ﷺ.
3. To you is owed the sweetness of the faith of the Holy Prophet ﷺ. The areas of Islam are strong just because of you.
4. Through your majesty and authority the Shariat Laws have acquired a high status and through your orders the splendor of Islam has risen high".

The above (translation of Persian) verses may not be quite appropriate for Sultan Abdul Hameed. But they depict a correct picture of the first ten Sultans of the Ottoman Dynasty.

the causes of fall of the great Ottoman Empire. According to her analysis, Suleman was ruling over three continents and two oceans and his forces – both at land and seas were powerful enough to meet effectively any challenge from his enemies. But, unfortunately, he was a slave to his Russian Queen, whom the Western people called Roxalane.[1]

This Russian queen of Suleman had borne a son who was a corrupt, drunkard and debauch. The Russian queen wanted her son to succeed Suleman but decision of his successor had already been taken in favour of another son of Suleman, Mustafa by name, who was borne of another wife. Mustafa rightly deserved his claim as the successor of Suleman, the great, because of his great qualities of head and heart and his administrative and military genius. But the Russian queen succeeded in creating bad blood between Prince Mustafa and his Emperor father and convinced him by her machination that Mustafa had plotted to depose the Emperor and get the throne in his lifetime. The result was that in 1553 AD when Mustafa was about to leave for Iran at the head of a large army, Suleman summoned him in his camp and got him strangled to death.

The Second brother of Mustafa, Ba-Yazid, also met a similar fate. Some well wishers advised Yazid to meet the threat of Salim (the son of Russian queen) should be met by armed resistant. Ba-Yazid took up this advice and declared war against Salim. But the empire's whole power under Suleman was at the support of Prince Salim. Ba-Yazid was defeated and took refuge with king Tahmasap of Iran. Suleman sent a threat of war to Tahmasap and also promised to pay him four hundred thousand gold coins for the head of Ba-Yazid and four sons. Tahmasap succeeded to this threat of powerful Suleman and handed to him his son Ba-Yazid his four sons who were all beheaded.

After the assassination of Prince Mustafa and Prince Ba-Yazid, the way was clear for Prince Salim to succeed his father Suleman. After the death of Suleman in 974 A.H. Prince Salim

---

1. Conflict of East and West in Turkey. P.36

Aal-e-Usman (The Children of Usman)

ascended the throne. As already stated he was the most incapable person who had no interest except in women and wine. The empire was run by the chief minister who was a well-trained beaurocrat. So long as he reigned over the Sultnate, there was no apparent sign of decay in the administration.

Sultan Suleman had, under the influence of his Russian Queen, spoiled the very basic structure of governmental machinery. As put by Khalida Adeeb Khanum, the incapability of the ruling figure could be compensated by a team of capable functionaries who had the will and capacity to run a smooth and just administration. But the Russian queen prevailed upon the Sultan to keep his princes bound to the four walls of the Palace where they had no chance of learning the social etiquette. The result was that princes who had no knowledge of steel-craft were coming out to rule over the empire. They were all easy going and fond of pump and show.

In the course of the 17th century AD, from beginning to end, there was a series of stupid, indifferent, and corrupt rulers who were either fond of pleasure or were unjust and tyrannical. The princesses began to sell out the big positions, corruption increased beyond all limitations. A Turkish proverb says:

"A fish starts decaying from its head".

This was true of the existing of Ottoman administration. Merit was no longer the criterion and everywhere corruption was rampant. The Ottoman palace was presenting the picture of Byzantine palace towards its unfortunate end.

During this century of decay, rebellion in the army units and removal of administration chiefs was the order of the day. Very few Sultans of this century died their natural death. Most of them were killed or removed by un-natural methods.[1] According to Khalida Adeeb Khanum, the decline of the Ottoman empire had started immediately after the death of Suleman, the great. But it would be more correct to say that the seeds of decline were inherent in the

---
1. Conflict of East and West in Turkey, P.36, 37

structure and mode of government given to it by Usman Khan Ghazi, the founder of the Ottoman dynasty. The causes of decline of the Ottoman empire may be enumerated under the following headings.

1. Institute of Heir-apparent:

As against the Islamic way the selection of ruler, the Ottoman had adopted practice of nominating the heir-apparent to replace a ruler. The flaw and weakness of this system was that the eldest son of the Caliph or the Sultan presumed that he would be the next ruler. As such, he never took pain to acquire the qualities of leadership for the difficult and onerous responsibility awaiting for him. This practice also created a team of flatterers around the prince heir-apparent who kept him bound in a psychological trap for their own nefarious aims. This gave birth to a multitude of plots and machinations within and without the royal palaces. At times these internal dissensions were responsible for the murder of the prince.

Sultan Ba-Yazid Yaldram killed his younger brother Yaqoob Chalsi who was in no way less courageous or capable. Similarly Sultan Salim I killed his two brothers Ahmad and Karkood. Sultan Muhammad Fateh, the conqueror of Constantinnople killed his foster brother by drowning when his mother, a princess of Serbia, was greeting the Sultan over his great success. He went to the extent of legalizing the murder of claimant brothers and his formula was later on was known as "law of blood shed".[1]

This arbitrary "law of blood shed" was hardly a legal provision of law and it was certainly derogatory to the Islamic Shariat. The killing of a small child by Sultan Muhammad Fateh unveiled his morality which was absolutely secular and worldly. The result of this so-called "law" was that Murad-III got five of his brothers killed and his son Sultan Muhammad III got nineteen of his brothers killed for the protection of his throne. The institute of heir-apparent or the law of heir-presumption was certainly an undemocratic, un-Islamic and unjust law which gave rise to

---

1. Daulat-e-Usmania Vol. 1, P.145

rebellions, dissensions and wide-spread differences with ruling family and the government functionaries.

2. Royal Marriages with Foreign Women:

The Ottoman Sultans were not at all serious in their matrimonial affairs. They did not see any harm in courting marriages with non-Muslim ladies and making them so free in government matters that they could change most of the policies of the government.

Oor Khan married Theodora, a daughter of Kantakozin who was a Christian ruler. He also allowed her to abide by her Christian faith. Sultan Murad I the successor of Oor Khan married a daughter of Sesman, the ruler of Bulgaria who was again Christian. Sultan Ba-Yazid Yaldram married Dispenia, the sister of ruler of Serbia, who was also a Christian. The Russian lady who became the queen of Suleman, the great, brought about real ruin of the Ottoman dynasty. These were the ladies who lived in royal palaces as queens of the Sultans and they considered it their right to influence decisions of the government. Apart from the princesses mentioned above, there were countless concubines and slave girls who adversely affected the Ottoman ruler's life style and policies.

The Christian women changed the original Ottoman blood of the Turks.[1] Salim II was half-Russian in his blood, because his mother was Russian lady. Muhammad III was half-Italian because his mother was an Italian lady who lived in Venus. Similarly Usman II, Murad IV, and Ibrahim I were half Romans and half Ottomans.

The sum total result of the increasing number of foreign ladies in the Ottoman palaces was that the original hardihood, bravery and lover for Islam of the early rulers of the dynasty, was changed to playfulness, pleasure-seeking and wide-spread indifference to the state affairs.

During the reign of Murad III (982 A.H. – 1004 A.H.)

---
1. Al-Islam-wal-Hizrat-ul-Arabia Vol.2, P.499

Suqulili Pasha was the Chief Minister for the first four years. Yet the influence of the ladies of palaces was tremendous. Four of the ladies had every say in the state affairs and things could take no shape without their intervention. One of them Sultana, mother of Noor Bano, the second was Sultana Saffiya, daughter of an aristocrat of Vennice (Baffo family). Due to her extraordinary intelligence and physical beauty, she was dominating the Sultan. She had a special hand in decisions about war and peace. Due to her interaction, the Sultan did not attack Vennice despite the insolence of its ruler. The third was Hungarian lady who had out-stripped Sultana Saffiya and was the center of Sultan Murad's attention. The fourth lady was Jan-e-Fida who was de-facto administrator of the Ottoman palaces. Due to her tactfulness and intelligence, she also had great influence on Sultan Murad. These four ladies were the real advisors of the Sultan and controlled the state affairs.[1]

There is no doubt that Islam allows marriage bonds with ladies who believe in Judaism and Christianity, yet facts vouchsafe that influence of such non-Muslim ladies on the Muslim society are always baneful. Hazrat Hozaifa Bin Al-Yameen had married a Jewish lady in Madain. Hazrat Umar ؓ wrote to him to divorce her at once. He wrote back to inquire if it was un-Islamic to marry lady believing in Bibles. Hazrat Umar ؓ replied that he should at once leave the lady and not enter into controversy. Hazrat Umar ؓ expressed his fears that common world follow his (Hazrat Hozaifa) example and marry non-Muslim Zimmi ladies because of their exceeding beauty and features and such a practice would ruin the future of Muslim ladies.[2] How true the fears of Hazrat Umar ؓ had proved to be are apparent from the history of the decline of the great Ottoman empire.

3. **Rebellion in the Army:**

The untoward conditions of the Royal Palaces proved possible for diluting the loyalty of the armed forces towards the

---

1. Daulat-e-Usmania Vol.1, P.24
2. Kitabul Asaar Imam Muhammad ؓ, Printed in India P.64

Aal-e-Usman (The Children of Usman)

Ottoman Sultans. Widespread disloyalty and a kind of anarchy began to appear in the state's affairs. Yeni Chri was the most trusted and selected army of the Ottoman Turks and, as a matter of fact it was the right hand and fighting instrument of the Ottomans. Due to pleasure-seeking habits of Sultan Murad, the third, his selected army called "Yeni Chri" began to rebel against him. In 1889 AD a great demonstration was staged before the royal palace. The Sultan had to hear their demands and fulfilled all the requirements. This encouraged the army who became habitual in demonstration for their demands. So much so that appointment of the Chief Minister of the state could not be made without the recommendation of the army leaders like the Abbasides Caliphs, the Ottoman Sultans became entirely dependent on and accountable to their armies.

4. Disloyalty and Corruption of Civil Chiefs:

The general atmosphere in the state had so much been poisoned that public morality had deteriorated beyond limits. Civilian chiefs and beaurocrates began to plot against the Ottoman government and had no conscience in betraying their rulers even in the battlefield. Russia was the worst enemy of the Ottoman Empire.

The Russian Emperor Peter, the great, left his capital at the head of a large army to invade the Ottoman territories and oust the Turks from Constantinnople. After crossing the Perth River, he came to know that the Turkish Chief Minister, Bultaji Muhammad Pasha had camped in the mountains in fort of Peter, the great with a force of two hundred thousand strong. Muhammad Pasha was in a position to capture Peter the great or even to kill him. Queen Catharine of the Ottoman Emperor planned to avert the catastrophe of the Russians. She sent gold and precious gifts to the Chief Minister Muhammad Pasha who er tered into a pact of peace with Peter and lifted the siege of the Russ an army which returned homes in peace and tranquillity.

A similar event took place during the reign of Sultan Abdul Majid. Ibrahim Pasha, son of Muhammad Ali Pasha Khadyu of Egypt, defeated the Ottoman Turks in the battle of Nasibain. This victory could advance the influence of Ibrahim Pasha in Asia Minor.

At this stage Ahmad Pasha Qayudan brought up the entire Armeda of the Ottoman and handed over to the Khadyu at Alexandria Port. But for the intervention of England, Khadyu of Egypt could have captured even Constantinnople and the Ottoman Empire could have faced most unfortunate end. During the reign of Sultan Abdul Hamid, the second, the English wanted to capture the Cyprus island. The Sultan did not like this. In 1878 AD when Safwat Pasha became the Chief Minister, he handed over the Cyprus to the British. He deceived Sultan Abdul Hamid by an assurance that the British would support them in Berlin Conference.

5. Economic Deterioration:

The Turkish people are by their nature the most hard working and hardy nation. Before the industrial revolution, they were a prosperous people who tilled their own lands and worked hard in industry and trade. After the industrialization, the Turks were not given due access to machinery and they had to lag behind the other nations, which used the machinery and earned much more. This caused the economic deterioration of the Turkish nation.

6. Inactivity and Lassitude of Religious Scholars:

The general atmosphere of deterioration effected the religious scholars also. Khalida Adeeb Khanum has described the apathy of the religious scholars in the following words:

> *"The religious scholars continued to perform their duties effectively till such times the theologians philosophy was having supremacy over public opinion. Madrasa Sulemania and Madrasa Fateh were the centers of the contemporary sciences and disciplines. With the advent of new branches of knowledge based on national thought and scientific investigation, the religious scholars were no longer capable of continuing their educational duties. This stupor of religious scholars continued till the middle of the 19th century AD."*

The religious scholars were rigid in their Catholicism and would not allow any change in the syllabus or curriculum of the educational institutions to include modern disciplines of knowledge and scientific subjects. Sultan Salim III (1203 A.H. – 1222 A.H.) wanted to introduce his scheme for educational and military reformations which aimed at setting up institutions of modern sciences and equipping and training the Turkish armies with modern weaponnery and methods of warfare. But Shaikh ul Islam Atta Ullah Afandi gave religious verdict that the modern types of military uniform were un-Islamic. The most capable units of the Turkish army: "Beni Chari" supported the Fatwa of the Shaikh ul Islam Atta Ullah Afandi and rose in rebellion against Sultan Salim III. They picked up all the supporters of the Sultan from among his chiefs and functionaries and killed them without mercy. This continued for two days and Sultan Salim III had to cancel his package of reformations. The military offices were not content with the cancellation of the Sultan's package of reforms. They attained legal justification from Shaikh ul Islam Atta Ullah Afandi and the grand Mufti and deposed Sultan Salim III.

In 1293 A.H. Sultan Abdul Hamid II ascended the throne. Like his predecessors he also wished to introduce educational and military reforms. But he met the same fate at the hands of the military who had attained Fatwa from the grand Mufti and Shaikh ul Islam.

7. Awakening in the Rivals:

When Turkish nation was fast sinking into degeneration of thought and action, the rival European nations were leaping to progress in education, scientific invention and military equipment. Seeing themselves better prepared and more prosperous, the rival nations of Europe considered effective measures to split up the Ottoman Empire into pieces and to strangle this "sick man of Europe" to slow death.

The Balkan States joined hands with England and France and began to attack the Turkish territories. The Ottoman Empire began to disintegrate and many parts of the empire slipped away from the hands of the Turks. As a result of the battle of Paloona, battle of the Balkan and the World War of 1914-18 AD the islands of Crete Cyprus and Malta slipped away from Turkish control. Later in 20th century all the possessions of Baghdad, Syria, Lebanon and Palestine right up to Mossil which were under Turkish control were forcibly taken away by European powers. The Balkan states which were under nominal control of Turkey became independent and Asia Minor was divided into pieces. After the World War of 1914-18 AD circumstances turned unilaterally against the Turks.

Rebellion of the Arabs (Hidjas):

The most pathetic feature of the World War 1914-18 AD was that the Arab political circles under the leadership of "Sharif" of Makkah played an ignoble role against the Turks who had been, since Sultan Salim I, calling themselves the "Servants of the Holy Places of Islam". The European enemies of Turkey beguiled "Sharif" of Makkah by giving him an idea of "Independent Arab State". He joined hands with the enemies of Turks who were also enemies of Islam and turned out the Turkish army units from Hedjaz (Arabia). This was a political and tactical blunder of the Arabs under the name of "Arab Nationalism" and they are repenting over this blunder to this day.

End of the Institution of Khilafat:

Turkey, which was dubbed as "the sick man of Europe", had reached a stage of weakness where death could overtake it any moment. But God, the Great, wanted it to continue living. The leadership of Mustafa Kamal Pasha and his colleagues came to the rescue of dying Turkey. Turkey has, under the wise leadership of Mustafa Kamal recovered its territories occupied by Greece and has also much progress at par with the European countries in the fields of industry, craftsmanship, education, science, military equipment and organization and social affairs. Unfortunately, the Institution of Khilafat was banned by Mustafa Kamal which had the effect of estranging the world of Islam from Turkey which now lives by itself and for itself. The Turkish nation has, perhaps, forgot the great losses of Muslim Brotherhood. The coming times may remind Turkey of its basic Muslim character.

Existing World of Islam:

The Muslim World, Turkey, Iran, Egypt, Pakistan, Afghanistan, Saudi Arabia, Libya, Syria, Sudan, Lebanon and Indonesia are all progressing in science and technology but the strength is non-secular than religious. The impression of Islam is weak but the public in the Islamic countries is keen for the revival of Islam in the political field also.

ANDLUSIA (SPAIN)

THE RISE AND FALL OF MUSLIM RULE

The conquest of Spain during the Banu Umayyas was a great achievement of the Muslim political power. They ruled over it for centuries with dignity and honour. But their political fall and ultimate expulsion for Spain has been an ignoble slur on the fair name of Islam.

Spain or Andlusia is a peninsula situated in the south west of Europe. Its area is 2,00,000 square miles and the climate is moderate. Wadi-ul-Kabir and Tagsi are two of its famous rivers. This is a fertile and prosperous country.

Before the advent of Islam, Spain was ruled by the Goth Dynasty. During the reign of Roderick when Walid Bin Abdul Malik was the Caliph of the Muslim World, Musa Bin Nusair, Governor of North Africa sought permission of the central government to conquer Spain.[1] He sent a batch of 500 persons to Spain to study the country and the inner conditions to assess possibilities of success in case of an armed intervention.

In 92 A.H. Tariq Bin Ziad led an army of 7000 Barbar warriors who entered the soil of Spain after crossing the strait of Gibraltar on many boats. They captured the coastal rocks on the eastern shores of Spain. This was later called "Jabal-ut- Tariq"

---

1. The famous historian Ibne Aseer has, in his book, "Tarikhul Kamil" (Vol. 4, P.269) narrated the inner story of the Muslim invasion of Spain. There was a custom among the royal and aristocrat families of Spain to send their young boys and girls to Toledo (the then capital) to learn culture and manners under the guidance of the King. An aristocrat, Yuleen by name, sent his daughter to King Roderick (Razreeq as put by Ibne Aseer). The girl was extraordinarily beautiful and King Roderick fell in love with her. He had illicit sexual relations with her of which the girl informed her father. The infuriated but helpless father persuaded Musa Bin Nusair, the Muslim Governor of North Africa to attack Spain and destroy the power of Roderick. The army sent by Musa for the invasion by led by Yuleen.

(Gibraltar) after the name of Tariq Bin Ziad. The Arab units advanced towards the north and, after reaching the desert, they conquered the island of "Khazra". Roderick who was busy with his army in another skirmish learnt of the Arab attack and moved with a force one hundred thousand strong to meet the threat. Musa Bin Nusair sent another detachment of 5,000 Muslim warriors to help Tariq Bin Ziad. Army units numbering twelve thousand were pitched against 1,00,000 soldiers of Roderick at the battlefield. The Arabs were in a foreign land and had crossed the sea by boats. Tariq Bin Ziad burnt all the boats to assure his fighting men that there was no going back and no escape. They had to win or die. He said:

> "O Muslims! The ocean is behind you and the enemy is in front of you. Now, you have to choose your course of action".

The Arabs fought with valour at the bank of Lakka River near the town of Shazoona. The forces of Roderick could not face the Muslim warriors and were utterly routed. Roderick himself fled for his life and his whereabouts were not known after the battle. Ibne Aseer opined that Roderick was drowned in the river.

Since Roderick did not belong to the royal family. He was not helped with earnestness. The members of the royal family were happy to see Roderick routed and killed. They thought the invaders would go back after loot and arson. But the Muslim forces under Tariq Bin Ziad continued with their advance and went on capturing towns after towns after the capture of Khazra. They ultimately reached the precincts of France after crossing the Pyranese Mountains. Musa Bin Nusair also came to Spain with an army to help Tariq Bin Ziad but the Muslims could not enter French territories.

Musa Bin Nusair and Tariq Bin Ziad were busy fighting the Christians in Spain and capturing towns after towns. The news of progress of the two commanders in Spain could not reach the headquarters of Caliph Walid Bin Abdul Malik who began to suspect the credentials of Musa Bin Nusair and instructed the Qazi of Damascus to invoke curses upon Musa Bin Nusair in his prayers.

Meanwhile a messenger of Musa Bin Nusair brought the glad tiding of conquest and looty to Walid who was overjoyed and repented over his misgivings about Musa B.n Nusair. He looked down in prostration and thanked Almighty Allah for his great favour and benediction on the Muslims.[1]

The fighting in Spain was still continuing when immediate call for return to Headquarters was received by Musa Bin Nusair who lost no time in obeying the Caliph. He made Abdul Aziz, his son incharge of the affairs in North Africa and left for Damascus in 94 A.H.

Exploits of the Muslims in Spain:

The Muslims ruled over Spain from 94 A.H. to 897 A.H. for a long period of 800 years. Their exploits and contributions to the welfare of human society and human knowledge are unique and shall ever be remembered by the mankind. The details of their wonderful deeds and courageous contributions to civilization, culture, etiquette, morality and human welfare are multitudinous and require volumes to describe. Famous Orientalist Professor Sadev's narrative in his history of Muslim Spain may be reproduced to give some account of the achievements of Muslims. He wrote:[2]

> "The Arabs were well versed in agriculture and commerce and know fully well the principles and practical details of these two important professions. Using their knowledge and expression, they changed the barren lands into flourishing fields and lifeless cities into blooming and prosperous towns. Using the principles of trade and commerce, they interjoined most of the cities into a network of habitation, one depending on another and one contributing to the prosperity of another. The result was that affluence and property reigned supreme in

---
1. Kitabul Imamat-o-Siasat Vol. 2, P.119, 120
2. Not from the cited book but from the Encyclopaedia by Fareed Wajidi.

the occupied Spain and the mutual rivalry and jealousy between the Arabs and the Barbars also disappeared."

The Arabs of Spain were far ahead of the European people in knowledge, skill, industry, etiquette, culture and civilization. The European monarchs were impressed by their moral superiority and gentleness. Due to their strict following of the teachings of the Holy Quran, the Muslims did not ban their criterion of advancement on colour, race and pedigree but on moral achievement and spiritual dignity. Even women were well-versed with logic, medicine, syntax, Algebra, Physics, Chemistry and Physical History. Their libraries were full of books, copied from books of ancient Greeks and philosopher of Alexandria. Towards the end of the 10th century AD the Roman Pope Gobert, benefited from the Arab libraries and presented wonderful disciplines of knowledge to his co-religionists so that, out of wonder, they began to call him a wizard.

In industry and skills the Arabs had acquired proficiency as they had done in different branches of knowledge and services. They had acquatinted themselves with the fundamentals of the developed nations like Romans and Phoenicians. They became well versed with different ores and discovered new ores like mercury and rubies. Near the coast of Andulisia, the Arabs dug out coral from the sea and near Targhoona they took out pearls from seawater. They also acquired proficiency in the weaving of the silk and cotton cloths. The people living in eastern Africa and the coastal areas very well knew that the best arrowhead spears were prepared in Toledo. The best silk comes from Granada and the best horse saddles and tunics come from Cardova. The Spanish Arabs sent or exported their manufactured commodities to different eastern countries and imported timber, cloves, camphor, Sable Skin (Samoor), and Persian carpets in exchange. To irrigate the barren and low-planed lands in Balnisha and Granada they evolved much contravene which testifies to their high intelligence. They constructed a dam to catch the water of river Tona near Walansa where it fell in the sea. The dam was built 6 miles before reaching the sea. They dug out and built seven canals as outlets of the stored water of the Tona river. This water was utilized to irrigate the fallow and dry lands. Every canal with its tributaries was shaped like an open manual fan. Apart from the canals ponds and reservoirs were also built to irrigate the barren lands. This new system of irrigation changed the country of Spain into a vast pasture and garden.

The system described above was so effective that no piece of land remained fallow for any part of the year. After harvest, the land was immediately used to sow a new crop. Thus three consecutive crops were reaped during a year.

The Spanish Arabs made agriculture a regular art by their proper use of knowledge about botany and agriculture. The Spanish tillers of the soil grew rice, sugar cane, Saffron, dates, pistachio, bananas, mulberry, pomegranates, peas, and many varieties of vegetables which were sent to every corner of Europe.

Historian Sadev has also given details on the civilization, urbanization, and expanding culture of the Muslim Spain. He wrote:

"The Muslim Spain comprised of six provinces, 80 big cities and 300 towns on small townships. In Cardova, alone there were 200,000 houses, 600 mosques, 50 hospitals, 80 public colleges, and 900 public baths. It had a population of 200,000 persons. Apart from one fifth of the booty in the battles and the (Jizyas) recovered from the non-Muslims, the annual income of the caliphs of Spain was 1,20,45,000 Dinars. This huge annual income was indicative of the affluence and prosperity of the Muslim Spain. Because of their fabulous wealth, they were able to erect buildings which had no parallel in the world. The mosque at Cardova is equal in grandeur and beauty to the Jame Mosque built by the Umayyads in Damascus. Its length is 600 cubits and the breadth is 250 cubits. There are 38 compounds on its right side and 29 compounds on its left side. It has had 193 pillars made of white marble. On the south it had 19 doors which were *covered with copper sheets. On the central building, the covering was much of gold. At the top there were 3 golden domes which had all above them a pomegranate made of diamonds. The mosque was illuminated with 4700 candles. The candle burnt in the principle arch made of pure gold. Every year 34000 "rattle" weight of olive oil and different fragrant items were used on it."*

Apart from the Grand Mosque of Cardova, Abdur Rehman III had constructed a glorious place for his Christian queen Zuhra at a few miles distance, from Cardova. Due to its grandeur and artistry in construction, it was a unique building. The historians have written that the domes of the palace were erected on 4300 pillars, which were made of marble of different colours. These pillars were painted with flowers of different kinds. Some of these pillars were sent to the Caliph Abdul Rehman, III, by the monarch of France and Constantinnople, as a gift. Some pillars were brought from African countries by selection by engineers. The roofs and the walls were also made of most precious stones and gold leaves. The vastness of the palace may well be judged from the fact that, in stead of "Zohra Palace", it was generally called "The City of Zohra". In the wide and spacious buildings of the palaces, there were ponds and fountains of pure and glittering water at every proper turn and place. The biggest of the fountain was made of gold, having most beautiful flowering over it. It was brought from Constantinnople and another fountain made of green marble was brought from Syria. It had images of many birds and beasts all of which ejected water from their mouths.

A part of the "Madina tuz Zohra" was called "Qasrul-Khulafa". Its roof was made of pure gold. Its walls were made of transparent marble so that one could see across the walls. In the middle of this "Qasar" there was a fountain with exquisite decorations. A pearl was fixed at the top of it. It was gifted to Abdul Rehman-III by the Emperor of Greece. Apart from this there was a fountain shaped wide plate, which was filled with mercury. All around the palace beautiful mirrors were fixed in stands of white ivory. Well-decorated doors made of wood were fixed in glass frames. When these doors were opened, the entire palace was filled with dazzling light and no body could cast a glance at the walls or roof. If the mercury was set in motion the entire building seemed to be quivering. People unaware of the technical arrangements became extremely fearful.

There were 13750 employees and 13382 slaves for the supervision and management of "Qasar-e-Zohra". Inside the private apartments of the palace, there were 6000 women employees for service. To feed the fish living in the palace ponds and reservoirs 12000 leaves of bread were thrown in waters. The cost on the construction of the "Qasar-e-Zohra" according to our times coinages, was equivalent of 20,500,000,0 rupees. The construction began in the year 325 A.H. and was completed in the next twenty years.[1]

Different Eras of the Muslim Governments in Spain:

The Muslim warriors conquered Spain in 92 A.H. during the Caliphate of Sulaiman Bin Abdul Malik of the Umayyads dynasty. Till 132 A.H. when the Umayyads rule came to an end, Spain had administrative relations with Damascus wherefrom the governors and government functionaries were sent. This relationship with the central "Khilafat" continued till the rule of Saffah, the first Abbaside Caliph of the Muslim world. When the second Abbaside Caliph, Mansoor ascended the throne, he began whole-sale slaughter of Banu Umayyads with a view to uproot the dynasty. Abdul Rehman, a person from the family of Abdul Malik Bin Marwan, somehow escaped the holocaust of the Abbasides and moving through Iraq, Syria, Egypt and Morocco, he reached Spain. He was warmly received by Banu Marwan who pledged loyalty and obedience to him in 138 A.H. The then governor of Spain, Yousuf Bin Abdur Rehman came out to fight but Abdur Rehman defeated him in a decisive battle and he became de-facto ruler of Spain in 141 A.H. The first step which Abdur Rehman took on coming into power was to delete the name of the Abbasides Caliphs from the Friday sermon.

---

1. Monthly Risala Ibrat Vol.5, Issue 3 by Maulana Akbar Shah Khan Najeeb Abadi.

He also was wise enough not to assume the title of "Ameer ul Momineen" for himself. Seven of his successor followed his practice. The eighth successor, Abdur Rehman Al-Nasir (who ruled from 300 A.H. to 350 A.H.) assumed the title of Ameer ul Momineen.

In 146 A.H. Ala Bin Mughis was nominated by Abu Jafar Mansoor for the Caliphate of Spain. He advanced from Africa to the soil of Spain when the armies of Abdur Rehman inflicted a crushing defeat on him in the sub-lands of Ashbilia. Ala Bin Mughis was killed along with most of his fighting soldiers. Abdur Rehman cut off the heads of many killed soldiers together with the head of Ala Bin Mughis and sent them to Qairwan and Makkah where the heads of the Abbasides defeated soldiers were placed in building along with the black banners (sign of the Abbasides) and the order of Mansoor appointing Ala Bin Mughis as the Caliph of Spain. When Mansoor came to know all the facts, he was over-awed by the strategy of Abdur Rehman and he said: "Abdur Rehman is a virtual Satan. God be thanked, who has placed the sea between us".[1]

During the reign of Abdur Rehman Al Nasir, Spain developed in culture, civilization and urbanization. He was a wise, brave and active ruler. When he ascended the throne, the entire country was burning in flames of turmoil and rebellion. He dealt with the evil elements and mischief – mongers with an iron hand and quelled the rebellion most effectively. Peace and tranquility were restored in the whole country. Allama Ibne Khaldoon wrote about Abdur Rehman Al Nasir: "Abdur Rehman Al Nasir witnessed the mischief and turmoil created in Spain by his opponents. He extinguished the fire lit by the miscreants and brought the rebellious elements under effective control. In a little less than 20 years of his rule, the whole of Spain regained peace and prosperity and came under his effective control.[2]

Ibne Khaldoon went on to write: "Abdur Rehman Al Nasir ruled over far nearly fifty years and the authority of Banu Umayyads

---

1. Tafh-ut-Tayyab Vol.1, P.165
2. Tafh-ut-Tayyab Vol.1, P.165

was firmly established in that country. He was eager of "JEHAD" and frequently advanced with his forces to fight against the infidels. In the 23rd year of his rule, he suffered a defeat after which he refrained from personal participation in the skirmishes. However, he continued to send military contingents to the European countries and inflicted losses on them. This step made the European rulers overawed and they began to advance hands of friendship and obedience to him. Valuable gifts were received by him from Rome and Constantinnople. Christian rulers of Qashnala and Nabluna came to him personally to pay homage".

"Abdur Rehman mitigated the taxes on the people which had the desired effect of complete peace and harmony in the country. Because of his positive administrative actions, famous writer, Ibne Abdur Raba praised him thus: "The crescent has reappeared on horizon and the country has regained its splendour and prosperity".

Abdur Rehman Al Nasir died in 350 A.H. after him there was wide spread anarchy and individual chiefs established their own governments in different parts of Spain. Ibne Ibad established his rule in Ashbilia; Ibnul Aftas and Ibne Zinnoon in Toledo; Ibne Abee Amir in Balniah and Ibne Hood in Sarqastah. This happened towards the end of the 4th century A.H. on 6th of Shawal 399 A.H., Suleman, a grandson of Abdur Rehman Al Nasir came to the throne. He adopted the title of Almustaeen Billah". He entered Cardova in 400 A.H. and added the words: "Az-Zaafir-o-bi-haul-Allah" to his title. Towards the end of this year he left Cardova at the head of Barbar forces and caused havoc throughout the length and breadth of Spain. He re-entered Cardova in 403 A.H. when the Barbar slaves left him alone and dominated all big cities of Spain and established their individual rule.

Ali Bin Hamood:

In Suleman's army there were two descendants of Imam Hassan ؓ Qasim and Ali – both brothers. Their father's name was Hamood. When Ali Bin Hamood saw a score of wide anarchy in the country, he thought of becoming the sole ruler of Spain. He wrote a letter to all the Chieftains who had camped various provinces of the country that "Hisham Bin Hikam" had nominated me as his heir in the course of his siege of Cardova". All the chieftains agreed to accept his claim and swore allegiance to him. Ali Bin Hamood advanced toward Cardova at the head of the Barbar slave soldiers. Suleman confronted them but was badly defeated. At last on 21st Moharram ul Haram, 407 A.H. Ali Bin Hamood beheaded him with his own hand. He also killed Suleman's father Al-Hikam the same day.

The circumstances in Spain began to result the events in Baghdad when the caliphate had become a tool in the hands of Turkish Slaves. Similarly in Spain the Barbar slaves became the controlling power in the country. The internal wars had destroyed the peace of the country and the government had lost its prestige. Ali Bin Hamood ruled over the country for a period of one year and 10 months. He had taken the title of "Al Nasir". But his avengers and hard men had turned his slaves against him. In 408 A.H. a slave chopped of his head when he was in a public bath. He had left two sons, Yahya and Idrees by name.

Qasim Bin Hamood:

Qasim Bin Hamood succeeded his brother Ali. He was a kind-hearted person who cared well for his people. The public was generally happy and satisfied with his rule. After four years, Qasim's nephew, Yahya Bin Ali rebelled against his uncle who ran away from Cardova to Ashbilia. Yahya entered the gates of Cardova without any resistance. He got himself proclaimed as "Caliph" and assumed the title of "Al-Motali". After some days, Qasim regained his sources and, with the help of Barbar tribes, conquered Cardova. Yahya ran away to Malika. He captured the island of Khazra where relatives of Qasim were living and his stores were also there. On the other hand Idrees Bin Ali, brother of Yahya who was the governor of Sibta, captured Tanjah. A section of the public in Cardova also became against Qasim who ran towards Ashbilia where two of his sons, Muhammad and Hassan were living. The people of Ashbilia turned out Muhammad and Hassan and handed over administration of the city to a council of three persons. Qasim now ran away to Shoraish. The Barbars now made Yahya Bin Ali their chief and laid a siege to the fort of Shoraish. Qasim was captured alive. He stayed in the captivity of Yahya for some days and was transferred to Idrees where he was killed by strangulation. His dead body was sent to his son. Qasim ruled for 6 years and was a captive for sixteen years.

After the capture of Qasim, Yahya had a free hand. But general anarchy in the country had deprived him of peace. He was wandering from place to place along with his army. He had laid siege to the fort of Ashbilia when a party of soldiers lying in ambush caught hold of him in drunken condition and killed him. This happened on 7th of Moharram 427 A.H.

The Banu Umayyads ruled over Spain from 138 A.H. to 407 A.H. for a period of nearly 275 years. After this there was turmoil and unrest in the country when Qasim and Ali, descendants of Imam Hassan ؓ opposed the Umayyads. After the death of Yahya, there were two or three rulers of the Hassan dynasty till 445 A.H. when Idrees, the last ruler of this dynasty died. Due to the weakness of this family, the people of Malka which was the Headquarter of their government, turned out persons of the Hassani family from all parts of Andolusia and the Barbars captured the Khazra island and its surrounding towns hills Karoona, Malka, Mankab, Granada and all the country around. Ashbilia was already in their possession. Thus the authority of the Hassani family was totally wiped away.[1]

The Last Days of Banu Umayyads in Spain:

After the defeat of Qasim in Cardova, the people selected a man Abdur Rehman Bin Hisham (who was from the Banu Umayyads) as their ruler. He assumed the title of "Al-Mustazhar Billah". He ruled only for a few months when there was a rebellion against him and he was killed on 27th Zil-Qadah, 414 A.H.

Abdur Rehman Bin Hisham was succeeded by Muhammad Bin Abdur Rehman. He was a dunce and weak person who had made Ahmad Bin Khalid, a weaver by profession, his minister. The people of Cardova were annoyed at this selection and, one day they

---

1. Khilafat-e-Moohideen, P.65, 66

Andulusia (Spain) The Rise and Fall of Muslim Rule

forcibly entered the house of Ahmad Bin Khalid and beat him to death. "Mustakfi" Muhammad Bin Abdur Rehman was caught and imprisoned in a cell where he was denied food and water for three days. He was then exiled from Cardova where he died at the border of the country by taking poison by one of his companions.

After "Mustakfi", Yahya Bin Ali became the ruler. At the end of his rule, his minister, Abu Muhammad Jamhoor Bin Muhammad Bin Jamhoor (who was a renowned chief of Cardova) pledged his loyalty to Hisham Bin Muhammad who assumed caliphate with the title of "Mo'ta'mid". This happened in the month of Rabi-ul-Awwal, 418 A.H. Hisham continued to roam about in the frontier districts where Ibn-e-Jamhoor advised him to reach Cardova where he entered in the month of Zil-Hajjah, 420 A.H. After his brief stay in Cardova his army rose in rebellion and he left Cardova for Larda where he died in 428 A.H. Hisham was the last ruler of the dynasty of Banu Umayyads.

At the end of Banu Umayyad's rule, the country was wrapped in complete anarchy. The Arabs, the Barbars and the Mawalis were divided into different sects and these heterogeneous elements began to rule over all such parts of the country where they could lay their hands. They also had the affront to assume the caliphate titles like "Mo'tazid", "Mamoon", "Mustaeen", "Muqtadir", "Motasim", "Motamid", "Motawakkil" and "Motawaqif". A poet of the troubled times disliked these childish assumption of titles and he said:

مما يزهدني في أرض الاندلس

سماع مقتـــدر فيها و معتضد

القاب مملكة في غير موضعها

كالهر يحكي انتفاخا صورة الاسد

"My hatred for the land of Andolusia and the reason of my leaving that country for good was that the

timely rulers had assumed titles of former dignified caliphs like "Muqtadir" and "Motazid". These titles were now misnomers and ill-suited and looked like cat expanding herself to imitate a lion".

The Christian government benefited from the general turmoil and anarchy of the Muslims in Spain. They would help one Muslim ruler to weaken his rival Muslim ruler and then annexed the territory of the ruler whom they had helped. Due to mutual enmities and rivalries the Muslim rulers had been deprived of the faculty of discernment between families and foes.

Murabiteen:

During 57 years of Muslim history in Spain from 428 A.H. to 485 A.H. the families which ruled the eastern and western areas of Spain were: Banu Jamhoor, Banu Ibad, Banu Zarin, Banu Azmari, Banu Zinoon, Banu Hamood, and Banu Aftas. At long last the family of Murabiteen was able to gain power and the general anarchy in the country came to an end.

This family belonged to Morocco (Africa) and had been ruling there since 400 A.H. The first ruler of this family who assumed power as sovereign of Muslim Spain was Yousuf Bin Tashfein. He was a monarch of great majesty and the whole of Africa was under his effective rule.

Yousuf Bin Tashfein and Battle of Zalaka:

The circumstances leading to the arrival of Yousuf Bin Tashfein may be explained. Motamid Ibne Ibad, ruler of Ashbilia crossed over to Morocco in 79 A.H. and asked for the help of Yousuf Bin Tashfein against the Christian rulers of Europe. Yousuf Bin Tashfein accorded most cordial welcome to Motamid and made a firm promise to help him. The same year he collected an army comprising 7000 cavalry and a large number of infantry, crossed the sea through the town of Sabta and reached Khazra Island in Spain. Al-Motamid met him with very precious gifts and invited him to Ashbilia wherefrom they could fight the enemies of Islam. But

Yousuf Bin Tashfein declined to have rest at Ashbilia and told Al-Motamid that he had come to fight the enemy whereever he may be

During these days, Alfanso, the 6th, (who was the king of Castilla) had laid siege to the Muslim fort of "His-nul-Lait". On hearing of this arrival of Barbars from Africa he lifted the siege to retreat and come back with better preparation. Alfanso sent message to all the Christian powers to send reinforcement and Al-Motamid also gathered all possible forces to fight under command of Yousuf Bin Tashfein.

On 12th of Rabi ul Awwal both the forces confronted each other in the battlefield of Zalaka which was adjacent to the frontiers of Rome. Alfanso played a psychological trick. He sent message to the Muslims that Friday was their auspicious day as Saturday was for the Jews and Sunday for the Christians. He, therefore, proposed that fighting should start on Monday when the three auspicious days had passed. Al-Motamid had felt that it was a deception but Yousuf Bin Tashfein agreed to the proposal made by Alfanso. The next day when Yousuf Bin Tashfein began his Friday prayers along with units of his army, Alfanso suddenly attacked the Muslims. Al-Motamid had already foreseen and had prepared to meet the situation. The forces of Al-Motamid contained the Christian forces of Alfanso and the Murabitoon also hastily reached the battlefield on their horses. S.P. Scott, the historian of the time described the encounter as under:

> "The numerical strength of the Christian forces was three times than that of the Muslims who were fighting to defend not only their houses but also their honour and religion. The Christians were also better equipped and had more powerful horses. The Christian soldiers had also more experience of fighting. The battle at Zalaka assumed the spirit of a crusade. The Christian priests gave hot sermons to the Christian forces on the eve of every new battle."

Yousuf Bin Tashfein himself was astonished to see the Christian superiority in every thing. The Christians attacked the army under Al-Motamid first of all and he was totally besieged. But he did not lose heart and displayed great valour and steadfastness. S.P. Scott described the encounter as under:

> "Al-Motamid fought so courageously that he reminded the enemy of the old days of the Arab rule in Spain. He and his army fought with the true spirit of the martyrdom. He got two wounds. Three horses died fighting under his legs. The armour he wore was shattered to pieces. His sword drenched with the blood of the enemies. Heaps of dead soldiers bore witness to their spirit of martyrdom and fearlessness". [1]

The King of Ashbilia was killing the Christians in large number and stood undoubted in the field when Yousuf Bin Tashfein arrived with heavy forces and attacked the army of Alfanso from behind. The attack was so heavy and so sudden that the Christian army was unnerved and took to flight. S. P. Scott has described the condition of the Christian army as under:

> "The Christians were smashed from all sides and felt they were helpless in the small battle ground. Their large number became a negative factor. Their horses and camels ran over their army soldiers. In utter confusion the soldiers began to kill their own comrades. The army lines become so close that the proper use of swords became difficult. The Christians who were surrounded by the Barbars could neither fight nor leave the ground. They were utterly routed and the Barbars chased them closely and killed many warriors". [2]

Allama Makri has written on the authority of some historians that in the battle of Zalaka the Christian army of three lacs

---

1. Akhbar-e-Andulus Vol.2, P212
2. Akhbar-e-Andulus Vol.2, P213

Andulusia (Spain) The Rise and Fall of Muslim Rule

was badly routed and majority of them was killed.[1] But S. P. Scott put the number of Christians at 60,000 out of whom 20,000 were killed. King Alfanso was badly injured due to a heavy strike of Yousuf Bin Tashfein but he made sure his escape.

The effects of this battle were positive for the Muslims. The Christian plans to re-conquer Spain were flouted. The Muslim anarchy and internal fighting also came to an end. The small chieftains of Muslim Spain were over-awed by the possibility of Yousuf Bin Tashfein and he was given the title of "Ameer ul Momineen".

Domination of Spain by Yousuf Bin Tashfein:

The internal warfare of the Arab chiefs of Spain and the general anarchy in the Muslim Spain had convinced Yousuf Bin Tashfein that the Christian would oust Muslims from the land leave no vestige of the Muslims rule in Spain. S. P. Scott has called him a usurper and, unfortunately Allama Abdul Wahid of Morocco has also expressed an adverse view of the exploit displayed by Yousuf Bin Tashfein. However, both Ibn-e-Khallakan and Abdul Wahid of Morroco have written that, in the beginning, Yousuf Bin Tashfein brought about a peaceful understanding between the rival Muslim chiefs, Al-Motamid Bin Ibad, the ruler of Ashbilia and Ibne Rasheeq, the ruler of Mercia. But the mutual hatred and enmity of the two Muslim rulers was so deep that, immediately after the battle of Zalaka, both the Muslim rulers, again became opponents of each other. Yousuf Bin Tashfein assumed the situation wisely and was convinced that the internal warfare of the Muslim chiefs of Spain could not be ended until Yousuf Bin Tashfein himself had captured the government of Spain. His love links are further strengthened by the fact that he called a meeting of the prominent scholars and asked their views if his capture of the government would be justified in the interest of peace and tranquility and defence of Islam and Muslims. They all agreed to the proposed domination by Yousuf Bin Tashfein. Thus in 485 A.H. the Muslim Spain came under the possession of

---

Nafh-ut-Tayyab Vol.1, P205

Al-Morabitoon of North Africa, and the general anarchy in the country came to an end. The Christian dream of ousting Muslims from Spain also became unreal.

Unfortunately, the peace and order in Spain brought almost by Yousuf Bin Tashfein was not lasting. The government of Al-Morabitoon was established in 485 A.H. It continued only uptill 523 A.H. When internal strife restarted and continued till 542 A.H.

Al-Mowahhidoon:

Meanwhile Abdul Momin lead his forces of Al-Mowahhidoon against Al-Morabitoon and captured Morocco from them. In 545 A.H. they also invaded Spain and captured it. Abdul Momin was called "Ameer ul Momineen" and he was a successor of Muhammad Bin Tomert.[1]

The government of Al-Mowahidoon continued in Spain from 545 A.H. to 620 A.H. IN 595 when Al-Nasir ud Din Ullah was ruler, Alfanso, King of Qustailah mustered a great army with the help of France and the Pope of Rome and invaded Spain. Al-Nasir confronted him but was badly defeated and the army of Alfanso chased the Muslims, looting and making many captives. But, not long after this defeat, the Muslims reorganized under Zakirya Bin Abee Hafas (who was a general in the army of Al-Nasir) and, in 609 A.H. he attacked the army of Alfanso and inflicted a crushing defeat on him. The routed army of the Christians left Spain and Muslim rule was again established.

Al-Nasir ud Din Ullah was succeeded by Yaqoob un Nasir who was fond of luxury and ease. The Europeans launched a very strong attack on Spain in 614 A.H. and began to annex the Muslim territories bit by bit. During this time, the Muslims in Spain had

---

1. Muhammad was resident of Soos (Morocco). He was a scholarly person who had the honour of being a pupil of Imam Ghazali. In 515 A.H. he had started a movement of reformation inviting people to abide by the injunctions of God and to avoid his prohibitions. He had a very large following and Abdul Momin was his successor and disciple. Latter on he laid claim to be the promised Mehdi.

been weakened and the government of Al-Mowahhidoon was also on its last legs. Till the end of this dynasty's rule, Cardova was the capital of Spain – a distance of about 125 miles from the fort of Gibraltar.

Ibne Hood:

During the general anarchy in Spain the name of Bani Hood was mentioned in the foregoing pages. A courageous upstart of this family, Muhammad Bin Yousuf who was commonly called Ibne Hood, benefited from the anarchic situation and took possession of Granada, Malika, Almiria, Jiaan and Cardova. Possession of vast limiting made him an awe-inspiring authority in the Peninsula. To add to his dignity, he sent an application to Abbaside Caliph Al-Mustansir Billah in Baghdad, stating that he had conquered the entire city of Spain in the name of the Caliph and he may be granted formal permission to rule on behalf of Khilafat.

The formal order was received from Baghdad and in 631 A.H. it was read out in a large gathering of people. This was also honour for the caliph of Baghdad who was able to write a "Farman" about Spain after 500 years.

Since the Caliphate of Baghdad was on its last legs, the people in Muslim Spain did not attach much importance to the orders received from Baghdad. A powerful defiant, Ibnul Ahmar (also called Nasar Bin Umar) rose in revolt against Ibne Hood and their armed dispute for power and sovereignnity continued for a long time.

Apart from the rivalry of Ibne Hood and Ibnul Ahmar, many selfish Christians had established their individual rule in different provinces in Muslim rule and were constantly fighting one another. In the province of Bolunsia, Marwan Bin Abdul Aziz, in Marsia, Abu Abdullah, in Almiriah, Ibne Rameemi and in Ashbilia Abu Marwan had become independent ruler, each challenging the authority of another to defeat their Muslim rivals they stooped low to join hands with the Christian chiefs (who were their common enemies) who gave them military help for territorial gains on the Muslim lands. Among the Christian chiefs, Froland I attained maximum land for the Muslim rulers. In the northern mountains, region of Spain Froland had already established his state. He extended the province of Jiaan (which was the most important and invincible part of Muslim Spain) from Ibne Umar for help against his rival Ibne Hood. Then Muhammad Bin Yousuf approached him for help against his rivals for which he demanded 30 Muslim forts, which Ibne Yousuf readily surrendered. Thus Froland began to weaken one Muslim chief against another and maneuvered that mutual fighting of Muslim chiefs should continue. Steadily he went on gaining lands from the Muslims till he had captured 2,25,000 square miles in the north of Spain and Muslims were left with only 60,000 square miles in the South.

The Muslim rulers of Spain kept quarrelling among themselves and the Christian chief (Froland) gradually became the king of Spain. In 627 A.H. the Christians captured the city of Maurida. In 628 A.H. they captured the island of Mureqa. In the month of Safar, 636 A.H., the Christians captured the province of Blunsia and in Shawal, 636 A.H. they occupied the Muslim capital of Spain – Cardova. In 645 A.H. Froland attacked Ashbilia and after a long siege, he captured it. By now, all the independent Muslim chiefs and rulers of provinces were shouldered by the Christians and nothing was left for the Muslims. The only Muslim ruler who survived the Christian attacks and machinations was Nasar Bin Omar who had the southern province of Granada under his effective control. Its area was about 60,000 square miles.

Nasar Bin Omar had no effective Muslim rival left in the country. He was also mindful of the rising power of Froland. He therefore, saw wisdom in making friends with the Christian monarch. Both being afraid of each other, Froland and Nasar Bin Omar made a pact for peaceful co-existence.

After this event, the Muslim capital of Spain was Granada in place of Cardova. With Granada as the capital of Muslim Spain, they ruled for about 250 years till 897 A.H. The monarch of

Granada mark the famous palace of "Al-Hamra" which gained the fame of being one of the wonders of the world.

Kingdom of Granada:

Like the kingdoms of Cardova and Ashbilia, the kingdom of Granada also had great glory and splendour. From the family of Banu Ahmar, there were two kings who performed praiseworthy deeds like the kings of Morabitoon and Mowahidoon families. The Banu Ahmar family made great development in the fields of politics, education and civilization. Their efforts made the Granada government a glorious and prosperous government. They built grand and splendid buildings, mosques and educational institutions. They built up a firm structure of police and army. They encouraged the development of literature, industry, craftsmanship and generally improved the economic conditions of the people. They also successfully fought the neighbouring Christian governments and retrieved several territories which belong to the Muslim rules of old. Unfortunately in Granada also circumstances began to take an adverse turn as had been done in Cardova and Ashbilia.

In 870 A.H. Sultan Hassan ascended throne of Granada. He was a monarch with awe and majesty. The Christian king of Castilla, Ferdinand arrogantly demanded tribute from Sultan Hassan who wrote back to him:

> "The mints in Granada are not minting coins of gold and silver. These are manufacturing steel swords and spears to pierce the hearts of Christians".

The reply of Sultan Hassan was not a mere a display of hollow words. He actually invaded in 886 A.H. the fort of "Sakhrah" belonging to the king of Castilla and conquered this strong fort in a single night. This conquest set a series of battles in motion.

In 887 A.H. the King of Castilla invaded the fort of "Al-Hamra" as it was denuded of Muslim army. He captured it and mercilessly killed thousands of Muslim men, women and young children. The same year in the month of Jamadi-ul-Awwal, King

Hassan learnt that the king of Castilla was advancing towards Granada at the head of a large army and had already laid siege to the township of Losha. Sultan Hassan hastened with his army to Losha. Both the armies confronted each other on 27th of Jamadiul Awwal and the King of Castilla was badly defeated. The Muslims captured all the equipment and goods of his army.

On one hand, the Muslim rulers were at war with the Christians and, on the other hand, they were involved in the internal differences and fighting among themselves. Sultan Hassan had a Christian maid girl whome he loved passionately. His own wife was a daughter of his uncle, Abdullah. She bore his two sons Abu Abdullah and Yousuf. The slave girl also had sons from him. His sons Abu Abdullah and Yousuf had fear that Sultan Hassan may not nominate their stepbrothers as his successor. Under this notion both the sons raised the banner of rebellion against their father, Sultan Hassan when was engaged in a war with King of Castilla at Losha. They captured a part of Granada. Sultan Hassan came to know of his son's rebellion and he sojourned at Malika to consider possible measures to quelling his sons rebellion. The Christians attacked Malika but were badly defeated. Many of their seasoned commanders were arrested along with a military force of 10,000.

Abu Abdullah attacked Malika to snatch it from his father. He was defeated and ran towards Granada. Then he attacked the town of Yushina in Rabi ul Awwal 888 A.H. He was coming back after loot and arson in Yushina when he fell in the hands of Christian army. He was arrested and taken to the king of Castilla. Sultan Hassan came from Malika to Granada. But was dejected at the rebellious activities of his son and he abdicated the throne in favour of his brother Abdullah Al Zaghal.

In 890 A.H. the Christians again attacked the province of Malika and captured a few forts at the border. Sultan Abdullah Al Zaghal had left Granada and was halting in a fort on the way but Christian army units attacked his fort unawared. But the Muslims fought the invaders with valour. The enemy was routed.

When Ferdinand, the king of Castilla saw the might and valour of the Muslims, he came to the conclusion that it was next to impossible to defeat the Muslims in a battle. He therefore, returned to tricks and machination. He called Abdullah (who was his captive) and persuaded him to attack Granada with his own help and oust his uncle, Abdullah Al Zaghal. He was now pitched against his own uncle and whatever he captured of the province of Granada, he went on handing it over to Ferdinand as per terms of the military pact with him.

Sultan Abdullah Al Zaghal left Granada for Malika where Ferdinand was slaughtering the Muslim population. Abu Abdullah heard this news and he hastily captured Granada. Abdullah Al Zaghal came to know of his nephew's exploit and did not choose to return to Granada. He stayed in the valley of Aash and did not reach Malika to save the Muslims from Christian massacre. Ferdinand was furious and he mercilessly killed Muslims and made thousands his captives. These events took place in 892 A.H.

Abu Abdullah was under illusion that Ferdinand would honour the pact with him and, after ousting Abdullah Al Zaghal (his uncle) from Granada, he would be able to rule over the capital. But, in 893 A.H. he realized that Ferdinand had played a trick with him to weaken the power of Muslims by helping one against another and to wait for the opportunity to capture Granada and undo the Muslim rule.

In 894 A.H. Ferdinand brought his forces against Abu Abdullah who did fight but was constrained to make peace with him at the condition of surrounding the province of Basta to Ferdinand. The peace terms did provide complete safety to the lives and properties of the Muslims but Ferdinand betrayed all terms of the peace pact and captured the properties and wealth of the Muslims by force.

Sultan Abdullah Al Zaghal became disgusted at the news of Abu Abdullah's surrender and he stayed on in the valley of Aash as its ruler. Here Ferdinand again played a trick with Abdullah Al Zaghal and by deception captured the province of Eliriah and then the valley of Aash also. Then he sent message to Abu Abdullah that Abdullah Al Zaghal had peacefully surrendered to him the areas of Eliriah and Aash and he (Abu Abdullah) might now surrender to him the fort of "Al-Hamra" in Granada province. In place of "Al-Hamra", Ferdinand deceptively told Abu Abdullah that he would give any amount of wealth he requires and also establish his government on any part of Spain desired by Abu Abdullah. Abu Abdullah replied that he had no hitch in agreeing to his demand but his public was against any such deed.

The to and fro messages between Abu Abdullah and Ferdinand were under exchange when Abu Abdullah, urged by his Muslim subjects, attacked some of the Christian fort and captured them. Ferdinand launched a direct attack on Granada but the Muslim forces displayed extraordinary valour beneath the walls of Granada and forced Ferdinand to raise the siege of Granada. Immediately after the departure of Christian forces from Granada, Abu Abdullah attacked the Christian forces left behind from the heights of Al-Basharat and captured the whole area by slaughtering the remnant of Ferdinand's force.

It was a painful reality that, due to the internal mutual differences and quarrels of the Muslim rulers of Spain, the vast empire of Spain had been reduced to a small area of Granada. The Muslim rulers were still sleeping and did not give up mutual rivalries. Abdullah Al Zaghal came to know how his nephew Abu Abdullah had captured Al-Basharat. He could not tolerate it out of deep malice and rivalry. He reached the area and began to create mischief to undo the victory of his nephew. The result was a civil war between the two Muslim rulers.

The king of Castilla was carefully watching the events and he did not lose the good opportunity to attack Al-Basharat and captured the fort along with a few other forts adjoining. Malicious and inimical as he was, Ferdinand killed Muslims as his general policy and indulged in large-scale loot and arson. He had no need to use Abdullah Al Zaghal as his tool for further advancement. He told him bluntly to go back to Africa and he would guarantee his save passage to that country. Abdullah Al Zaghal saw no better alternative and came to Africa where he settled in Talsman where he died after some times. Now Abu Abdullah was the only Muslim ruler left in Spain.

Ferdinand was persuaded by his clever and cunning queen, Izabella, to attack Granada. He launched an attack at the head of a large army. Queen Izabella laid the foundation of a new city in front of the gates of Granada which was indication of the Christian's intention that they would never go away without capturing Granada.

The siege of Granada continued for seven or eight months. The public of Granada bore all the hardships patiently. However, when winter set in and cold and snows arrived, all the arsenals of reinforcement and help were closed to Granada. The people sought permission to go out in the open fields and fight the enemy. Abu Abdullah had lost courage. He could not confront 100,000 strong Christian army with his meager 20,000 soldiers.

The hardship of the siege obliged the Granada Muslims to seek foreign help of Muslim rulers. In the name of Islamic brotherhood they wrote pathetic letters to the Muslim rulers of Africa and Constantinnople to save their souls. The letter written to Ba-Yazid-II read as under:

"For centuries the Christians have been pressing us hard. Now we are unable to defend ourselves. We are suffering all sorts of losses and making every possible sacrifice. Our brothers have been made slaves. The troubles and affliction we are facing may eventually result in the disappearance of Islam from this land and the extinction of Muslims".

Mr. S. P. Scott has written in the following lines the immediate effect of those letters on Ba-Yazid-II:

"The appeal of his co-religionists had an effect on Ba-Yazid who sent two French marks to the Pope in Rome and threatened that the Christian population in the Turkish Kingdom was enjoying all civil rights. If the repression of the Spanish Muslims continues

at the hands of the Christians rulers, we shall take Vengeance from the Christians in our country. The Pope must intervene to dissuade his follower kings to stop cruelty".

The Pope sent both the missionaries of Ba-Yazid with his own letter to Ferdinand. But he had made recommendation in his letter for the kind treatment of the Spanish Muslims. Ferdinand and Izabella were too clever to be influenced even by the Pope. They wrote back to Pope: "The whole Peninsula of Spain belonged to them of right. The forefathers of these Muslims had usurped their lands which they claimed as their own. They (Muslims) shall soon loose this land as our forefathers had lost it to them". He further wrote that all non-Christians in his territories had equal social rights with the Christians".

On the other hand Sultan Ba-Yazid-II was at war with the Amir of Egypt. Ferdinand displayed his cleverness and offered Ba-Yazid to help him with men and ships to cope with the Egyptians. Ba-Yazid accepted this offer and took no further heed of the Muslims suffering in Spain. S. P. Scott wrote: "Ba-Yazid left his co-religionists to their fate".[1]

Abu Abdullah held a general meeting in the Palace of "Al-Hamra" which was attended by all prominent scholars, shaikhs, aristocrats and ministers. Some of the participants displayed great courage and gave their fine view that Granada may not be surrendered to Ferdinand at his arrogant demand and Muslims must fight to defend their land, their homes and town. But the majority of the participants were timid people who talked of peace. Abu Abdullah nominated his minister Abu Qasim Abdul Malik for peace talks with Ferdinand. At long lost a Peace Contract was drawn up which was signed by Ferdinand and Abu Abdullah and, under this contract, the 800 years old Muslim rule in Spain came to a pathetic end.

---

1. Akhbarul Andulus Vol.2, P292

This peace contract was a document of long misfortunes for the Muslims of Spain. Amir Shakaib Arsalan has explained this contract in detail in his book "Akhir Bani Siraj". The salient features of the fatal contract signed by Abu Abdullah are reproduced below:

"All small and big Muslims will be provided perfect peace. Their properties, wealth and estates shall be protected. Their religious affairs and mosques will function independently without any duress. The disputes of the Muslims will be decided by their own courts headed by Qazis. The properties and wealth so far falling in the hands of the Muslims will not be recovered from them. They will not be called upon to pay any taxes over and above the tax mutually agreed by the contract signing authorities. No Christian convert to Islam shall be asked to give up Islam and no Muslim will be forced to accept Christianity. Any Muslim intending to leave for Africa will be sent there at government expense. No Christian shall enter the house of any Muslim or scale the walls of his house. The Muslims shall not be forced to arrange feast for the Christian armies. The Muslims shall be free in the choice and wearing of their dresses. They shall not be forced to use any particular sign or insignia (like the cross). No Christian shall ever join at or give names or demoralize or look down upon a Muslim. If one insulting a Muslim shall be punished. Any Muslim war prisoner shall be immediately released. If a Muslim slave fled from his master (especially a Christian) and reach Granada, he will be given protection and the king shall pay his cost to the owner of the slave".

The unfortunate peace contract between king Ferdinand of Castilla and king Abu Abdullah of Granada was signed on 30th December, 1491 AD Corresponding with 1st of Rabi ul Awwal, 897 A.H. apart from king Ferdinand, his queen Izabella, all the princes and princesses of the royal family of Ferdinand, Christian priests, aristocrats and ministers had also signed it. Both Ferdinand and Izabella had sworn to abide by every word and every letter of the contract. They also made it obligatory for their successors, their children, their government functionaries and the coming generation of their families not to flout or deviate from any clause or part of this contract".

The above contract was of general input regarding rights and obligation of the Muslims, there was a separate contract signed for the benefit of Abu Abdullah. This contract had 14 clauses wherein king Ferdinand and queen Izabella had agreed to given some lands, some estates and the town of Albasharat to Abu Abdullah. It was also promised that Abu Abdullah shall be given an amount of 1,40,50,000 of the local currency as soon as king Ferdinand and queen Izabella entered the fort of "Al-Hamra". It was also promised that Abu Abdullah will not be liable to any taxes so long as he continued to live in Spain. If he wished to leave Spain, his lands and properties shall be bought at reasonable cost. If he wished to leave behind an administrator of his estates and properties, their income shall be ensured to be sent to Abu Abdullah. If Abu Abdullah wished to undertake a voyage, the ships or boats shall be arranged by king Ferdinand". According to the research of Amin Shakaib Arsalan, the second contract was signed on 25th December 1491 AD.[1]

It is worthy of note that Abu Abdullah entered with the above contracts without the knowledge or the consent of the people of Granada, who were angry and disgruntled. At the incitement of Hamid Bin Zararah, 20,000 people of Granada armed themselves and came out to fight the Christians. But unforeseen circumstances failed their intention to fight on the second day of this event, Abu Abdullah came out of the fort of "Al-Hamra" with a body of elite of the city and addressed the Muslims:

> *"O Muslims! I admit that no one is to blame for this dishonour and disgrace accept myself alone. I disobeyed my father and rose in rebellion against him and I called upon the enemies to attack our country. God has punished me for my sins. I have accepted and agreed to this contract solely to*

---
1. Hazar-ul-Aalam-ul-Islami Vol. 2, P.7

> *protect your lives and honour so that wives and women are not made slave girls and maidservants and your Islamic laws and your properties are duly protected by them (Christians). Kings would be a decidedly better human beings than this unfortunate Abu Abdullah".*

Ferdinand had given Abu Abdullah a period of two months and 10 days within which the fort of "Al-Hamra" was to be handed over to him. But Abu Abdullah was so much confused and overstricken that, long before the scheduled time, he sent a message to Ferdinand only after a day of his address to the Muslims of Granada to take possession of the city. Ferdinand appointed a Christian priest to enter "Al-Hamra", remove the sign of Islam from the highest pillar in Granada and fix the cross their on so that, on seeing the cross, the king and the queen may be inspired with Christian jubilance and enter the city in victory. Preparations went afoot for exit of Muslims and entry of Christians into the city. During the whole night wretched Abu Abdullah and his family kept preparing to leave. "Al-Hamra" and Ferdinand and his queen rejoicing in their camp and preparing to enter next morning.

Early next morning Abu Abdullah left "Al-Hamra" along with his kith and kin. The priest sent by Ferdinand met him on the way along with a body of his attendants. Abu Abdullah handed over the keys of "Al-Hamra" to the priest and said to him:

> *"Go and take possession of this fort which Allah, the Great has taken away from us due to our bad deeds and handed over to you".*

The priest entered "Al-Hamra" and, in accordance with the instructions of the Ferdinand, removed the banner of Islam and put up the banner of cross. When Ferdinand, Izabella and their army saw the big change, their joy knew no bounds. Both the king and the queen fell down on their knees to thank Almighty God. All the armed forces also followed their king and fell down on knees in gratefulness of the Great Creator. Then they left for entry into

Granada. On the bank of the river, there was a small mosque where Abu Abdullah met them. Abu Abdullah saw King Ferdinand and intended to get down his mount out of respect. But both the king and queen prohibited him. Abu Abdullah wished to kiss the king Ferdinand and queen Izabella but both of them declined to stretch their hands. Seeing the anxiety of Abu Abdullah both the rulers gave solace and spoke words of comfort. Abu Abdullah's son who was held as hostage by king Ferdinand was restored to him. Then he handed over to him the keys of the city of Granada and said wistfully: "These keys are the last symbol of the Arab occupation of Spain. You take these. God has so willed that our country and our belongings and even our bodies be in your possession. I hope you will treat my people with compassion and mercy as you have promised". Ferdinand replied: "No doubt we shall abide by our promises". Then Ferdinand handed over the keys to the queen who passed on the keys to Prince John who gave them to Count Tandal who was made the commander of the Christian army of Granada.

Now king Ferdinand, his queen Izabella and their army proceeded to take their possession of Granada. Abu Abdullah proceeded to the place in the valley of Barshana which had been allotted to him. After walking a little he stopped and cast a wistful glance on the city of Granada, its population, the fort of "Al-Hamra", its domes and minarets. All his companions joined him in looking at the city left by them. All of these were dumb forwarded and no body could speak a single word out of remorse and utter sorrow. They were busy looking at the lost grandeur when cannons began to roar from the fort of "Al-Hamra", indicating the Christians had defeated the Muslims whose government had come to an end and the Christians were Victorious over the land of Spain which they had conquered. At this stage Abu Abdullah was overpowered by sentiments and he burst into weeping. He wept profusely when his mother Ayesha (who was a wise lady) said to him:

> *"Now you are weeping like women. You had occasion to defend Granada but you failed to defend it and did not have the dare to fight".*

The minister of Abu Abdullah also tried to console him but the tears ran from his eyes like a stream. He could not find peace of mind. The hillock of Al-Bashraat on which Abu Abdullah stood weeping and cast his last wistful glances at Granada came to be remembered as: "The last breath of the Arabs". Ameer Shakaib Arslan wrote that he had seen the place during his visit to Spain.

Death of Abu Abdullah:

As stated above, Ferdinand had fixed Al-Bashraat for the residence and stay of Abu Abdullah. But after capture of Granada, Ferdinand failed to honour any of his commitments with the result that the vast land of Spain became narrow and inhospitable for Abu Abdullah and his family. Ferdinand purchased the land of Al-Bashraat with nominal price and Abu Abdullah said good bye to Spain forever. He came to Africa and took up service with the king of Morocco. He died in Morocco in 940 A.H.

Abu Abdullah had left two sons – Yousuf and Ahmad as his heirs. In the city of Fames (in Morocco) when Abu Abdullah had died, his progeny continues to him. Ameer Shakaib Arsalan met the children of Abu Abdullah "who were living in abject poverty. They used to feed from public kitchens where the poor and needy persons are invited for sustenance".

Repression and Tyranny on Granada Muslims:

At the fall of Granada, the Muslim rule of Spain, which had continued for nearly 800 years, came to a sad end. With the end of Muslim government, the Muslim citizen of Spain were subjected to untold tyranny and oppression. There was no mode of repression and injustice which was not perpeturated on the Muslims. When the terms of the agreement signed by Ferdinand are compared with the untold tyrannical measures adopted by the Christian government of Ferdinand, one is drawn to the natural conclusion that a nation which cannot guard its honour and existence, vainly hope for and look for kindness, sympathy and fair deal from the nation dominating them.

The first thing which Ferdinand and Izabella did on entering Granada was to turn the biggest Muslim mosque into a Christian church and said their prayer of thankfulness in that church. Then they made efforts through government agencies that Muslims may voluntarily give up Islam and embrace the Christian faith. When soft and persuasive measures failed to convert the Muslims to Christian faith hard and cruel measures were taken without any reason or any regard of the pact signed by the Ferdinand. The first governmental order forbade the acceptance of Islam by any Christian citizen. As against this, if a Muslim gave up Islam to become a Christian, he was heaped with wealth and favours. In 1499 A.H. a circular order was promulgated that any citizen of Spain who was not prepared to accept the Christian faith, must leave Spain. The result of this order was that very weak and poor Muslims who had no support and power to resist the unjust order, were seen visiting the churches and performing the Christian ritual to save their skins. The Muslims who took courage to refuse forced conversion to the Christian faith, they were maltreated and annoyed in several ways and, whereever the government agencies found it possible, Muslim children were given forced baptism.

When the Muslims complained of atrocities before the royal court in 1524 A.D., their complaint was handed over to the department of religious investigations. In accordance with the decision of this department, thousands of Muslims were burnt alive. Then the lord bishop of this department proposed that once a year the Muslims may neither perform their religious duties nor put on their particular dress, nor they should talk in their particular language. During the reign of king Phillip-II, the lord bishop of Granada promulgated with the permission of the king that the Muslims shall not take a bath either to remove dirt of their bodies or after co-habitation when a bath was compulsorily enjoined on them. It was also made obligatory for the Muslims to join the western dances in the ball rooms and the speaking of the Arabic language as well as wearing of the veils for the Muslim women was made unlawful and punishable.

Andulusia (Spain) The Rise and Fall of Muslim Rule

The atrocities and sanctions did not end as described above, the Muslims were forced to change their names. Ameer Shakaib Arsalan has written in part II of his book "Hazir ul Aalim ul Islami" that many of the names of the struts and public places which are now Spanish were originally Arabic and those were attributed to prominent Muslim chiefs who were forced to give up Islam and convert to the Christian faith. On that account their original Arabic names were caricatured.

Apart from the Muslim historians, the European Christian historians have also described the atrocities and human torture perpeturated on the Muslims in reasonable details. The famous author of the "Arab Culture" (Tamaddun-e-Arab), Mosseu Leban says:

> "The torture and atrocities on the poor, helpless Muslims of Spain has no parallel in the history of the mankind although the self-same Muslims never did any injustice and had never been unfair towards the Christians subjects when they ruled over that country. Had the Muslims chosen to be unjust and coercive the entire Peninsula of Spain would have been denuded of Christians".

In the end of the 15th century A.D., after the death of Lord Bishop Mandora, Francisco Shcemens DeSeosoz was made the lord bishop. This man was extremely bigoted and inimical to Islam and the Muslims. He has been described by S. P. Scott as under: "The life story of this man, his social contacts and his educational background made him a narrow minded, prejudicial and bigoted person of the times. He had neither tolerance nor kindness nor any feeling of human mercy. His job as understood by him was to follow blindly and implement the orders given by the church authorities". His above-normal condition has been described by S. P. Scott as under: "He availed for himself all moral and immoral facilities. His favourite women belonged to the elite of government circles. They were either the daughters of the Christian aristocrats or the maidservants of the queens. Pope Innocent, the VIII in 1486 A.D. and queen Izabella in 1487 A.D. declared the bastard children of Lord Bishop Scheemens as lawful children. Despite his moral corruption this Lord Bishop was so much influential that he practically ruled over the country in the name of the King. He had obtained a royal order from the king whereunder he investigated the cases of Muslims according to his own whim and fancy, and inflicted any kind of punishment of his choice". S. P. Scott has narrated the tyrannical tales of his torture and atrocities on the Muslims which cannot be described. We are constrained to reproduce below a summary of the atrocities on the Muslims as described and written by S. P. Scott:

> "After the surrender of Muslim rulers in Spain to king Ferdinand and queen Izabella, the Muslims were going towards the suburbs of all Al-Baseen Mosque where they were caught and 4000 Muslims were baptized on the pretext that they were sick of their religion (Islam). The mosque was turned into a church. The forced converts were under such restraints that they could not do anything against Christian religion without intention. The Muslims who scolded and blamed the converts for their apostasy, they were tortured and punished in different ways and were imprisoned".

Burning of Books on Islam:

After usurping power by trickery and cunningness, the Christian rulers of Spain turned their attention to the annihilation of literacy and cultural monuments of the Muslims. All the Muslim houses of Granada were searched and ran-sacked and all the available Arabic books were confiscated. About 10,00,000 books were collected which included very precious copies of the Holy Quran and the old precious documents of the times of Banu Umayyads which were held in great esteem from generation to generation. Some of those precious books were translations of the old Greek books of wisdom which had been in the libraries of Alexandria. These had reached Spain from far away coast of Nile and were wonderful specimen of Muslim calligraphy. Their pages had been decorated with gold and silver linings. Some of those books had leather covers while some other had on them ivory works and pearls studded in a golden background".

The valuable treasures of knowledge Science and wisdom were heaped up with the crossing of "Bab ur Rohlah" and they were burnt to ashes. S. P. Scott described this tragedy in his own words:

> *"The loss which the entire human race suffered on account of this religious fanaticism may well be guessed from the fact that such a precious treasure of knowledge, science and wisdom did not exist anywhere else in the world – which Lord Bishop Scheemens burnt to ashes in the historical crossing. The human posterity suffered incalculable loss because treasures collected over centuries were burnt to ashes. The research scholars can never lay their hands on the sources of Saracens culture and civilization which had played a leading role for the humanity of their times".*[1]

The European historians had estimated that the number of precious books burnt to ashes by Scheemens was 80,000 [2]. If the number of books burnt in other cities of Spain may also be counted, the volume of human loss would appear as colossal.

Muslims Burnt Alive:

S. P. Scott has written that the crossing of Bab ur Rohlah where Muslim books were burnt was also notable for the burning alive of the Muslims who had been accused of crimes known to Scheemens alone.[3]

Massacre of Muslims:

Professor Kurd Ali wrote on the authority of the western historians and research scholars that the era of repression and torture

---
1. Akhbarul Andulus Vol.3
2. Al Islam-wal-Hizara-tul-Arabia Vol.1, P.252, 253
3. Akhbarul Andulus Vol.3, P.275

of Muslims started in 1499 A.D. The Spanish Christians caught hold of Muslim children and baptized them forcibly. The pretext was that they were originally Christians. They were put up before the officials of religious research who burnt alive those unfortunate children. Since conversion to the Christian faith on a large scale was not possible, the Lord Bishop who wanted to cleanse the Spanish soil of the Arabs, he gave general orders that any Arab who did not accept the Christian faith may be put to death.

The famous French reformer Volteer said:

> "When the Arabs conquered Spain, they did not force Islam on a single Christian. But, it was unfortunate that, when the Spaniards captured power in Spain, Lord Bishop Scheemens decided that all the Muslims must forsake Islam and accept the Christian faith. He forced 50,000 Muslims to put on the sign of cross on their bodies which they did not believe".

In 1566 A.D. a general order was promulgated forbidding the Muslims to use the Arabic language and to give up their national Islamic dress and all the rituals which gave them the resemblance of Islam. Being annoyed at those forcible measures, the Muslims in "Al-Basharaat" took to rebellion. Skirmishes continued for years till 1604A.D. when Muslims were defeated and it was broadly declared that the Muslim population of Spain must vacate the land of Spain. In pursuance of this governmental order the Muslims to the turn of 5,00,000 left Spain in about 2 years. Some of them went to Africa while others sought asylum whenever they could go. The historians have estimated that, since the occupation of Granada by Ferdinand till the final order of 1604 A.D. no less than 30,00,000 Muslims had left Spain. One historian has stated that three forth of the Muslims who had fled to take asylum in Africa were killed on their way to Africa. By the beginning of the 17th century A.D. not a single Muslim was left in Spain.

---

1   Al Islam-wal-Hizara-tul-Arabia Vol.1, P.252, 253

RISE AND FALL OF MUSLIMS IN INDIA

As history tells the Muslims were able to establish their rule in many parts of the world. The establishment of the Muslim rule was important event in the history of the world. They ruled over India for nearly 800 years after which circumstances so changed that their governments ceased to exist and, while examining the rise and fall of the Muslims in the world scenario, it appears to be necessary to have a glance on the rise and fall of the Muslims in the Indian sub continent.

During the days of caliphate of Hazrat Umar ؓ, the governor of Bahrain, Usman Bin Abil Aas ؓ had sent an army to the Indian coast via Amman. This army came upto Tana (Thana near Bombay). Hazrat Umar ؓ was angry over this expedition and wrote to Usman ؓ: "If the Muslims had suffered any loss of life in this expedition, I would have taken revenge from your people". Usman had also sent his brother Al-Hakam to Bharoouch and another brother, Mughira to Daibal where both had had a skirmish with the local infidels. They came victories in the fighting.

When Hazrat Usman ؓ rose to caliphate, he appointed Abdullah Bin Aamir as governor of Iraq and wrote to him to send a suitable man to India who may study the circumstances and life conditions of that country and report to us. He selected Hakim Bin Jablah Al Alvi for the survey of India. On return from India Hakim Bin Jabla narrated the circumstances in such a manner that Hazrat Usman ؓ considered it improper to send any body to India.[1]

During the caliphate of Hazrat Ali ؓ and Ameer Moawiyya ؓ there is a mention in the history books of the Muslim units of army having visited Makran, Qabqan and even Lahore and Bannu. But those were only skirmishes.

---

[1] Futuh-ul-Baldan by Balazri

A regular expeditions to attack the land of Sindh was undertaken by the renowned Muslim General Muhammad Bin Qasim during the caliphate of Walid Bin Abdul Malik.

Attack on Sindh by Muhammad Bin Qasim:

The ruler of Sindh, Raja Dahir was inimical towards Muslims. He had granted asylum to the culprit Arabs who had killed Saeed Bin Aslam, Governor of Makran. Another event took place in between. The ruler of Ceylon (Lanka) wished to build up friendly relations with the Muslims. He sent a few ships loaded with costly presents to Hajjaj Bin Yousuf, the famous governor of Iraq. These ships had on board some Muslim pilgrims and a few women of the Arab traders, who had passed away in Ceylon. Perchance these ships reached the port of Daibal, 24 miles from Thatta, which was part of the territory belonging to Raja Dahir.[1] The pirates (sea robbers) looted all the precious goods on the ships and made the women and the children of the Arab traders their captives. Hajjaj Bin Yousuf came to know of it. He was furious and wrote to Dahir to set the women and the children free and restore the goods taken by pirates without further delay. Dahir expressed his helplessness to prevail upon the pirates. Hajjaj Bin Yousuf was already aware of the enmity of Raja Dahir towards Muslims and he now decided to teach him a lesson.

After seeking permission of the central caliphate, he sent an army under the command of Ubaid Ullah Bin Nabaan. He was killed. Then Hajjaj Bin Yousuf sent Budail Bin Tahfah Al-Bijli. Unfortunately his horse remained sulky and he was surrounded by enemies and killed. Then Hajjaj Bin Yousuf selected Muhammad Bin Qasim, his nephew and son-in-law who were then in Iran. He was sent to Sindh at the head of a large army, which included 6000 Syrian soldiers alongwith others.

Muhammad Bin Qasim reached Makran first of all. After stay of a few days he advanced to Qarrabou which he conquered and

---

1 A seaport twenty four miles in the south west of Thatta.

moved on to Armail which was also conquered by him. Then he advanced towards Daibal which was a sea port about 24 miles from Thatta. This was under Raja Dahir. Muhammad Bin Qasim himself came by road but a big army, well equipped, joined him by sea. At Daibal, the Muslim army camped and started preparation for encounter with the army of Raja Dahir. In Daibal there was a big temple where a red flag was hoisted on a very high pole. According to the historian Blazri, when the wind blew this flag began to circulate and covered the whole city of Daibal. Muhammad Bin Qasim tactfully used his carriage carrying the cannon and fired at the flag from an oblique angle, uprooting the pole and downing the red flag. This event made Raja Dahir very furious. Both the armies fought a pitched battle which ended in victory for the Muslims. Muhammad Bin Qasim stayed at Daibal for 3 days and in disregard of the Islamic code of warfare, indulged in large scale massacre, killing even the priests of the big temple.

The conquest of Daibal demoralized the Hindu ruler and his subjects. Muhammad Bin Qasim advanced towards Nairon and Sehwan and conquered them without fighting. When he reached Mehran, Raja Dahir prepared well for the defence of his land. Muhammad Bin Qasim sent a unit of army under the command of Muhammad Bin Mosaab to Sadosan which was surrendered by the priests without any fighting. When Muhammad Bin Qasim returned, 4000 Jats accompanied him who all joined the army of Muhammad Bin Qasim, who crossed the Indus River at Talhat and turned to the capital of Raja Dahir. Raja Dahir confronted the Muslim army at Klab Gucheri where Dahir suffered a bad defeat. Muhammad Bin Qasim now advanced to the city of Alore where Dahir confined himself into the fort.[1] The siege laid by Muhammad Bin Qasim continued for 10 days during which there was fighting between the two armies for 7 times. On the 10th of Ramzan, 93 A.H. Raja Dahir came out of the fort at the head of 10,000 armoured soldiers and 30,000 infantry. One unit of tall and heavy elephants also attended the Raja who was himself riding a well-decorated elephant.

---

1 So is the statement of Syed Muhammad Masoom – Tareekh-e-Masoomi, P.24, but according to Chuchnama, Dahir was in the fort.

The two armies confronted each other. Muhammad Bin Qasim personally advanced at the head of a unit of his army to fight the enemy. At this time, a unit of Muslim army began to discharge fire works, which made the elephants frightful and they took to their heels stamping under their feet soldiers of their own army. Suddenly an arrow shot by the Muslim artillery struck the throat of Raja Dahir who died instantly.[1] The defeated army of Raja Dahir ran towards Bahman Abad where Muhammad Bin Qasim chased them and conquered Bahman Abad also. Now the entire land of Sindh had come under the control of Muslims.

After the conquest of Sindh, Muhammad Bin Qasim proceeded to Multan which was called in those days "the house of gold" because of its prosperity and wealth. In Multan there was a big idols temple. The Muslims had to face great trouble and tired in their fight for the conquest of Multan. Their provisions were totally finished and they were forced to eat the flesh of monkeys/asses to keep the body and soul together. Anyhow, they fought with endurance perseverance and valour and came out successful in expedition.[2]

Sad End of Muhammad Bin Qasim:

The exploit of Muhammad Bin Qasim in his having conquered Sindh and Multan was by no means less honourable than that of Musa Bin Nusair or Tariq Bin Ziad in their having conquered Spain. If this event had taken place during the regime of one of the Khalifa-e-Rashid (one of the first four caliphs) and the Muslims had not fallen a prey to tribal and family prejudices, the Indian sub-continent would certainly have emerged as an entirely Muslim country like Egypt, Syria and Iraq.

Muhammad Bin Qasim had hardly been on the Indian soil for four years when Walid Bin Abdul Malik died in 96 A.H. and his brother Suleiman Bin Abdul Malik came to occupy the throne of caliphate. Certain events had made him inimical towards Hajjaj Bin

---

1   Tareekh-e-Masoomi
2. Futuh-ul-Baldan P.427

Yousuf, the famous governor of the Banu Umayyads regime. Muhammad Bin Qasim was a nephew and son-in-law of Hajjaj Bin Yousuf. He, therefore, earned the wrath of Sulaiman Bin Abdul Malik. Sulaiman made Yazid Bin Abi Jaisha, the governor of Sindh and removed Muhammad Bin Qasim from his post. Not only that, he also ordered that Muhammad Bin Qasim may be sent to Iraq under fetters. On reaching Iraq, the governor Salih Bin Abdur Rehman imprisoned Muhammad Bin Qasim in the city of Wasit. He was tortured in various ways and, at long last, the conqueror of Sindh was slain along with a group of persons belonging to the family of Ibne Aqeel. [1]

General historical statements reveal that Muhammad Bin Qasim was very harsh and coercive with the enemies in his battles in Sindh and Multan. Even after the cessation of hostilities and his victories, he continued general slaughter of the enemy for several days. He demolished temples and idols houses and killed many priests and religious scholars (Pandits). But the harshness in his attitude was short-lived and, after the matter was settled down, he was a kind and considerate ruler. How he had befriended himself with the local people may well be judged from the fact that, when Muhammad Bin Qasim was leaving Sindh with fetters (as per command of Sulaiman Bin Abdul Malik), the local population wept bitterly and they raised statue of Muhammad Bin Qasim. [2]

Doctor Tara Chand has compared the administration and the mode of government adopted by Raja Chach (father of Raja Dahir) and Muhammad Bin Qasim. He writes: "Raja Chach was a bigoted ruler. He had promulgated prejudicial laws for the follower of Budh religion who were forbidden to wear arms, to wear silk, and to ride horses with saddles. They were also required to walk bare footed and bare headed and to keep always dogs with them". As against the above, he wrote about Muhammad Bin Qasim:

"The Muslim conqueror treated the conquered

---

[1] Futuh-ul-Baldan P.428
[2] Futuh-ul-Baldan P.428

people with ease and kindness. They allowed the old public servants to continue their service. Hindu priests and Brahmans were absolutely free to follow their way of worship in the temples. They had only to pay a very meager tax (Jizya) which commensurate with their income. The disputes of the Muslims were decided in the Qazi courts while the disputes of the Hindus were decided by the Panchayats. Hindus were holding some very high offices of the government. So much so that the Prime Minister of Muhammad Bin Qasim was the self-same Hindu who had served as Prime Minister of Raja Dahir".

Acceptance of Islam by Hindu Rajas of Sindh:

After Muhammad Bin Qasim, Yazid Bin Jaisha was made the governor of Sindh. But he died after only eighteen days of his arrival in Sindh. Now Habib Bin Al-Mohallab was made the governor. By the times, governor Habib reached Sindh, the Hindu Rajas had re-captured their respctive areas. The son of Raja Dahir, Jaisha came back to Brahman Abad to rule. During this time, Sulaiman Bin Abdul Malik died and Hazrat Umar Bin Abdul Aziz (99 A.H. to 101 A.H.) became the caliph. His mode of government was strictly on the pattern of Khalifat-e-Rashida (i.e., like the government of first four caliphs). He was not inclined to capture lands or to accumulate wealth. He, therefore, wrote letters to the Indian Rajas to embrace Islam. The Rajas had already known the fine sentiments of Hazrat Umar Bin Abdul Aziz and his impersonal way of government. Many Rajas, including the son of Raja Dahir accepted Islam willingly. Jaisha son of Raja Dahir, chose his Islamic name from Arabic names. [1]

After the death of Hazrat Umar Bin Abdul Aziz, governors for Sindh were duly appointed by the Khalifa at Damascus. Nothing extraordinary happened till 105 A.H. when Hisham Bin Abdul Malik

---

1. Futuh-ul-Baldan P.429

appointed Junaid Bin Abdul Rehman as governor of Sindh. He was a very courageous and daring man. He organized the administration of the Sindh province on a sound footing and then planned to annex more Indian areas to his administration. He sent one army to Ujjain and another army to Malwa under the command of Ujaib Bin Marrah. Allama Blazri stated that no land was conquered due to those skirmishes but substantial looty was collected to the Muslim armies.[1] The last governor of Sindh under the Banu Umayyads was Mansoor Bin Jamhoor al-kalbi who came to Sindh during the regime of Banu Umayyads caliph Marwan al Himar (127 A.H. to 132 A.H). He is reported to have laid the foundation of a new city "Mansurah". In 132 A.H. the Abbasides came into power.

Sindh under the Abbaside Caliphate:

Among the Sindh governors appointed by the Abbaside caliphates, Hisham Bin Amr –Al-Tughalbi was the most courageous ruler. He was appointed during the caliphate of Abu Jafar Mansoor (136 A.H. to 158 A.H.). on reaching Sindh, he re-annexed all those territories of the Province which had been receded due to rebellions and turmoil during his predecessor's rule. He also made an attack on Bharaich and Kandhara on reaching there by sea with a fleet of boats. Then he turned towards the North and made an attack on Kashmir when he collected much wealth as looty.[2]

Till the times of Mamoon-ur-Rashid Abbasi the dignity of the Arabs was uphold in Sindh. However, during the caliphate of Mo'tasim Billah differences became acute between the Nizaris and Yemenites. The prejudices of the old "Jahiliyya" made the two families inimical. The governor of the time, Imran Bin Moosa was more inclined towards the Arabs which the Nizaris disliked. This gave a chance to the local Hibari family to rise up. Umar Bin Abdul Aziz Al-Hibari availed an opportunity and killed the governor Imran. The governors of Sindh continue to be appointed by the caliph till the times of Wasiq Billah and Mutawakkil Billah. After him, the

---

1. Futuh-ul-Baldan P.430
2. Futuh-ul-Baldan P.431

relations between Sindh and the central caliphate remained only nominal.

In 240 A.H. the Hibari family came into power in Sindh. Their government continued till 290 A.H. when Banu Samah of Multan declared their independence. Now on-ward two separate Muslim states – Multan and Mansurah – came into existence.

By the end of the 1st century, A.H. the Muslim rule in Sindh was breathing its last. However, Islam began to enter the sub-continent from the North Via Khyber Pass. We shall soon study.

Amir Sabukta-Gin:

The first caravan of Islam entered the Indo-Pak sub-continent in 980 A.H. the leader of this caravan was Amir Sabukta-Gin, the then ruler of Ghazni. The person who paved the way for the advent of the Islamic forces was Raja Jay Pal, the then ruler of Punjab, Peshawar and Kabul. Being fearful of any Muslim advance from Ghazni, he prepared to check any possible Muslim advance in their own territories. In 369 A.H. (979 A.D.) Raja Jay Pal advanced towards the Muslim kingdom of Ghazni at the head of a very large army assisted by a battalion of elephants.

According to the research of Bargz, Amir Sabukta-Gin came out with a large army to meet the challenge of Jay Pal. At Taghan, both the armies were pitched against each other for many days.[1] After sever fighting Jay Pal proposed peace. Amir Sabukta-Gin's son Mahmood (later known as Sultan Mahmood Ghaznavi) also joined the parleys for peace but advised continuous fighting. However, peace was concluded. But Jay Pal was dislodged to the terms of the peace. In stead of handing over articles promised in the peace talks, Jay Pal imprisoned the men of Amir Sabukta-Gin who had gone to Lahore to fetch the promised things. This infuriated Amir Sabukta-Gin who left for India at the head of a large army. Jay Pal mustered support of the rulers of Delhi, Ajmir, Kalanjar and Qannuj and came to Peshawar to meet the Muslim army from Ghazni.[2] Jay Pal was

---
1. Tareekh-e-Farishta Vol.1, P.10 (under translation)
2. Ibid P.56

routed in the encounter near Peshawar and the areas of Kabul and Peshawar were captured by the Muslims. Amir Sabukta-Gin left 2000 cavalry with his deputy and returned to Ghazni.

The role of Amir Sabukta-Gin was no less heroic than that of his son, Sultan Mahmood because he had opened the doors of Indian soil for Islam. According to Historian Farishta, Amir Sabukta-Gin was a person of high character, good at heart and a just ruler. He died at Trimz near Balkh at the age of 56 years in 387 A.H. corresponding to 997 A.D. He ruled for 20 years.

Sultan Mahmood of Ghazni:

At the death of Amir Sabukta-Gin his elder son Sultan Mahmood was in Neshapore. As such, in accordance with the dying will of his father, the younger son, Amir Ismail succeeded his father in Balkh. But the army and the people did not accept his rule. Sultan Mahmood came to know of the difficulties and he advised Sultan Ismail to accept the rulership of Balkh and Kharasan in exchange for Ghazni and the capital areas because an experienced and elderly ruler could control the circumstances.[1] Amir Ismail did not agree. Sultan Mahmood, much against his wish, confronted his brother in the battlefield. The army of Amir Ismail was defeated and Besieged itself in the fort of Ghazni. Sultan Mahmood negotiated with the army and peacefully took them out of the fort. He captured the Treasury and appointed reliable men to control the capital and himself left for Balkh. After a few days Amir Ismail was imprisoned in the fort of Jarjan.

Sultan Mahmood Attacks Punjab:

Right from his childhood Sultan Mahmood had a desire to conquer India. After freedom fron the expeditions of Kharasan and Turkistan, he left Ghazni at the head of 10,000 cavalry and reached Peshawar in 1001 A.D. Jay Pal was not unaware. He mustered a heavy force of 12,000 cavalry, 30,000 infantry and 300 elephants to meet the Sultan. There was a pitched battle at the banks of the

---

1. Tareekh-e-Farishta P.63, 64 (Urdu translation)

Attock river in which Sultan Mahmood was Victorious. Jay Pal and some of his relatives were arrested but Mahmood made him his tributary (tax-payer) and released him. According to the Hindu belief Jay Pal had become unfit to rule because of his repeated defeats. He, therefore, abdicated in favour of his son, Anand Pal and burnt himself to death.

Sultan Mahmood Attacks Multan:

A Hindu named Baheara Rai ruled in Bhatia near Multan. He was so arrogant that he would submit neither to Jay Pal nor to the governor of Amir Sabukta-Gin. In 395 A.H. Sultan Mahmood attacked Bhatia. After a few days' deadly battle the Raja was defeated and killed. Next year Sultan Mahmood wanted to punish Abul Fateh, the Ruler of Multan who had become arrogant and sought alliance with Anand Pal to face Sultan Mahmood. Anand Pal came to Peshawar to block his march to Multan. Sultan Mahmood fought the Rajputs and Anand Pal fled towards Kashmir. Then Sultan went to Multan, punished Abul Fateh and returned to Ghazni.

Battle at Peshawar and Conquest of Nagar Kot:

In 399 A.H. Sultan Mahmood again attacked India. Anand Pal rejoined his strength and was also helped by the rulers of Ujjaun, Gowaliar, Kalinger, Qannouj Delhi and Ajmir. Even Hindu women had sold away their ornaments to help Anand Pal against the Muslim invaders. There was a great enthusiasm among the Hindus. Sultan Mahmood was very confused in his preparations for the war with the collective forces of Hindu Rajas. He got a ditch dug out on both sides of his army to avoid the attack by the Hindus. The Muslim artillery started the operation and flung arrows at the enemy who came closer to fight. When face to face fighting began 20,000 Hindu soldiers crossed the ditch and went right into the midest of the Sultan's army. This resulted in the killing of the three to four thousand Muslim soldiers. The Muslim army was un-nerved at this un-expected attack. Perchance Anand Pal's elephant was frightened at the roar of the cannon balls and took to flight. The Hindu army thought their leader had left the battlefield for his life and a general rout took place. The Muslims chased the large Hindu army for two days and two nights. About eight thousand enemy soldiers were killed. Sultan Mahmood was Victorious.

Siege of Nagar Kot:

After his victory at Peshawar, Sultan Mahmood made up his mind to conquer the strong fort of Bhim in Nagar Kot (Dt. Kangrah). This fort had been made by Raja Bhim at the top of a hill. It was reported to be a Treasure Loan of idols and wealth. Sultan laid siege to the fort which continued for three days. On the fourth day the besieged Hindu army opened the gates and let the Sultan's army in. He gave assurance of life to every one in the Fort and collected all the fabulous wealth which had been accumulated since the reign of Raja Bhim. With the huge volumes of wealth he left for Ghazni. This victory was gained in 401 A.H. or 1010 A.D.

Conquest of Thanseer:

In 405 A.H. corresponding to 1014 A.H. Sultan Mahmood attacked Thanesar and accumulated lot of wealth as looty by demolishing Temples and idols at Thanesar. He returned to Ghazni. He then thought of capturing Delhi but his courtiers advised him not to consider to conquest of Delhi until he has captured Punjab which was not possible due to his pact with Anand Pal. The Sultan Mahmood accepted the advice and gave up idea of conquering Delhi. He returned to Ghazni with nearly 200,000 slaves and maidservants.

Attack at Kashmir:

In 406 A.H. the Sultan proceeded to conquer Kashmir. He laid siege to the mountain fort of Lohkot which was famous for its invisibility. Due to heavy snows and the rigours of inclement weather, he had to lift the siege and turned to Ghazni. On the way the army lost the route and went astray resulting in awesome difficulties and loss of valuable lives.

Conquest of Qannouj:

In 409 A.H. the Sultan attacked the fort of Qannouj where Raja Jay Pal was the ruler.[1] The Raja surrendered without fighting. Then the Sultan went to Mathra and conquered it without resistance.

Conquest of Som Nath:

After Qannouj, Sultan Mahmood conquered the fort of Kalinger. In 415 A.H. or 416 A.H.[2] (Ibne Aseer and Muhammad Qasim Farishta differ about the year), Sultan Mahmood left for the conquest of Som Nath Fort which had great reputation of unprecedented wealth in it. On his way he conquered Pattan and Ajmir.

He reached the fort of Som Nath which was built high on the bank of a river. As a matter of fact the the waters of the river reached its rampart. The Muslim soldiers managed by ladders to get at the top of the fort and made a sever attack on the besieged Hindus from all sides. After a pitched encounter the Sultan was Victorious. Some historians have narrated fabulous stories about the fort and the Sultan's encounter. Hakeem Sanai of Ghazni wrote a poem on the victory of Som Nath. "Like the heavens Ka'ba (The House of Allah in the city of Makkah) and Som Nath (Indian Temple of great reverence) was purified of idols by Holy Prophet ﷺ and by Mahmood (Sultan of Ghazni). He (the Holy Prophet ﷺ of Islam) threw out the idols from the Holy Ka'ba while he (the Sultan of Ghazni) completed the process of purification in Som Nath."

When Sultan Mahmood conquered Som Nath, Al-Qadir Billah was the Abbasides caliph in Baghdad. He was overjoyed at the heroic performance of Sultan Mahmood and in token of his appreciation, he sent to Mahmood an "Alqaab Nama" calling him

كهف الدولة والاسلام

---

1. Allama Aseer has also written the same name of the Raja of Qannouj.
2. Tareekh-ul-Kamil Vol.9, P106. Farishta recorded the year 415 in Tareekh-e-Farishta Vol.1, P.15.

"The protecting cave of Empire and Islam".[1]

He also granted him the "Banner of government" for Kharasan, India, Neem Rose and Khwarism.

Sultan Mahmood's Death:

In the month of Rabi-us-Sani, 421 A.H. Sultan Mahmood was sick with dysentery and stomach trouble and died. He was born in 360 A.H. As such, he lived for nearly 60 years. He ruled for 35 years and was burried in Qasr-e-Feeroze of the city of Ghazni.

Life and Character of Sultan Mahmood:

The personality of Sultan Mahmood is confused on account of his conduct and life character. Some Historians have doubted him as an avaricious and greedy man whose sole aim in all his expeditions was to grab wealth of all kinds and carry these home. Some historians have held an opposite view calling him "Ghazi" (i.e.) fighter in the way of Allah and Islam). They have argued that his name gives the immediate impression of The smasher of idols. The truth lies between the two extreme views quoted above. Allama Ibne Aseer has praised the heroic exploits of Sultan Mahmood; but he has also written about his aviarice:

ولم يكن فيه ما يعاب الاانه كان يتوصل الى اخذالاموال بكل طريق

"The Sultan had no other defect in him except that he tried to accumulate wealth by all possible means".

Ibne Aseer has quoted an incident in support of his view about the Sultan. He had of a very wealthy man in Neshapore. He called him to Ghazni and said to him: "I have been informed that you held the religious views of 'Qaramti' (who are apostates). The man read out the mind of the Sultan and said: "I am not at all a

---

1. Tareekh-e-Farishta Vol.1, P.116

Qaramti but I have lot of wealth which I can pass on to you, if you like". The Sultan took away all his wealth and gave him a certificate of being a true Muslim.[1]

Despite allegation of greed against the Sultan he can hardly be accused of being a mere bandit or a decoit. He had carefully studied the political circumstances of India and the wide-spread enmities and mutual rivalries of the Hindu Rajas encouraged him to attack their forts and particularly the Temples which were famous for fabulous wealth. He had an innate hatred for the idols and wanted to discourage idol-worship as a true Muslim. Ibne Aseer praised his conduct of being an anti-idol warrior.

The Hindu nation had developed an idol-phobia. They considered that every happening in the world was the result of the will and intention of the idols. The profit and loss of human beings and honour and dishonour of the son of Adam and Eve were determined by the idols. Sultan Mahmood wished to demolish this mental picture. Allama Ibne Aseer faithfully explained the monotheistic trend of Sultan Mahmood and his inimical approach to the polytheistic trends in India and the psychological grip which the habit of idol worship had taken of the Hindu people. He wrote:

> "Whenever "Yemin ud Daula" Mahmood Ghaznavi gained a victory or broke an idol in a captured fort, the Hindus would openly say: "Som Nath is angry with those people otherwise it would have punished the people who smash the idols". Sultan heard this story and made up his mind to smash Som Nath itself to see and to demonstrate that Som Nath was as powerless as all other idols and their devotees and worshippers would see the wisdom of monotheism and the blessings of Islam which granted intellectual emancipation to the human beings".[2]

---

1. Tareekh-ul-Kamil Vol.9, P.139
2. Tareekh-ul-Kamil Vol.9, P.118

It is wild thinking that Sultan Mahmood was more of a dacoit than conqueror. He honoured and respected the teachings of Islam. In the midst of severe fighting he would bow down in prostration before Almighty God and pray for his victory against idol-worshippers. He honoured his peace pact with Raja Anand Pal and did not attack Delhi. In Toos Sultan Mahmood re-built the masoleum of Hazrat Ali Bin Musa Raza which had been demolished by his father Nasir-ud-Din Sabukta-Gin.[1]

There is also an allegation against Sultan Mahmood that he wanted to conquer the lands controlled by the caliph of Baghdad. The reality of this allegation is that the Sultan submitted an application to the caliph of Islam at Baghdad that Samarqand may be given to him which the Abbaside Caliph rejected. The letter received by Mahmood was full of threats and undiplomatic language. Sultan was enraged at the contents of the letter and told the Messenger from Baghdad bluntly: "Do you wish that I should advance upon the capital of the Khilafat with a thousand elephants, trample it to dust and return to Ghazni with the dust of Baghdad loaded on the elephants". The caliph of Baghdad wrote back to draw attention of the Sultan to the contents of "Surah-i-Feel" in the Holy Quran and admonished him to take lesson from what happened to Abraha, the leader of the Elephant forces who was wiped out by an act of God". The Sultan was deeply moved by the reference to the Holy Quran and was deeply in sorrow at his mistake. He sent back the messenger with precious gifts and regrets for his blunder. He actually wept bitterly.[2]

The positive result of the seventeen successive attacks of Sultan Mahmood on the Indian sub-continent is to be seen in the fact that he paved the way for the establishment of a Muslim government by the Muslim forces for the future. He had weakened the military power of the Rajput rulers of India and annexed the Punjab with the Ghazni state. He left his deputy and a military detachment in the Punjab.

---

1. Tareekh-ul-Kamil Vol.9, P.139
2. Tareekh-e-Farishta Vol.1, P.118

Sultan Mahmood did not e tablish any stable or regular Islamic system in India. However some local persons embraced Islam without duress. On the whole the Indian society did not accept any impact of Islam.

Sultan Mahmood was a great patron and supporter of knowledge, sciences, Art and literature. His court presented the replica of the court of Abbaside's caliph Mamoon ur Rashid. The fabulous wealth he had carried from India to Ghazni gave him the means to make Ghazni a beautiful and well-furnished city. It had a Museum, a university and a big public Library.

Decline of the Ghazni State:

After the death of Sultan Mahmood, the state of Ghazni began to show signs of decline. Various sons of the deceased Sultan began to fight with one another for successors. After good deal of fighting, Masood succeeded in capturing the throne of his father. But the throne had become a bed of thorns for Sultan Masood. Saljuq and Turks were ravaging the kingdom of Ghazni and Turkish and Indian slaves were creating turmoil and anarchy within the country. After some time the Masood was deposed and his brother, Muhammad was put on the throne by the powerful underlings. The Ghaznavis throne kept changing the monarchs very quickly and the monarchs lost their prestige. The effect on India of this anarchy was Nagar Kot was taken away by Rajputs from the governor of Punjab appointed by the King of Ghazni.

The Ghauri Dynasty:

The days when the decline of the Ghazni dynasty has started, were also the days when a rival power in the area of Ghour (near Qandhar) was developinng fast to take its place. In India two rival Rajput powers had weakened each other. Qannouj under Raja Jai Chand and Delhi and Ajmir under Raja Prithvi Raj were at daggers drawn. In North India the elements which had political say were siding with either of the two Rajas. Judging the political atmosphere of North India as helpful Shahab ud Din Ghauri attacked Bhatinda in 1191 A.D. and captured it. Prithwi Raj came to know this and he came out at the head of a large army to oust the Muslim forces under Ghauri. At a distance of 14 miles from Thanesar the two armies confronted each other and there was a pitched battle in which both sides displayed abnormal bravery. The Muslims were routed and Sultan Ghauri was saved by a loyal slave who rode on his horse and ran away with the wounded Sultan from the battlefield. After recovery of his wounds, Sultan Ghauri came to Ghazni and prepared for a second round with the Indian Rajputs.

After two years Ghauri attacked the kingdom of Prithwi Raj who himself met him in the battlefield and fought with courage. But he was arrested while fighting in the fore-front. At his arrest, the Rajputs were routed and the area upto Ajmir was captured by Ghauri. Sultan Ghauri left Qutbud Din Aibak, his trusted slave, to look after the Indian territory captured by him and himself left for Ghazni. The next year Qutbud Din Aibak captured Delhi also.

In 1194 Shahab ud Din Ghauri attacked Qannuj and defeated Raja Jai Chand. He went back to Afghanistan but his deputy, Qutbud Din Aibak captured Gujrat and his second deputy Bakhtiar Khilji captured Oudh, Bihar and eventually west Bengal. No doubt Shahab ud Din Ghauri had captured a major part of India but he could not consolidate his victory by proper administration. There were frequent rebellions and turmoil in the country. In north India the Khokhars had conducted un-predicted unrest.

In 1206 A.D. Sultan Shahab ud Din Ghauri personally came to India to quell the rebellions. At the bank of the River Jhelum at Wameek an apostate Ismaili attacked the Sultan so vehemently that he died. Historians considered his death as a very sad event in the history of Islam. Haji Az-Zubair JozJani said: "The Holy Prophet ﷺ was asked as to when the Doomsday was likely to occur. The reply was a little after 600 years". Then the Historian opined that the death of Sultan Ghauri in 602 A.H. was the first sign of Doomsday. The onslaught on the world of Islam by Jingiz Khan starting in the same year was considered as the second sign of the Doomsday.[1]

---

1. Zafar-ul-Wala BaMuzaffaro Aala, Vol.2, P.682

Sultan Shahab ud Din Ghauri was courageous and brave but, unlike Sultan Mahmood Ghaznawi, he was a very generous man and man with open heart and amiable disposition. Allama Ibne Aseer wrote:

> "*Sultan Ghauri was a brave soldier of Islam. He acted on the Laws of Shariat and gave his decisions strictly under the Shariat Law*".[1]

Sultan Shahab ud Din Ghauri had great respect for the soldiers of Islam. Imam Fakhuruddin Razi, to whom the Sultan was greatly devoted, used to visit the palace and deliver sermon to the Sultan and his family members. In one of his sermons, Imam Razi said: "O Sultan! Neither your authority will live for ever nor shall the mockery (sermons) of Razi continue for ever. We are all to return to Allah (at our appointed times)". This sermon had such a moaning effect on the Sultan that he burst into tears and wept so bitterly that on-lookers had pity on his condition.[2]

The Sultan had no son. His only legacy was a daughter. But he had a wonderful habit of purchasing slaves and took pains in their education, training and moral and intellectual development. He had purchased forty slaves who were shaped into learned and capable administrators. They were appointed as governors or chiefs over the territories under control of the Sultan. They were his real children and successors of his worldly position.[3]

The governors/slaves trained by Sultan Ghauri were so capable that they successfully administered the territories to which they were appointed. After the death of the Sultan, his kingdom disintegrated and various parts assumed independence. Qutbud Din Aibak who was governor of Delhi assumed an independent role and laid the foundation of the Slave Dynasty.

---

1. Tareekh-ul-Kamil Vol.12, P.84
2. Ibn-e-Aseer Vol.12, P.84
3. Zafar-ul-Wala BaMuzaffaro Aala, Vol.2, P.683

The Slave Dynasty:

Qutbud Din Aibak was the founder of the Slave Dynasty which ruled from 1206 to 1290 A.D. his successors were slaves in reality.

Qutbud Din Aibak was a Turk by blood. The word "Aibak" in Turkish language means "benumbed". He was called "Aibak" because one of his hands was benumbed. He was brought from Neshapore and sold away to Qazi Fakhuruddin Abdul Aziz Al-Kufi who was a descendant of Imam Abu Hanifa. He brought him up as his own son. Qutbud Din Aibak was admitted to a religious school where he learnt the Holy Quran, the Hadith and Islamic jurisprudence. Then another man purchased him and presented him as a gift before Sultan Shahab ud Din Ghauri. The Sultan was a great psychologist and he easily judged the high personality of Qutbud Din Aibak. The Sultan gave him military and administrative training. According to "Tabaqat-I-Nasiri", Qutbud Din Aibak was not handsome. But he had find fine demeanour, good habits, wisdom, skill, bravery, generosity, truthfulness and people generally praised him".[1]

Qutbud Din Aibak ascended the throne of Delhi in 1205 A.D. Later on he snatched away Lahore from Tajuddin Yalzer. Then he went to Ghazni. After 40 days he returned to Lahore. He was playing Polo one day, fell from the horse and died. This happened in 1210 A.D. only four years after his power. He was buried in Lahore in a street of Anarkali Bazar where his tomb stands as a reminder of the mortality of man.

After Qutbud Din Aibak his son Aaram Shah ascended the throne. But he was unfit for ruling. Shams ud Din Altmush who was in Delhi (he was also the son-in-law of Qutbud Din Aibak) came to oust Aaram Shah. There was fighting between the two rival claimants near Delhi. Aaram Shah was arrested and sent to Badayun.

---

1. Zafar-ul-Wala BaMuzaffaro Aala, Vol.2, P.684

Qutbud Din Aibak was not only a brave and doubtless warrior. He was also a wise statesman. His greatest achievement in the political field was that he cut off the connection of the Indian Muslim government from Ghazni which had continued from two hundred years. The slave rulers were independent of Ghazni and, according to Fakhuruddin Mubarak Shah, "Qutbud Din Aibak abolished all taxes which were not legal accordinng to the Shariat Law. Ushr was charged and sometimes even half of Ushr was charged". "Dr. Tripathy (a Hindu Historian) wrote:

> "The government policy of Qutbud Din Aibak was generous. He followed a definite code of Law and his government was systematic".

The slave dynasty ruled for 84 years only. This was a novel ruling dynasty of the world which the teachings of Islam created. No other society of the world can claim such high status for slaves.

SULTAN SHAMSUD DIN ALTAMASH

In 1210 A.D. Sultan Shamud Din Altamash ascended the throne after Aaram Shah. He was an emancipated slave and a son-in-law of Qutbud Din Aibak. He was a very intelligent, wise and brave statesman who had great qualities of administration and successful warfare. He quelled the rebellions of the governors of Sindh and Bengal and then conquered the Rajput states of Ranthambore, Gowaliar and Ojjain (the capital of the Rajput state of Molwa). Dr. Tripathi praised him as the first founder of an independent Islamic state.[1]

Apart from his secular qualities mentioned above, he was also a deeply religious personality who had mystical trends.[2] He was rigid in his prayers and lived the life of an ascetic. He was fond of listening to religious scholars and, after Friday prayers, he used to hold a meeting of prominent scholars who delivered useful lectures on the teachings of Islam and points of jurisprudence to which he listened very carefully.

He was a contemporary of Khawaja Usman Harwani (spiritual guide of Hazrat Khawaja Moeen ud Din Ajmiri). Khawaja Usman Harwani praised Sultan Shamud Din Altamash as a "perfect man". During his regime scholars and mystical personalities of Islam came in large number to India from the North. He went on foot for miles ahead to welcome the incoming dignitories. When Hazrat Khawaja Qutbud Din Bakhtiar Kaki came from Multan to Delhi, Sultan Shamud Din Altamash greeted him in a grand way and requested him to stay in the royal palace. On his expression of inability to stay in the palace, he used to visit him frequently in his Zawia where Hazrat Bakhtiar Kaki was staying. Hazrat Qutbud din Bakhtiar Kaki narrated a story about him:

> *"One night Sultan came to me and caught hold of my feet. I asked him if he had any trouble or any*

---

1. Some Aspects of Muslim Administration
2. Islamic Culture Vol.2, P.166

need. The Sultan said he had no trouble and no need. He only wanted to know if he would be with those who attain salvation on the Day of Judgement".

On one occasion Hazrat Khawaja Mueenuddin Chishti wanted to take Khawaja Bakhtiar Kaki along with him to Ajmir. Sultan Altamash accompanied the great multitude of people who went with the saints to see them off on their journey to Ajmir. When Hazrat Ajmiri realized the concern and grief of Sultan Altamash due to separation of Hazrat Bakhtiar Kaki, he allowed Khawaja Bakhtiar Kaki to continue living in Delhi. Sultan Altamash was so much overwhelmed that he kissed the feet of Khawaja Ajmiri and brought back Khawaja Bakhtiar Kaki to Delhi with utmost respect and regard.

He was a unique culmination of a Saint and a warrior in the cause of Islam. After the Khulafa-i-Rashideen he was perhaps the only personality who combined in him the qualities of a statesman, a warrior, a scholar, a saint and as administrator. The kings feared his dominant sword. But he wept all nights for fear of accountability before the Tribunal of God. On 14th Rabi-ul-Awwal 633 A.H. Hazrat Khawaja Qutbuddin Bakhtiar Kaki died and he left his dying will that:

> *"Only a person who had been chaste all his life and never missed the four Sunnah prayers of "Asr" and the Takbir-e-Tahreema may lead his funnel prayers". The Sultan was present with the funeral procession. He kept waiting for the desired person to come out and lead the prayer. But, no body advanced. After sufficient time, the Sultan himself stepped out to the prayer carpet, saying: "I never wished to make my worship habits public but the will of Hazrat Khawaja has to be fulfilled".[1]*

He went with the funeral procession to the graveyard.

---

1. Khazain-ul-Asfia, P.275

Sultan Shamsud Din Altamash

Sultan himself died after a few months of the death of Hazrat Bakhtiar Kaki. He kept sending food for the "Fathia" of Hazrat Bakhtiar Kaki regularly to the Khanqah of Qazi Hamid ud Din Nagori, a successor of Hazrat Khawaja Kaki.

Sultan Shamud Din Altamash was the first Muslim monarch who was honoured with grand Robe (Khila't-e-Fakhirah) from the court of Khilafat in Baghdad. The auother of "Tabaqat-e-Akbri" – Nizam ud Din Ahmad said that the Sultan was jubilant on receiving the grand robe and he wore it with utmost pleasure. A function was held in which robes were distributed to all the chiefs of the kingdom.

Sultan Altamash died in 633 A.H. and was buried near the mosque Quwwat ul Islam in the precincts of the Qutub Minar along a highway.

After Altamash, his son Ruknud Din Feroze Shah came to the throne. But he was incapable of running the affairs of the state. Soon he handed over the authority to his mother – Shah-e-Turkaan and lost himself in wine and pleasure. Shah Turkaan was a Turkish maid who had an impure and malicious heart. She misused authority and got many of the surviving wives of Altamash killed with ignominy and dishonour. Many of the beautiful maids and ladies of the palace were driven to live life of poverty and need due to the tyranny of Shah Turkaan. The younger son of Shamudd Din, Qutbuddin was also killed at her behest. Due to the aforesaid circumstances there was wide-spread unrest in the country. After only six months of his coming into power, Ruknuddin was deposed and then slain. Sultan Altamash's wise and capable daughter Raziyya was raised to the throne.

Raziyya Sultana:

Historian Farishta praised Sultan Raziyya as a paragon of virtues. She had all the qualities of a great ruler except that she was a woman. She was intelligent, wise, statesman-like, prudent, and a most scholarly person. She recited the Holy Quran with great respect and devotion. Even during her father's life, she had great say in important state affairs and her opinion was always respected.

Altamash had appointed her as his successor on the occasion of his victory over Gowaliar. He praised her great qualities of head and heart and explained her preference over her brothers who were given to life of pleasure and ease.[1] All historians have agreed that Sultan Raziyya was a perfect ruler. She wore male dresses, rode upon horses like a warrior and worked hard for the consolidation of her kingdom. Some of her Turkish chiefs became jealous of her and took to rebellion. After having ruled for three years and a half she was deposed and then killed.

Nasir ud Din Mahmood:

After Sultan Raziyya, two kings – Bahram Shah and Ala-ud-Din sat on the throne of Delhi within two years. Both were incapable and pleasure loving. Behram Shah was slain after two years of his reign while Alauddin was, after four years rule, arrested and put in prison. He died in the prison.

All the chiefs and dignitories of the court unanimously selected Nasir ud Din Mahmood, the youngest son of Sultan Altamash to rule the country. In his character, demeanour and habits Nasir ud Din Mahmood was an exact replica of his father. In bravery, worship and generosity he was just like his father. He got no money from the Public Treasury for his expenses. He earned his livelihood by writing the Holy Quran.[2]

Nizam ud Din Ahmad wrote in his "Tabqat-I-Akbri": "Sultan Nasir ud Din used to write two copies of the Holy Quran in a year which gave him sufficient income for his sustenance. In his palace there was no maid servant to help his queen in the household. Tired of the rigors of the household, the Queen once demanded that a slave girl be purchased for her help. The King replied: "The Public Treasury belongs to the people and I am not authorized to get money for my perosnal comfort".[3]

Since Sultan Nasir ud Din Mahmood was by nature inclined

---

1. Tareekh-e-Farishta (Urdu translation) Vol.1, P.257
2. Ibid Vol.1. P.268
3. Ibid Vol.1, P.277 and Zafar-ul-Wala Vol.2. P.726

to like a life of an ascetic and wished to spend his maximum time in seclusion and worship, he selected Ghias-ud-Din Balban, the emancipated slave of Sultan Altamash (as well as his son-in-law as stated by Historian Farishta), and made him minister plain potentially to look after the affairs of the state. After appointing him as Minister of State, he said to him: "I have appointed you my deputy and put the reins of the people in your hands. Do not do any thing which may render me answerable before the Tribunal of God and which may earn my shame".

Balban was a Turk of the Farakhtai race and belonged to Al-Bari tribe. When the Mughals advanced like a tornado and entered the frontiers of Turkistan, Balban was captured by a Mughal soldier who sold him to a trader. The trader took him to Baghdad and sold him to Khawaja Jamal ud Din who was a God-fearing religious man. Khawaja Jamal ud Din took Balban along with a few other slaves to Delhi and presented them all before Sultan Altamash for sale who purchased all the slaves at high price.

Finding signs of goodness and virtue in Balban, Altamash took special pains in his education and breeding. He was a "Bazdar" or a "Khasadar" during the reign of Altamash. During the days of Ruknuddin, Balban was appointed commander of the Indian Turks and was engaged in quelling the rebellion of disgruntled elements in the Punjab. During the reign of Raziyya Sultana, he was arrested by the Royal army and confined to prison. He was released after some time and appointed as "Mir-e-Shikar". During the rule of Muiz ud Din Baharam Shah, his state was raised to the position of "Mir-e-Akkhor". He was granted the districts of Hansi and Rawari as estates. He brought under control the troublesome Mewatis who used to creat turmoil in the capital.

The suppression of the Mewati's trouble raised the prestige of Balban and he became a distinguished courtier of Bahram Shah. When Alauddin Masood became the ruler, Balban was further raised in status and became the Amir-e-Hajib which gave him power to run the administration. When Nasir ud Din Mahmood came to power, Balban continued to rule, the country in a reasonable way. As a matter of fact, he ruled in the name of Nasir ud Din Mahmood.

Ghias-ud-Din Balban had, apart from his inherent ability and genius, given his daughter in marriage to the king which made him further reliable and dear in the eyes of the King. He was wise and farsighted. He gave many positions of trust and responsibility to his relatives. His younger brother Kishlu Khan was appointed as Amir-e-Hajib and his cousin, Sher Khan was appointed governor of Lahore and Bhatinda. But for a short period when Balban and his men were removed from positions at the backbiting of Imad-ud-Din Rehan, Balban continued to be an important pillar of the government of Nasir ud Din Mahmood till the end of the regime.

In 1266 A.D., Balban ascended the throne at the death of Nasir ud Din. He had now to face two kinds of troubles. Inside the country many of the governors became arrogant and rebellious and Balban dealt with them with an iron hand. The Mughals were attacking the Punjab repeatedly but he dealt with their menace effectively and did not allow them, like Shamsuddin Altamash, to create disturbance on a wide scale as they had n Baghdad and Neshapore.

Ghias-ud-Din Balban was prudent and did not take hasty steps. When the provinces of Gujrat and Malwa (which had been annexed to the Muslim state by Aibak and Altamash) raised burmones rebellion and many of his chiefs advised him to repress them, he did not move into action because to leave Delhi would have cost him the whole of his kingdom.[1]

In his character and habits, Balban was a combination of opposite qualities. He was genius by nature and welcomed all princes and chiefs of Turkistan Mawra-un-Nahr, Kharasan, Iraq, Azerbaijan, Faris, Rome, and Syria who had lost their honour and position due to the recurring attack of the Mughals and came to India. They were appointed as his important courtiers. Two of such princes who belonged to the Banu Abbaside family, were placed nearest to the throne. He had a deep love and respect for the guests. Historian Frishta has studied that he rejoiced at the arival of a guest

---

1. Tareekh-e-Farishta Vol.1, P.288

and, some times, named the streets of the city after the names of new arrivals in his capital. He has mentioned 15 such streets.

Balban also respected the scholars very deeply. After Friday prayers he used to visit the contemporary scholars like Shaikh Burhanuddin Bilji, Maulana Sirajuddin Sanjri and Maulana Najam ud din Dimashqi. The company of religious personalities has made him very considerate of the troubles of common people. He liked to join the funeral prayers and attended even the burial of certain people. He sympathized and helped the widows and orphans. He used to attend the sermons of preaching scholars and profusely wept on hearing the injunctions of God and his Holy Prophet ﷺ.[1]

Despite all the tenderness of heart, he did not tolerate any attempt at rebellion or trouble. The prestige of his state was maintained at all cost. Some relatives of Shamuddin appeared to creat trouble for him and he immediately sent them to the next world. Respect of law was forcefully introduced by him and high and low were equal in his eyes. Once Malik Lagheeq, the conqueror of Badayun, killed a person by beating him with whips. When Balban visited Badayun, the widow of the person complained to him of the tyranny perpetrated by the governor. Balban gave orders that the governor may be whipped and sent to join the deceased husband of the widow. This was a unique example of social justice. After death the body of the deceased governor was allowed to hang at the gate of the city.

How high his principles of state-craft were is evident from the fact that; once he called all his sons in his presence and said to them: "Sultan Shamsuddin Altamash used to say: "Twice in the meeting of Mu'izuddin Muhammad Bahauddin Sam I heard Syed Mubarak Ghaznawi say: Most of the actions of rulers reach the precincts of polytheism and most of their deeds are against the Sunnah of the Holy Prophet ﷺ. If they can, despite above lapses, to act with courage and care on the following points, they can save their skins: (i) A ruler must use his prestige and authority with

---
1. Tareekh-e-Farishta (Urdu translation Vol.1, P.286

utmost care for the benefit of the people and act with mercy and compassion to earn the pleasure of God; (ii) He must not allow any kind of lowdown or obscurity to spread in the country and should always act with stern-ness to subdue the immoral and bad people and keep them in constant terror of the state (iii) He should entrust the affairs of the state to honest and God-fearing people who have the intelligence and wisdom to run affairs with utmost capability (iv) He must himself act with justice and fair play and keep watch and full control over his functionaries so that they do not act with prejudice and injustice. His control should be so effective that injustice and tyranny may be totally wiped out from the kingdom". Then Ghias-ud-Din Balban addressed his sons by way of advice: "You are part of my body and soul. You must act always with justice and fair play. If any one of you acts with tyranny and is unfair to the weak and helpless people, I shall certainly punish the unjust and the tyrants".

Ghias-ud-Din Balban was not kind and just to any particular section of his people. His justice and kindness was widespread without any distinction of cast, colour or creed. Dr. Ishtiaq Hussain Qureshi, Professor of History, Delhi University, has written: "An old epitaph in Sanskrit language has been discovered which is partly in Sanskrit language and partly in Heriana languages. It relates to the year 1280 A.D. when Ghias-ud-Din Balban was the ruler. The Muslim rulers in general and Balban in particular have been praised. It is specifically written about Balban that: "Under the peaceful and kind government of this ruler the country from Ramehwaram to Ghour presented the sight of a flourishing meadow. His forces are a guarantee for peace and order. The King is so vigilant and active for the maintenance of peace, that it appears that VISHNU god has ceased to look after the world and has gone away to retire in sleep near the ocean of milk". [1]

Balban made the drinking of wine unlawful and himself did not drink. He was regular in his prayers and said the extra prayers

---

1. Administration of Delhi, P.228

like Tahajjad, Ishraq and Chasht. He was always in purity and cleanliness of ablution.[1]

Ghias-ud-Din Balban died in 685 A.H. after ruling the country for 40 years. When the funeral left the Royal palace in the morning, the high ranking chiefs of his government and the servants of the Royal palace were in utterly deep grief and mourning. They were all bare-headed and tore their shirts in excessive grief. There was not a single person who did not put dust on his head. People wept profusely and made the on-lookers weep. Malik ul Umara Fakharuddin was most grief-striken. After Balban's death he slept on bare ground for six months. There was no one in the capital city of Delhi who did not give away something in charity for the departed soul.[2]

Successor of Balban:

After Balban his grandson Qaiqabad ascended the throne. He was son of Bughra Khan, governor of Bengal. He was a most incapable man and was given to luxury and indifference. In his court there was always a gathering of beautiful singers and actors. Fun-artists and eunuchs were appreciated and were in demand. Bouts and dancing parties come to the court for display of their art and for earning.[3]

Bughra Khan advanced with an army to Delhi to teach his mis-guided son a lesson. But Qaiqabad promised to abide by the commands and preaching of his father and warfare was avoided.

After his father had left to go back to Bengal, Qaiqabad returned to his old habits and remained in power for three years and a half. He fell ill with pralysis and some Turks killed him in his last days of illness. With the consent of the elites of the country, Jalal ud Din Khilji, governor of the Punjab, was selected to rule over the country. Thus the Slave Dynasty came to its end after 84 years of rule.

---

1. Tareekh-e-Farishta Vol.1, P.286
2. Zafar-ul-Wala BaMuzaffaro Aala, Vol.2, P.737
3. Tabqat-e-Akbari Vol.1, P.104

The Khilji Dynasty:

The Khilji people originally belonged to the Tartar race but the Khilji tribes had settled in Afghanistan for a long time. Nizam ud Din Ahmad Bakhshi, compiler of "Tabaqat-e-Akbar." wrote that these people were actually the progeny of Qalij Khan, a son-in-law of Jingiz Khan. Thus they came to be known as Qaliji which changed into Khilji as Qalji in due course of time.[1]

The first Khilji King of India was Jalal ud Din who ascended the throne at the murder of Qaiqabad. The best part of his life was spent in repelling the repeated attacks of the Mughals at the Punjab. He ascended the throne of Delhi in old age. At first he was under impresssion that people did not like him. As such, he did not enter Delhi, the capital of India but built a new city at Kelo-Kheri. Later on when people came to know of his godliness, virtues and high character, they pledged deep loyalty to his person.[2] He entered the capital city with great pump and glory. He dismounted from his horse at the gate of the Royal palace and fell down in prostration to thank the Almighty Allah who had raised him to the high status. He said: "For years I have lowed my head in respect before this throne but today I am stepping up on it to sit in authority. How can I offer my gratitude to God for His bounty and kindness".

Jalal ud Din was a tenderhearted, humble and God-fearing ruler. After ceremonies of ascending the throne, he reached the gate of the Palace known as "Koshak-I-Lal", he put off his shoes in accordance with his old habit when Balban was in power. Umda-tul Malik Ahmad Hajib Barbak was accompanying him. He said: "Now this Koshak belongs to you. How is it that you are dismounting out of respect?" The Sultan replied: "It is must and proper to respect and pay homage to the memory of my past master". Then Malik Ahmad again said: "You should now stay and live in this Koshak which is the State House". Jalal ud Din Khilji said: "This Koshak Palace was built by Ghias-ud-Din Balban during his government.

---
1. Tabqat-e-Akbari, Vol.1, P.116
2. Ibid Vol.1, P.117

This now rightly belongs to the children of Sultan Balban. I have no moral right to occupy it". Malik Ahmad again retorted: "In state matter there seems no room for such delicate signs of piety and assignment of rights". The Sultan again replied firmly: "How can I ignore the standing and permanent rules of Islam for transitory gains of the state? The common source of man and the law of jurisprudence do not favour the giving up of moral values for short lived worldly gains".

In the second year of his ascension to power, the nephew of Jalal ud Din, Malik Jhajju rose in rebellion against his uncle and assuming the title of Sultan Mughis ud Din, got the Friday sermon read in his name and circulated the new currency under his name. Many chiefs supported him. Then he turned towards Delhi to oust Sultan Jalal ud Din who appointed his son Akbar Khan Khanan as temporary incharge of the capital and himself marched to fight the rebellious nephew out of Delhi. There was pitched battle and the enemy was badly defeated. Malik Jhajju and his companions and supporters were all arrested and put up before Sultan Jalal ud Din Khilji who set them all at liberty. Some of the very high officials who had served under Sultan Balban were given great respect despite their support of Malik Jhajju. He sent them to the VIP baths and, after bathing, gave them new dresses ammoniated with perfumes. All the persons were extremely repentant at their audacity and rebellion. The Sultan said to them: "You had picked up the sword to support your master. This is hardly blame-worthy". Malik Jhajju was sent respectfully to Multan and provided every means of gay and happy life. Malik Ahmad Hajib and other chiefs said: "The rebellious Malik Jhajju and his companions deserve to be beheaded. To treat them so kindly and bestow favours on them was against the rule of state-craft". Sultan Jalal ud Din replied: "Whatever you have said is absolutely correct. But I have spent 70 years in the Islamic faith without shedding blood of any body. Now that I have become old, I do not want to shed the blood of any Muslim".[1]

---

1. Tabqat-e-Akbari, P.121

In 689 A.H. the Sultan advanced upon the Ranthambore fort with intention to capture it. Siege was laid by the Raja. After a few days, Sultan Jalal ud Din Khilji lifted the siege and decided retreat of the army, saying: "This fort is not so important that human life may be stalked for its capture. If I capture it after killing of some human beings what shall be my condition when widows and orphans of the killed soldiers appear before me in helplessness. The joy of capturing the fort shall be changed into bitterness". [1]

Once it occurred to the Sultan that he had successfully fought against the Mughals and it would be proper if he is announced in the Friday Sermons as:

الـــمجاهدفى سبيل الله

i.e. A warrior in the cause of Allah.

He spoke to his wife Malika-e-Jehan to suggest to the chiefs who visit the palace to mention it for his permission. When Qazi Fakharuddin (who was the greatest religious scholar of his time) mentioned it to the Sultan by way of suggestion, the Sultan was, as it were aroused from deep apathy and said: "You are making this suggestion at the instance of Malika-e-Jahan. I have re-considered that non of my fighting loots was purly for the defence of Islam or for the sake of God alone". He repented and gave up the idea altogether".

The above events go to prove that the Sultan was a tenderhearted man, pure of nature and very soft at heart. But this trait of his character was out of turn and misused on occasion. Nizam Ahmad Bakhshi wrote: "His misplaced sense of mercy and generosity resulted at times in granting bounties to culprits who deserved to be punished". This extreme softness on his part resulted in creation of turmoil and mischief in the country. Decoits and thieves were arrested and brought before the Sultan who, in stead of punishing them effectively, let them off at mere repentence and

---

1. Tabqat-e-Akbari, P.127, 128

promise of betterment. People spoke wild language against the Sultan under intoxication of wine. But the Sultan connived at such serious happenings. People were caught for reviling and creating unrest in the country by disparaging the Sultan, but he let them off. At times he would even bestow rewards and positions on such people who were his bad enemies and ill-wishers. A man named "Manda Hari" had inflicted a grievous injury on the face of Jalal ud Din when he was a governor. The man was arrested and brought in his presence when he was the monarch. But the Sultan did not punish him and let him off.

It is rather strange and paradoxical that, on one hand the Sultan said: "Why should I act against the injunctions of Islam for this short-lived authority and rule". On the other hand wine was freely used in his own palaces and drinking parties were freely held in which handsome persons participated. Amir Khusrao used to compose a fresh lyrical poem and sing it in such meetings. Zia ud Din Barni has mentioned such meetings in a laconic style. The stories of the King's misplaced and extreme leniency and softness spread in the country and the public did not like or approve it. They used to say openly:

این مرد جهان داری و بادشاهی نمی داند

i.e. "This man is not at all aware of statesmanship or the rules of conduct of a monarch".

A very pathetic event took place which shook the very foundations of the kingdom. A great Saintly person, Syedi Maula who had a big "Khanqah" (monastery) in Delhi, was murdered at the instance of Jalal ud Din Khilji for creating a plot against the King. Jalal ud Din had already lost much of his popularity for his leniency and his lack of effective control over mischievous elements. On the other hand his nephew Alauddin Khilji had gained many victories in India and had become very powerful. He called his uncle at Karrah under some pretext but in reality under a deep conspiracy and got him murdered mercilessly when he was fasting and the sun was setting in the west. He was so callous that he got the head of Jalal ud Din raised on a spear and circulated it in the lanes and the streets of the town. The reign of Jalal ud Din lasted for 7 years and 4 months.[1] He died in the month of Ramzan in the year 695 A.H.

The wife of Jalal ud Din badly handled the situation. The elder son of Jalal ud Din, Urkely Khan (who was a capable deceased statesman) was at Multan. Instead of calling him to Delhi to succeed his discerned father, Begum Malika Jahan put her younger son, Ruknuddin Ibrahim at the throne. He was too young and too inexperienced to rule. Thus, owing to the short intelligence and hasty action of an un-wise woman, the circumstances became worst.

---

[1]. Tareekh-e-Farishta, Vol.1, P.352

ALAUDDIN KHILJI

When Alauddin learnt about the events in Delhi, he made up his mind to attack and capture the capital. He left for Delhi with his army, on the way, spent generously on his army raising their morale and number. He fought 2 or 3 skirmishes and entered Delhi victoriously on 23rd of Zil Haj, 695 A.H. corresponding to 1296 A.D. He sat on the throne and decorated the city. For 3 days there were public rejoining and people held functions of dance, dinner and drinking. He lavishly spent money and gave gifts to all and sundry so that the idea of brutal murder of Jalal ud Din was almost washed away from the minds.[1]

Alauddin kept his chiefs and ministers in good humour by grants, gifts, promotion and positions. At the same time, he was cruel and callous beyond imagination in hitting his two cousins, Arkat Khan and Ruknuddin Ibrahim and the two sons of Arkali Khan as well. He was so hard of heart that he blinded his cousins before putting them to death. He also did not spare the royal women. He imprisoned Begum Malika Jahan and her two daughters-in-law in Delhi. He also punished the chiefs who had betrayed Jalal ud Din and helped him to gain the throne. He killed the entire families of the elite who were in power during the regime of Jalal ud Din Khilji and looted their entire wealth to the tune of 10 million rupees which Alauddin deposited in the royal treasury.

The first two years of his rule were spent in fighting the Mughals whom he turned out from the Punjab. In the 3rd year of his rule, he attached Gujrat. The Raja of Gujrat, did not have the courage to fight and fled away. Gujrat was annexed. Then he turned his attention to the Rajputs who had built up principalities in Rajputana after leaving north India under pressure of Muslim forces. They had united into one confederation headed by Rana of Chittor. He laid siege to the fort of Ranthambore but could not capture it

---

1. Tareekh-e-Farishta, Vol.1, P.357

capture it even after 6 months of siege. Peace pact was agreed upon with the Rana of Chittore.

Alauddin ruled for 20 years. During this period, he had, due to his military genius, conquered and annexed to his kingdom vast areas which no one of his predecessors had done.

Arrogance and Egotism of Alauddin:

His conquests and larger kingdom made him arrogant. He decided to assume the title of second Alexander. He directed that his titled may be mentioned in the Friday Sermons. In his ambition to be called "Skindar-e-Sani", he also intended to get out of India and conquered Kharasan Mawra un Nahr, Turkistan and later on Rome, Persia, Iraq Mesopotamia, Syria and even Abyssinia.

Alauddin was illiterate and uneducated person. He had no knowledge of religion. It got into his head that he may, like the Holy Prophet ﷺ of Islam he may promulgate a new religion so that he may acquire the splendour and glory of religion and state together like the Holy Prophet ﷺ and his name may become immortal in history.[1] This indicates that behind all this action, there was only an ambition of having a high name and fame and there was no such lofty idea of godliness or other worldliness. Many of his ideas resembled the ideas of Akbar. Fortunately he had around him persons with correct thinking and courage to tell him what was wrong and what was right. Kotwal Alaul Malik and Qazi Mughis prevented him from promulgating a new religion. Alaul Malik took courage in both hands and spoke out to the King: "The matters like religion and Shariat Law relate to Prophets and Prophet-hood is connected with divine revelation. This position was last by enjoyed by the Holy Prophet ﷺ after whom there can be no religion. If you talk of a new religion, the public opinion shall become vehemently against you and people would start disliking you. This may create turmoil and unrest in the kingdom. You are already aware that Jingiz Khan and his progeny tried hard to efface the true religion of Islam and to

---

1. Tabqat-e-Akbari, Vol.1, P.144, 145

impose the ancient religion of Turkistan on the people. In their attempt they killed millions of Muslims but their efforts failed and eventually they themselves became Muslims".[1]

The truth spoken by Alaul Malik had the desired effect and Alauddin Khilji agreed with him and said: "Whatever you have said is absolutely correct and is in the fitness of things. Henceforth I shall not indulge in such talk".[2]

Then Alauddin asked him: "What is your view about our conquering the whole world?" Abul Malik replied: "This idea of the king is correct. The power and sources which the king commands can help him to realise in his ambition. But there is a difficulty involved in the plan of conquest. When the king is far away from his capital in the distant regions of the world, who will perform the duties of the state. Another problem may arise about the conquered lands. When the king leaves the conquered land and appoints his governors to govern on his behalf, there is no guarantee that the governor will remain loyal to the king who had conquered. The case of Alexander the great was different. During those days, people had better word sense and did not become disloyal to their benefactors and rulers. Moreover, Alexander had in Aristotle a great statesman as his ministers who had the wisdom to control things for the conquerors".

Alauddin asked him: "If I give up the idea of world conquest and become contented with the present kingdom with Delhi as its headquarters, what will be the use of this huge wealth and the armies which I am commanding?" Alaul Malik replied: "Presently there are two such expeditions which may involve huge expenses from the Royal Treasury. The first is the conquest of cities situated in the North, in the South and in the East of the Indian frontiers. The second expedition relates to the effective stoppage of the Mughal attacks on our territories. After successful completion of these two momentous tasks, the King would be well-advised to stay on in the

---

1. Tareekh-e-Farishta, Vol.1, P.365, 366
2. Tabqat-e-Akbari, Vol.1, P.145

capital and dispatch his loyal and trusted chiefs for conquests around his kingdom". Towards the end of his wise talk, Alaul Malik said: "All these ambitious programmes can be implemented only when the king controls his habits of drinking, hunting and pleasure-seeking and personally suppresses his plans".

Alauddin Khilji was deeply impressed by the wise and sincere speech of Alaul Malik and praised his wisdom and correctness of opinion. He gave him great gifts and all the chiefs who attended that meeting also gave him thousands of coins and two fine horses in reward. Hazrat Nizam ud Din Aulia who was a contemporary of Alauddin Khilji was deeply purturbed at the arrogant ways of the King. When he came to know of the speech delivered by Alaul Malik, he was very happy and prayed for the welfare of Alaul Malik.[1]

A similar inter-change of ideas also took place between Alauddin Khilji and Qazi Mughis. After reading the discussions of Qazi Mughis, one is impressed by the courage with which the true scholars of Islam put up correct views before the despotic rulers and kings. The Historian Farishta stated: "Alauddin was forced to learn reading and writing because he had to read and reply in writing.. the money petitions and applications submitted to him by his chiefs. He read certain Persian books and learnt how to read handwriting and how to write. He gradually developed a sort of liking and love for the religious scholars. He began to sit in the assembly of scholars and listened to their discourses patiently. He called Qazi Mughis and expressed his intention to ask him certain questions. At first Qazi Mughis expressed fear and bluntly told the King to behead him if he had that intention because whatever Qazi Mughis said, that may annoy him and the result would be the death of Qazi Mughis. But Alauddin assured him that he will have no harm at his hands and he may give replies strictly in accordance with the Shariat Laws.

The King put four questions to the Scholar, Qazi Mughis, for replies:

---

1. Tareekh-e-Farishta, Vol.1, P.366, 367

(i) Q. Which Hindu can be called a "Zimmi" under the Shariat law?

A. Islam calls such non-Muslims as "Zimmis" when they voluntarily pay the nominal tax of Jizya to the government functionaries of the Muslim government.

(ii) Q. If a government functionary takes illegal gratification while collecting government dues, will it be called theft or stealing.

A. If the government official extort extra money from the tax-payers, they should be compelled to return it but the penalty of cutting a hand will not be applicable to such persons.

(iii) Q The wealth which I acquired from Dev Garh before ascending the throne at Delhi shall legally belong to my person or to the Public Treasury?

A. The Muslims who helped the king in the acquisition of wealth at Dev. Garh are co-sharers of that wealth.

Alauddin Khilji was displeased at the above answer of Qazi Mughis and said: "The wealth which I got during my governorship and which was not deposited in the Public Treasury, how can it be treated as Public money?" Qazi Mughis replied: "The wealth which the king earns by self effort rightly belongs to him but the wealth which he acquires with the help of armed forces it has equal right of all in it, the king as well as the army soldiers". Then the king asked: "In such wealth what is my share and what is the share of my children?" Qazi Mughis was frightened at this question and he thought his death was fast approaching because the previous answer had also infuriated the king. Alauddin Khilji read out from his face the condition of his heart and said: "Do not fear for your life and give a correct reply".

Qazi Mughis said: "There are three ways for the division of such wealth. If the law of equality is followed and the practice of the first caliphs of the Holy Prophet ﷺ is kept in view, the share of the King will be the same as that of the common Muslims. If middle course adopted, the King will get a share equal to the share of his chiefs. The third way would be to give the King a share equal to the share of the highest dignitories of the state". Then the king said: "My practice is that I got back three years wages from the soldiers who do not join marshal expedition. Secondly when I meet the rebels, I kill them all and capture their wealth and deposit it in the Royal Treasury". On hearing this, Qazi Mughis got up from his seat and went to a corner in the room, put his head on his hand and said: "All these things are against the injunctions of the Shariat Law". The king was infuriated at this reply and, in his fury he left the courtroom and went inside his house. Qazi Mughis also immediately left for his house to tell his people that he was going to face death shortly.

Fortunately, much against his expectation, the king called Qazi Mughis and confered on him many precious gifts in appreciation of his truthfulness and spoke out: "Although I am an uneducated person and know little about the injunctions and prohibitions laid in the Shariat Law. Yet I am a born Muslim and the son of a Muslim. I fully realize that whateveer you have said is absolute truth but the peculiar circumstances oblige me to deal with situation in my own way. My intention is always good and my aim is welfare of the people.[1]

Respect for Hazrat Sultan Nizam ud Din Aulia:

A stage had come when Alauddin Khilji developed great respect for Hazrat Nizam ud Din Aulia. Whenever he had to embark on an expedition, he would come in the audience of Hazrat Nizam ud Din Aulia. During the days when Alauddin was busy conquering the fort of Chittor, a strong Mughal army numbering 1,20,000 headed by Turgi approached Delhi and camped near the river Jamna. The Sultan had his best army deployed in Deccan and found himself helpless to defend Delhi when reinforcement from Aligarh and Buland Shehr also could not approach for fear of the mughals. Sultan was upset and requested Hazrat Nizam ud Din Aulia for help. The spiritual powers came into action and the commander of the

---

1. Tareekh-e-Farishta, Vol.1, P.377-381 and Tabqat-e-Akbari, Vol.1, P153-157.

Mughals, Turghi was overpowered by imperceptible fear. He raised the siege of Delhi and left for his own country all of a sudden. This was considered to be a miracle of Hazrat Nizam ud Din Aulia by the people of Delhi.[1]

Another occasion for spiritual help arose when Alauddin was in Delhi but his forces were in Warangal (Deccan) fighting to conquer the fort. For many days there was no news of the army and Alauddin was perturbed. He sent Qazi Mughis and Malik Qara Baig to the audience of Hazrat Nizam ud Din Aulia who gave good news of victory. The same day a harbinger came to the Sultan in the afternoon and gave glad tidings of victory. This event further increased the respect and dedication of Alauddin for Hazrat Nizam ud Din Aulia. Alauddin repeatedly wrote letters to Hazrat Nizam ud Din Aulia for spiritual help.[2]

Public Reforms:

Continuous victories and annexation of conquered lands gave Alauddin a vast empire which was bigger than the Indian British Empire as opined by Shaikh Muhammad Akram, author of "Chashma-e-Kausar". He was brave and dauntless in the battlefield and at the same, his statesmanship, organizational genius and administratitive ability made him a unique ruler. He had so tactfully organized his intelligence network that he was fully aware of whatever happenings took place in various place of his empire. Law and order situation was ideal and the whole country from Lahore to Deccan was like a peaceful inn.[3] Travelling and trading was easy and without fear. The big government officials fear the Sultan because of his effective intelligence. He had made drinking out of law and punish the drunkards most severely. There was a well in Badayun where the wine addicts were imprisoned. The result of sever penalties was that drinking was totally stopped in the country.

Alauddin had administration wisdom and foresight. He took

---

1. Tabqat-e-Akbari, Vol.1, P.158
2. Tareekh-e-Farishta, Vol.1, P.401-403
3. Ibid, Vol.1, P.374

measures to have equitable distribution of wealth. He seized all estates from the chiefs and made the part of the Royal properties. He took away all surplus wealth for Muslims and non-Muslims and made them to work hard for their livelihood. Farishta (Historian wrote that Alauddin introduced measures for equal distribution of wealth among the financially weak and financially strong people in urban and rural areas. He stopped corruption with an iron hand. He introduced a system of inspection of revenue offices where any illegal wealth, if discovered, was confiscated.

The second important administrative measure was the fixation of rates for all articles of eating, drinking, wearing, houses, cattles and even different types of lands. Government servants' pays and salaries were graded and permanently fixed. Even skilled, semi-skilled and artisan types of workers were given a fixed rate of their wages for work or performance beyond which they could not charge any thing. The traders who came from abroad they could not sell any thing at arbitrary rates. A department called "Sarai-Adl" controlled all the rates of imported merchandise. Wheat, Barley, grains, rice, and pulses had fixed rates of sale and these rates were stable during the regime of Alauddin Khilji.

During his regime there was an evil sect "Abahiya" who had no moral taboos or restrictions. They used to hold a function once in a year in which they indulged in all kinds of immoral activities, so much so, they molested even their own sisters and mothers. Alauddin came to know that a group of the "Abahiya" sect was present and active in Delhi. He got them totally annihilated so that not a single person survived.

Alauddin Khilji had an extreme psychology. If some one peleased him, he was given the highest gifts and honour. If some one displeased him or had indications of doing him harm, he would take the most sever action against him. A great grandson of Jingiz Khan Alghou Khan (who was also the son-in-law of Jalal ud Din Khilji) professed Islam along with 4,000 Mughal men and women. All of them had settled in India. Alauddin came to know that some people from among those new converts had hatched a plot to kill Alauddin when he went on hunting. Alauddin got all the new

Muslim converts mercilessly killed and he renewed the tyranny of Zahak and Pharos.

Alauddin was fond of new buildings and constructions. He got new mosques, monasteries, and safety enclosures in such a large number that no other king in history could equal him. He also encouraged men of art and literature. The Historiann Farishta wrote: "Men of art and literature, skilled persons and experts in each branch of knowledge and human activity had gathered around the king in such a large number that such a gathering was never seen before or after him. Justice, truth, peace and perfect law and order prevailed. A large gathering of religious scholars and mystical dignitories was seen in Delhi during the regime of Alauddin. It was unique and was never paralleled in any other regime in the Indian history. Forty six great scholars of Islam have been mentioned who used to teach and were listened in the religious institutions.

End of Khiljis:

Alauddin ruled with great pomp and splendour for 20 years after which such circumstances came into existence which resulted in the tragic end of the Khilji dynasty.

The foremost reason for the downfall and decline of the Khilji dynasty was the newly converted ex-Hindu Prime Minister of Alauddin. Malik Kafoor fell into the hands of Alauddin while conquering Gujrat. He was initially a Hindu but his handsomeness and graces so much impressed Alauddin that he purchased him as a slave and after his conversion to Islam, made him a commander of his forces. Kafoor achieved tangible successes in the expeditions in the Deccan and was raised to the status of Prime Minister. He became so close to Alauddin that he never took any action without consulting Malik Kafoor.

Alauddin's son Khizar Khan, born of Malika Jahan, was nominated as successor to the throne. Kafoor wanted to oust him from the position of Royal successor. Khizar Khan had gone to Amroha for hunting while Alauddin was ill. He returned to Delhi without informing his father. Malik Kafoor concocted a story of plot against the king, involving Khizar Khan therein. As per advice of Kafoor Khan, poor prince was imprisoned in the fort of Gowaliar for plotting against his father. Kafoor also got Alap Khan, brother of Malika Jehan , killed after calling him from Gujrat. Thereafter, Alauddin himself died, perhaps as reported by some historians, due to poison given by Malik Kafoor.[1]

On the second day after the death of Alauddin Khilji, Malik Kafoor showed a writing of the dead king to the senior most organs of the government, replacing the nomination of Khizar Khan with the nomination of his younger brother, Shahab ud Din as the heir-apparent of the deceased king. So Shahab ud Din was placed at the throne and Malik Kafoor ran the affairs of the government in his name. Malik Kafoor had the meanness to get Khizar Khan and his brother, Shadi Khan blinded in the fort of Gowaliar when they were imprisoned. He also captured all the wealth of Malika Jahan: wife of Alauddin who was also a prisoner in the fort of Gowaliar. Shahab ud Din was mere a child at the time of his occupation of the throne. "Tabaqat-e-Akbari" has described the henious strategy of Malik Kafoor in the following words:

> "*Kafoor called out Shahab ud Din from inside the palace for an hour or two and made him sit on the Bam-e-Hazar Satoon and all the chiefs and dignitories of the state to stand before the "King" with folded hands. When the court was over, he sent the child king to his mother in the palace and himself got engaged in playing chess with his trusted eunuchs.[2] Kafoor, the infidel was so daring in his evil actions that he married the mother of Shahab ud Din although he was impotent.*"[3]

Kafoor was so diloyal to the Royal family that; after blinding Khizar Khan and Shadi Khan, he arranged to get a third prince Mubarak Khan also blinded by paid servants. When the servants reached Mubarak Khan with evil intention of blinding him,

---
1. Tabqat-e-Akbari, Vol.1, P.172-173
2. Ibid, Vol.174
3. Tareekh-e-Farishta, Vol.1, P.414

he made them realize the great benefits and benedictions which his father, king Alauddin had bestowed on them. They were deeply impreessed and made up their minds to take vengeance from the disloyal rogue. The same night they entered upon Malik Kafoor's private chamber and killed him along with all his supporters and friends. This happened only after 35 days of the death of Alauddin Khilji.

After the murder of Kafoor and his supporters, Mubarak Khan ran the affairs of the government as the deputy of his brother Shahab ud Din for a period of two months. At the end of two months he took the reins of the government independently and stepped up on the throne under title of Sultan Qutbud Din Mubarak Shah. He imprisoned prince Shahab ud Din in the fort of Gowaliar.[1]

Qutbud Din Mubarak ascended the throne on 8th of Moharram, 717A.H. His attitude was positive and constructive in the beginning. He annihilated the mischief-rogues and the rebels in the country. He gave six months advance pay to his servants and reduced the taxes which Alauddin had imposed. He also increased the monthly stipend of religious scholars and mystics who were borne on the official list. After only a few days Qutbud Din Mubarak Shah became fond of pomp and pleasure which resulted in his gross indifference towards the affairs of the state. He was frequently seen in the assembly of singers and dancers and even wore female clothes. Like Malik Kafoor, a low caste Hindu, Malik Khasro, had nominally converted to Islam. He was ruling over the nerves of Qutbud Din Mubarak who had made him Prime Minister of the state and given all affairs in his hands. He was a cunning hypocrite who appointed his favourites in all offices and departments of the country.

---

1. Historian Farishta wrote that, when Kafoor was planning to get Mubarak Khan blinded, his mother Bibi Maahak sent a man to the audience of Shaikh Najmuddin, son of Hazrat Shaikh Ahmad Jam, a saint of great spiritual powers and made a request for help. The Shaikh said: "Do not worry in the least and be hopeful of Divine help". Then the Shaikh put off his cap and put it upside down with remarks: "I shall put on this cap only after Mubarak Shah has ascended the throne".

When Malik Khusrao (Hindu convert) had established his supremacy over the country by giving all key posts to his trusted men, he arranged through his men to murder Qutbud Din Mubarak most mercilessly and got his bodiless head thrown under the palace. After the murder of Qutbud Din Mubarak, Malik Khusrao assassinated all the sons of Alauddin as well as their mothers. He was so mean and audacious that he married the widow of Khizar Khan. The evil treatment meted out to the queens and princes of the ruling Khilji family has been described by Historian Farishta in the following words:

> "Malik Khusrao gave his brother (who was a low caste Hindu convert) the title of Khan-e-Khanan and handed over the daughter of Alauddin Khilji to him. Himself Malik Khusrao took over the widow of Qutbud Din Mubarak Shah. Apart from these important ladies, Malik Khurso audaciously distributed the princesses and widows of the Khilji family to the chiefs of his army. He assassinated all the loyal servants and slaves of Alauddin and Qutbud Din Mubarak and handed over their women and children to the Hindus of Gujrat. This callous Hindu hypocrite who was from a low caste, did every thing possible to efface the remnants of the Khilji family. So much so that a nephew of Alauddin Khilji, Malik Mussarat Khan (who was a recluse and had taken to solitude) was also assassinated by Malik Khusrao".

During those times there was a mystical mad man, Shaikh Bashir by name. He was asked as to why the entire troubled and family of Alauddin Khilji was being ransacked and wiped out. He replied: "This is the result of the thanklessness on the part of Alauddin who mercilessly killed his uncle and benefactor, Jalal ud Din Khilji. This act had displeased God".

The author of Tabaqat-e-Akbari has also written that "Qutbud Din Mubarak Shah used to despite Hazrat Nizam ud Din Aulia and bore deep malice against him which he openly expressed".

The rise and fall of the Khilji dynasty was due to manifest circumstances and reasons which have been explained in detail. Khusrao Khan was a Muslim only in name. In the heart of his hearts he continued to be a bigoted Hindu of low caste. According to Zia ud Din Barni: "His real aim was to establish a strong Hindu government in the North India. After killing all the young and old members of the family of Alauddin, Khusrao Khan began openly to express his malice and hatred against Islam. He got the institution of Islam closed by order and converted the mosques into Hindu temples".

Historian Farishta said: "The Hindus had the meanness and courage to sit on copies of the Holy Quran as they used to sit on chairs".[1] Khawaja Nizam ud Din stated: "Since all big functionaries of the government were Hindu, the institution of Islam suffered and the Hindu system and institutions gained ascendancy. The idols were worshiped and the mosques were ran-sacked.

---

1. Tareekh-e-Farishta, Vol.1, P.427

THE TUGHLAQ DYNASTY

The Khiljis were punished for the misdeeds they had performed during their rule of India. Their name was effaced from the world scene. But the spiritual power of Hazrat Khawaja Nizam ud Din Aulia and Hazrat Khawaja Qutbud Din Bakhtiar Kaki came into action against the forces of evil and Hindu tyranny against Islam. The lamp of Islam lightened by Shahab ud Din Ghauri and Qutbud Din Aibak could not be extinguished by the puffs of evil mongers like the Hindu Malik Khusrao. Hardly five months had passed after Malik Khusrao ascended the throne when Ghazi Malik Fakhruddin, the then governor of Punjab advanced upon Delhi like a violent tarnish and wiped out all vestiges of anti-Islam forces, killing Khusrao Khan and all his comrades and confederates.

All small and big persons in Delhi were happy over this great performer of Ghazi Malik Fakhruddin. The elite of the capital city came to his audience and congratulated him on his great achievement. Next day a grand meeting was held in the Koshak Hazar Satoon Palace where the chiefs of civil and army counted his golden deeds for the revival of Islam and made a favourite appeal to him to take up the reins of government. Ghias-ud-Din Tughlaq (that became the title of Ghazi Malik) delivered a very impressive speech in reply which Amir Khusrao quoted in his own words: "My crown and my throne in reality are my sword and arrow. On hearing the inhuman tyrannies of Khusrao Khan (Hindu convert), I was pain-stricken and my heart wept with grief. I became ashamed of my life and make up my mind to perform three important tasks --

1. To revive the Divine religion of Islam in this heretic land of India;

2. To snatch away the government from the diabolical and cursed Hindu child (Khusrao Khan) and bestow it on some of the living princes who may be deserving it; and

3. To annihilate the tyrants who had mercilessly effaced the royal family from the country.

The Tughlaq Dynasty

All the three intentions were entertained for the pleasure of God and I am grateful to the Almighty that He has granted me courage and strength to perform all the three tasks successfully. I am not a seeker of throne and, except for the defence of Islam, I shall not unsheathe my sword. If any descendant of Khilji Royal family is alive, this throne of Delhi rightly belongs to him. If there is no one alive, then you may choose from among the great chiefs and leaders presently available in Delhi. As for myself I love my horse and wilderness of Dipalpur to which I belong".[1]

After the above speech, many elderly chiefs fell at the feet of Ghias-ud-Din Tughlaq and kissed them devotedly, seeking with favour and humility that he may step up on the throne as he was the most deserving person for it. At long last he agreed to take up the rein of the government. On the 1st of the month of Sha'ban, 720A.H. he ascended the throne and adopted the title of Sultan Ghias-ud-Din Tughlaq.

Sultan Ghias-ud-Din Tughlaq:

A new ruling dynasty stepped in with the enthronement of Sultan Ghias-ud-Din Tughlaq. Ghias-ud-Din Tughlaq born in a poor family who rose to the position of monarchy by dint of his personal character and perfection. Historian Farishta spoke highly of Ghias-ud-Din Tughlaq. He stated: "This king was cool-hearted and tolerant. He was intelligent and generous by nature. He was pure-hearted and chaste in character. He regularly said his five times prayers in congregation. He spent his full time from morning to evening in his public chamber, considering multiferious social, administrative and financial problems".[2]

After ascending the throne he got beheaded all the supporters and confederates of Khusrao Khan. As for the person of

---
1. Masnavi Tughlaq Nama. P.141
2. Tareekh-e-Farishta. Vol.2, P.2 (Urdu Translation)

Khusrao Khan, he was killed precisely at the spot (in the Qasr-e-Hazar Satoon) where he had mercilessly killed his master and benefactor, Qutbud Din Mubarak Shah. His head was likewise chopped off and thrown down the palace.[1]

After effective annihilation of mischief-mongers in the country, he diverted his attention to administrative reforms, and, according to Nizam ud Din Ahmad Bakhshi, what other rulers could not do in years he got them done in one week's time only.[2] If he saw any one in trouble, he would inquire after his affairs and render effective help to solve the problem. He avoided all actions which could displease or annoy the public.[3] He appreciated and rewarded men of real humanity and integrity.

Ghias-ud-Din Tughlaq brought about reformation in the economic system of the country as well. His policy was moderation. If any government official got more then the official dues, and the charge against him was proved, he was severely punished. Khusrao Khan had lavishly distributed public money to win good wils of the people. Ghias-ud-Din recovered the money from all such persons as he knew them and deposited vast accounts in the Treasury.

He appointed religious scholars and mystics. On any function of rejoicing in the palace, he also invited mystics and scholars to attend along with high ranking government officials. The result of this good-naturedness was that people felt equal and equitable treatment at the royal hands and rivalries stopped making the country heaven of peace. The Mughals who were repeatedly attacking Indian territories were totally stopped by Ghias-ud-Din Tughlaq and, during his regime, they could not make any inroads. Besides great qualities of statesmanship and administration, he was also fond of erecting beautiful buildings. Tughlaqabad fort in Delhi was made under his orders. In his day-to-day administration he was very careful to implement the injunction of Shariat.

---

1. Masnavi Tughlaq Nama. P.151
2. Tabqat-e-Akbari. Vol.1. P.191
3. Ibid. P.192

The Tughlaq Dynasty

The public opinion about Sultan Ghias-ud-Din Tughlaq may well be judged from the remarks of Zia ud Din Barni who wrote in "Tabaqat-e-Foroz Shahi" "I have heard from most seasoned and experienced elderly persons that no monarch on the throne of Delhi was so just, considerate, well-wishing of his people and peace-loving as Sultan Ghias-ud-Din Tughlaq".[1]

He had hardly ruled for four years when suddenly the message of his heavenward journey arrived. He was returning from Bengal after effectively dealing with the tyrannical governors there when the roof of the newly constructed palace (under which he had taken the feast arranged by his son) collapsed and he died instantaneously. This unwholesome event took place in the year 725 A.H. corresponding to 1325 A.D.[2] It was a coincidence that Hazrat Amir Khusrao also passed away during the same year.

After Ghias-ud-Din Tughlaq his son Muhammad Shah ascended the throne. His personality proved to be an enigma for the historians. He was wise, intelligent, mentally alert, brave and statesman-like. "He was, as it were, born for the decoration of the monarch's throne",[3] said Zia ud Din Barni. He was so that he gave away large sums to any needy person and yet would be sorry for not having given much. To religious scholars and men of art and literature he gave away munificently. Distinguished persons from Khrasan, Iraq, and Mawra un Nahr came to his court and were given so such favours that they needed no more of any thing all their lives.[4] His knowledge of psychology was so deep that on his first sight of a person, he could tell his vices and virtues.[5] He was also very leaned in history. His memory was exceptional. He never forgot any event of his life. He was also well-versed in rational sciences like medicines, philosophy, astronomy, mathematics, logic and spent much time in study of books. He spoke with eloquence.

---

1. Tareekh-e-Feerozshahi
2. Ibid. P.452
3. Ibid. P.457
4. Tabqat-e-Akbari, Vol.1, P.199
5. Tabqat-e-Akbar, Vol.1, P.200

His letters written in Arabic and Persian were so well written that men of letters wondered at his expertise. His hand-writing was fine and pure and the calligraphists admitted his great art and skillfulness.[1]

He was also sincerely dedicated to the rituals of Islam. He said his five times prayers regularly in congregation and never missed the obligatory fasting. He also said many supererogatory prayers like Tahajjad, Ishraq, Awwabin etc. He never took any drugs. He also made his people strictly follow the injunctions and prohibitions of Islam. Ibne Batoota wrote: "The Sultan had ordered that any Muslim avoiding congregational prayers must be punished. He had appointed certain scholarly persons to teach the details and methods of prayers to the common Muslims. There was also a spy network and any one not offering his prayers in conjugation was caught and brought before the king. People were seen committing to many problems about the prayers.[2] Even singing girls had become regular in saying their prayers". Ibne Batoota went on to write: "I have never seen a ruler more just and loving of justice than Sultan Muhammad Tughlaq". Once a Hindu put up petition that the king had killed his brother without reason. The king appeared before the Qazi without any army and any protocol. He saluted the Qazi and displayed great respect for the court. The Qazi announced the verdict that the king was guilty and he must satisfy the appellant or else get ready for punishment under the Shariat Law. The Sultan made a compromise with the Hindu and the Qazi then set him at liberty.

A yet more strange incident has been noted by historians faces the son of an aristocrat accused the king of having beaten him with a stick. The case went up before the Qazi who gave a decision that the king may compromise with the boy or get the punishment. Ibne Batoota wrote: "I have seen with my own eyes that the king called in the boy, gave a stick in his hands and asked him to take his revenge. He gave him an oath of his head that the boy may beat him

---
1. Tareekh Farishta. Vol.2, P.10
2. Travellogue of Ibn-e-Batuta. Vol.2, P.131

with same force with which he had beaten him. The boy took up the stick and inflicted 21 strokes on the king so much so that at one stroke, the cap of the king fell down from his head".[1]

He was courageous and very large-hearted so that even an empire of seven countries was insignificant in his eyes. He sent a large army of one hundred. thousand strong to conquer China. He sent an equally strong army to Iran for conquest. Both the expeditions failed.

In a short duration of time, he was successful in giving his people perfect law and order. All the provinces were free from any trouble and at the revenue system was of high standard. The king was keen to avoid any source of unlawful income. In 741 A.H. he gave orders that all taxes were abolished except the Islamic taxes of Zakat and Ushr.[2]

For two days in a week -- Monday and Thursday – the Sultan had public audience in an open ground where people submitted their applications through four high officials who were appointed for this purpose. All complaints were reduced to writing and the Sultan read them minutely to understand particularly the nature of each complaint which was decided on merit.[3]

Waywardness and Cynical Attitude:

Muhammad Tughlaq was a problem personality. Combined with the countless virtues described above, he was an extremist in his attitude and was never stead fast to any course of action, always vacillating. It occurred to his mind that the capital of the kingdom must be located in the heart of the goverened territories. During discussion the name of Ujjain was suggested to him for the capital. But he proudly liked Dev Garh for its good climate. He gave immediate order that all residents of Delhi may migrate to Dev Garh.

---

1. Travellogue of Ibn-e-Batuta, Vol.2, P.130
2. Ibid, P.131
3. Ibid

Royal order was implemented and Delhi became a desolate city with no glamour while Dev Garh, which was re-named Daulat Abad, became a splendid town.

Historian Farishta described the repercussions of the change of capital. He wrote: "This change had unwholesome effects on the public and the administration. There was turmoil and rebellion in the Punjab and in Multan. The king himself advanced to the troubled areas to meet the disturbance. Now he realized that change of capital was a blunder. He therefore, again ordered people to return to Delhi at their discretion. Many people came back after great hardships and the city was again well populated".

Historians are divided over the rationale of the transfer of the capital from Delhi to Dev Garh. Some have called it lunacy while some others have called it lack of balance. However, Professor Khaleeq Ahmad Nizami has taken a different view, which are opposite to the common views of the historians. In his research thesis, he has stated that his motive was the preaching and propagation of Islam. He wrote: "Muhammad Tughlaq had great political insight which made him realize that foundations of an Islamic government cannot take a firm root unless there is substantial Muslim population in the particular area. Muhammad Tughlaq sent preachers to Deccan areas for the propagation of Islam". His research pointed out that Muhammad Tughlaq never changed the capital. He only sent religious scholars and mystical saints to Deccan for systematic preaching of Islam. There was no such thing as the change of capital. His army, Treasury and government offices continued to function in Delhi. The purpose of his sending the selected scholars and elderly persons to Dev Garh is further classified by the fact that, on the eve of departure to Dev Garh, the Sultan delivered an eloquent lecture in which he impressed upon the people the necessity of "Jihad" i.e. struggle in the cause of Islam. This meeting was attended by dignified scholars and mystics like Maulana Fakhruddin, Maulana Shamsuddin Yahya, and Shaikh Naseer ud Din Chiragh Delhvi.[1] It is also established by research of

---

1. Sier-ul-Aulia. P.239

The Tughlaq Dynasty

Doctor Mehdi Hassan that only Muslims were sent to Dev Garh.

There is no reason left to doubt that the action of Muhammad tughlaq was purely for the preaching of Islam. Its aim was laudible but the modus operendi was devastating. Due to change of population, there was lot of unrest and the central position of Delhi was adversely affected.

During his regime there was a sever famine in and around Delhi so that one seer of wheat cost Rs.17/- or more. Countless people died of hunger and many cattle also gave up life. The king made efforts to mitigate the calamity and gave many concessions to the peasants. Unfortunately the Royal Treasury was almost empty due to military expeditions of the king and he increased the revenue inordinately, particularly for the Hindu peasants. The result was that people were desperate due to unbearable hardships. They burnt their houses and ran away to seek shelter in the jungles. To meet this financial hardship, Muhammad Tughlaq circulated copper coin (instead of regular silver and gold coin) which was not accepted by foreign traders. The result was that commerce came to a stand still and the markets became empty. There was large increase of beggars.

This uneasiness and administrative anarchy had bad political effects. Many provinces rebelled against the central government of Delhi. In South India three provinces seceded from Delhi and could not be conquered again. The vast Hindu State of Vijya nagar and the Muslim Bahmani State of Deccan were founded during the time of Muhammad Tughlaq. As compared with the vast area of the Khilji empire during the period of Alauddin Khilji the kingdom of Muhammad Tughlaq was greatly reduced in area.

The attitude of the Sultan was unwholesome towards the mystical personalities and the religious scholars. He wished to get the services of the saintly persons for his personal and private affairs. The most prominent personality of the time, Hazrat Naseer ud Din Chiragh Delvi refused to accept his unreasonable demands and was imprisoned. The most unfortunate event, which took place at the time, was that Hazrat Shaikh Shahab ud Din (who was a descendant of Shaikh ul Islam Jam Zinda Peel), among the greatest of spiritual personalities, had taken asylum in a cave, 6 miles from Delhi. He was called by the king but he declined to appear before him and said that he could not see the cruel monarch. He was forcibly brought and the king asked him: "Do you call me cruel?" The Shaikh replied: "Yes; you are cruel and you have performed such and such acts of cruelty". Sultan Muhammad Tughlaq unsheathed his sword and gave to the Sadr-e-Jahan (Prime Minister).. he said to the Shaikh: "Prove my cruelty and chop off my head if I am guilty".

The Shaikh said: "Who testifies to your tyranny, he will be beheaded, yet you yourself know so well that you are a cruel ruler". The king got the saint hand cuffed and put chains in his feet. For 14 days this state of cruelty continued and the Shaikh did not take any food. On the fourteenth day the king sent some food to the Shaikh which he refused to take and he said: "My sustenance on the earth is finished now". He was then forcibly made to eat the cow's dung and the next day he was beheaded.[1]

The cruelty and inefficiency of the king had brought his downfall very near. He himself said to Zia ud Din Barni: "All the organs of my state are unhealthy. If I treat one disease, another arises. Can you give me good advice for improvement? Zia ud Din Barni replied: "When people dislike a ruler and there is wide spread unrest and turmoil, the best course for the ruler is to abdicate in favour of his brother or his son, and himself take to life of solitude and prayers. If cannot abdicate he must avoid the things which breed hatred in his people".

Under the unwholesome circumstances explained above, the king became ill with fever and 21st of Moharram, 752 A.H. and died (1351 A.D.).

Sultan Feroze Shah Tughlaq:

Muhammad Shah Tughlaq was succeeded by his cousin, Sultan Feroze Shah Tughlaq who was the son of commander Rajab,

---

1. Travellogue of Ibn-e-Batuta, Vol.2, P.137-139

a real brother of Sultan Ghias-ud-Din Tughlaq. His mother was a Hindu convert lady and was the daughter of Raja Rana Mal Bhatti. Her Hindu name was Bibi Nalah but in the Royal family she was named Kad Bano. Feroze Shah was born in 709 A.H. and his father died when he was only seven years old. He was brought up under the care and guidance of his uncle, Ghias-ud-Din Tughlaq, who always kept him in his company and taught him good conduct and good character.[1] He appreciated his virtues and gave him title of "Naib Barbak" after appointing him Naib Amir Hajib.

Feroze Shah served Sultan Muhammad very assiduously during his illness and the king gave him dying will for his appointment as his successor. After the death of Sultan Muhammad Tughlaq, the state dignitories and scholars came to him with the request to ascend the throne. Feroze Shah said: "I have made up my mind to visit the Holy Ka'aba and the Holy Shrine of Madina. You may select some one else for the kingdom".

The country was facing great troubles. There was great unrest in the country and the Mughals had created widespread trouble in Delhi and other parts of the country. There was no better person available for the throne of Delhi than Feroze Shah. Under the circumstances scholars and saints like Hazrat Shaikh Naseer ud Din Chiragh Delhvi and Makhdoom Zada Abbasi, along with great dignitories of the state announced the kingship of Feroze Shah and, Amir Tataar Khan who was the most elderly person in the meeting, caught hand of Feroze Shah and forcibly put him on the throne. When the king saw that kingship was being thrust upon him, he asked the elderly dignitories to wait till he had performed ablution and said two prostrations of prayers. He prayed and in his prolonged prostration, begged of Almighty Allah to help him with His Divine help to discharge these difficult duties of rulership for the benefit and favour of the public.[2]

Sultan Feroze Shah Tughlaq ruled from 1351 A.D. to 1388 A.D., for nearly 38 years. As a Muslim monarch, his rule was ideal

---

1. Tareekh-e-Feerozshahi, Preface I & II
2. Tareekh-e-Feerozshahi, Preface III

and exemplary. He was not as much fond of more as he was of preaching and spreading Islam.[1] Due to complete peace and order and welfare actions and institutions for the public, his period was considered by historians as a golden period of Muslim rule. He set at liberty who were put behind the bars by Muhammad Tughlaq without any crime. He gave monetary compensation to the dependants of all those persons who were killed without any fault. He restored all the properties and estates which were unlawfully usurped by the former rulers. He also abolished all the unbearable taxes.

The provinces and territories which had declared independence during the regime of Sultan Muhammad Tughlaq were not disturbed. Feroze Shah recognized their independence. He, however, tried to re-conquer the province of Bengal but did not succeeded. His policy was to rule under strict Shariat Laws over whatever territory was under his jurisdiction. With this aim, he performed the following actions:

1. He abolished all cruel laws under which the Muslims were surrendered. He appointed all servants strictly under regular salaries. He made a regulation that the son of a dying official must replace him in the office of the state. If there was no son, the son-in-law will replace him. If there was no son-in-law, then the slave or the servant of kin must replace. The result of this welfare rule was such that people became prosperous and population increased. Every body had heaps of gold and silver in his possession.

2. The names of the Muslim rulers were not announced in the Friday sermons. Sultan Feroze Shah Tughlaq gave orders that they must be announced.

3. He abolished all unlawful taxes and severely punished all officials who took any unlawful money.

---

1. History of India by Dela Fass

The Tughlaq Dynasty

4. Previously only one fifth of the war looty was distributed among the fighting forces and the rest was deposited in the royal treasury. He gave orders that only one fifth of the looty be deposited in the treasure and four fifth be distributed among the fighting forces.

5. He severely punished all those persons who were spreading apostasy and lewdness in the country and burnt their literature.

6. He strictly prohibited and made unlawful all evil social customs, like photography, visit of tombs by women, use of gold and silver vessels in houses, he threw out all such vessels and pictures from the royal palace.

He was also keen to build useful buildings like mosques, schools and public places of utility. He appreciated religious scholars and mystics. He encouraged the spread of useful knowledge and got many useful books translated from Sanskrit into Persian. Famous books on Islamic jurisprudence like "Fatawa-e-Tatar Khania" and "Fiqah-e-Feroze Shahi" were written under his jurisdiction. He himself wrote a small booklet of 32 pages under caption, "Fatoohat-e-Feroze Shahi" in which he narrated all his reformatory measures and his useful performance. He also got these engraved on a pole in Kotla Feroze Shah. Apart from these, he built dispensaries at many places, inns and public reservoirs of water, and constructed roads and performed countless acts of public welfare.

Historian Farishta has given the statistics of the welfare buildings erected under rule of Feroze Shah:

1.	Water reservoirs (Bandjoe)	50
2.	Mosques	40
3.	Madrassas (schools)	30
4.	Public Monasteries	20
5.	Mansions and Palaces	100
6.	Dispensaries	5
7.	Tombs and Shrines	100
8.	Public Bath Rooms	10

9.	Water wells	1500
10.	Bridges	100

Historian Farishta wrote that; besides the above mentioned works of public welfare, Feroze Shah got a large number of gardens made for the people. Every building of public welfare was registered and a suitable trust was established for its day-to-day maintenance and expenses. With the advice of Muslim scholars he imposed the Jizya tax on Non-Muslims and granted them all civil rights and liberties.

After having ruled for 38 years, this great ruler died at the age of 90 years in 799 A.H. (1387 A.D.)

Amir Taimoor

After the death of Feroze Shah Tughlaq, the entire land of India was in the grip of anarchy and turmoil. During, period of 9 years many claimants to the throne rose to position and were killed one after another. First of all Tughlaq Shah, a grandson of Feroze Shah Tughlaq rose to power and began to rule under the title of Ghias-ud-Din Tughlaq. Within a year of his ascendancy he was killed. His cousin, Abu Bakar Shah rose to power. After 18 months, Nasir ud Din Muhammad got him killed and captured the throne. He ruled for almost 6 years and 7 months. His son Humayun Khan succeeded him on the throne under title of Sultan Sikandar Shah. After only 45 days he fell seriously ill and died. For 15 days the elders of the state could not decide about the successor of Sultan Sikandar Shah. At long last, through the efforts of a senior chief, Khawaja Jahan, the youngest son of Nasir ud Din Muhammad, Mahmood was placed at the throne in the month of Jamadi ul Awwal, 796 A.H. He took the title of Nasir ud Din. A courageous chief, Saadat Khan, rebelled and made efforts to place Nusrat Khan, another grandson of Feroze Shah, at the throne. Saadat Khan was killed but the aristocrats of Feroze Abad recognized Nusrat Khan as the ruler. Mahmood Khan ruled in Delhi while Nusrat Khan ruled in Feroze Abad. As such, two monarchs ruled over India simultaneously. This situation weakened the authority of Delhi. There was widespread rebellion and turmoil. The provincial

The Tughlaq Dynasty

government of Bengal, Jampur, Sindh, Gujrat, Malwah and Deccan were all Muslim. But they became independent out of Delhi. In Rajputana and South India, the Hindus had established strong governments. The authority of Delhi was, therefore, negligible.

The invasion of Taimoor, the lame, in 800 A.H. totally finished the authority and prestige of the Delhi government. Taimoor wrote in his memoirs that the purpose of his invasion was to fight for Islam against the idol worshipers of India who were enemies of Islam and to capture wealth for the soldiers of Islam. But the cruel deeds of Taimoor such as reckless murder of civilians in Delhi for day together, the merciless murder of Muslims in Iran and Angora, the arrest of the great Mujahid of Islam Sultan Ba-Yazid Yaldram and his imprisonment in a cage, - are all indicative of the fact that Taimoor had nothing to do with Islam and all his military exploits were for worldly purposes and for the gratification of his ego.

When Taimoor attacked Delhi, Mahmood Tughlaq fled for his life to Gujrat a day before the attack. The citizens of Delhi accepted the authority of Taimoor to save their lives. Despite this compromise, the descendants of Jingiz Khan displayed his sense of cruelty and there was massacre of citizens in Delhi and the great city was ruined and became desolate. Taimoor left Delhi after 15 days and a minister of Mahmood Tughlaq, Mallo Iqbal captured Delhi and began to rule.

In 1405 A.D. there was a rebellion against Mallo Iqbal and he was killed. Mahmood Tughlaq was recalled from Gujrat and asked to rule. He was left with small territory of Delhi City and the area around it. As such, he did not take the title of king. He ruled uptil 1412 A.D.

The Sadaat Dynasty (1414 A.D. – 1450 A.D.):

After the death of Mahmood Tughlaq, there was widespread anarchy till Khizar Khan, governor of Sindh, reached Delhi and conquered it in 1414 A.D. Three of his successors ruled over Delhi which had shrunk in jurisdiction. Most of their time was spent in defending Delhi against attacks of Muslim chiefs who had set up independent principalities around Delhi. Khizar Khan was the son of Malik Suleman who claimed to be a Syed. As such this dynasty came to be known Sadaat family. Historian Farishta has quoted two arguments in support of this claim but both the arguments are absurd.

The last ruler of Syed family was Sultan Alauddin Bin Sultan Muhammad Shah. Like his father, he was incapable and fond of rest and recreation. He went to Badayun and so much liked its climate that he decided to stay on there despite great unrest in Delhi calling for his attention. The state of Delhi was already a small state. As such the governor of the Punjab, Bahlol Lodhi reached Delhi and captured it in the absence of Sultan Alauddin. He wrote to Alauddin at Badayun that he had set right every thing in Delhi and had not allowed his (Alauddin's) name to be omitted from the Friday Sermon. Alauddin wrote to him: "My father had called you his son and, as such, I consider you my elder brother. I give you the state of Delhi with pleasure and shall continue to stay in Badayun.[1] As such, in 855 A.H. corresponding to 1451 A.D. Bahlol Lodhi became the regular ruler of Delhi and the Afghans began to rule.

Lodhi Dynasty:

Bahlol Lodhi was a capable ruler. He tried his best to restore the past splendour of the Delhi government. He conquered the areas around Delhi and, in 1478 A.D. annexed Jampur. He died in 1489 A.D.

Sultan Sikandar Lodhi:

After the death of Bahlol Lodhi, his son Sultan Sikandar Lodhi ascended the throne. His kingdom comprised Delhi, Punjab and united provinces. He added the province of Bihar to it, and made Aagra as his capital and seat of government.

Skindar Lodhi was a capable ruler. He was brave, courageous and lover of knowledge. He attained the Quranic lectures of Sheikh Abdullah who was a great religious scholar of his

---

[1]. Tareekh-e-Farishta, Vol.2, P.123

time. He was so sensible that, to avoid any commotion and disturbance in the lecture (due to the presence of king in person), he sat in a hidden corner of the mosque to avoid any sights. When Maulana Rafi ud Din Shirazi, a great scholar of Hadith came to Aagra from Sheraz, Sultan Sikandar Lodhi gave him very great respect and Maulana continued to teach Hadith in Aagra for a long time. Sultan Sikandar Lodhi was regular in prayers and fasting and did his best to act on the injunctions of the Shariat. He was also fond of poetry and himself composed verses. Persian language was greatly developed in his time and many good books were written under his supervision.

Unfortunately he was hard of temperament and, during his time, a Hindu Budhan Brahman, was killed due to religious verdict of some scholars which made the Hindu community against Sultan Sikandar Lodhi. He ruled for nearly 30 years and died in 923 A.H. (corresponding to 1517 A.D.) after a sever illness and was buried in Aagra.

Sultan Ibrahim Lodhi:

After Skindar, his son Sultan Ibrahim Lodhi came to the throne. Unfortunately, turmoil and anarchy gripped the country and, taking advantage of the wide unrest, Babar who was then the ruler of Kabul, came with a large army at the invitation of Daulat Khan, governor of Punjab, and, after trespassing Punjab, advanced towards Delhi and Aagra. Sultan Ibrahim Lodhi left at the head of a large army to defend the empire. At Panipat there was a pitched battle in which 15000 soldiers along with Sultan Ibrahim Lodhi himself were killed and Babar was victorious. This happened in 1526 A.D.

Advent of Babar and the Mughal Rule:

After the Panipat battle, Babar advanced to Aagra and captured it. He arrested the family of Sultan Ibrahim Lodhi. The Afghans tried to establish their government at Jampur. But Babar and his son, Humayoun defeated the Afghans.

In 1527 A.D. Rana Sanga advanced towards Aagra at the head of a high Rajput army. Mahmood Lodhi, a brother of Sultan

Ibrahim Lodhi, had also joined Rana Sanga with a large army to fight the Mughals. A sever battle was fought in Fatehpur Seekri, near Aagra. On this occasion Babar had taken a vow never to drink wine again if God granted him victory. The Rajputs fought with great courage and they were about to win. But suddenly the Mughal army got control of the battlefield and inflicted a grievous defeat on Rana Sanga and his allies. Babar chased the Rajput recklessly and did not give up th pursuit till he had captured their centers of power and activity.

In 1529 A.D., Babar captured Bihar. Now his empire extended from Bukhara to Multan and from the Arabian Sea to East Bihar. In 1530 A.D. Babar died in Aagra after a short illness. His dead body was taken to Kabul for burial.

The Character and Perfection of Babar:

Among the famous personalities of the Mughal family, Zaheer ud Din Babar was conspicuous for his versatile capabilities, comprehensive qualities and attractive personality. He became a king at the age of 12 years and ruled for 38 years. He was a brave and courageous warrior who was so well versed in the art of fighting. He was also well educated and loved art, literature and music. He also learned **calligraphy and** invented a style of handsome handwriting called "Khat-e-Babri". He wrote copies of the Holy Quran in this peculiar handwriting and sent them to the Holy City of Makkah Moazma. He wrote the events of his time and his own biography in his book "Tuzk-e-Babri". It was translated into Persian by Abdur Rahim Khan-e-Khanan under order of king Akbar. He was also a poet besides being a man of battles and a calligraphist. His own verses appear engraved at the edge of a water reservoir in Kabul.

During his stay in India, he did not have a chance to rule regularly yet he learnt the golden rule that no stable government was possible in India unless the religious sentiments of the Hindu population were duly respected. At his death, he issued the following points of advice to his son, Humayoun:

The Tughlaq Dynasty

"India is a land of many sacred religions. As such he should carefully bear in mind his following commands:"

1. Never entertain prejudice in your mind against any religion Bearing in mind the religious sentiments of all religious groups, he should deal with justice and fair play with all.
2. He should avoid the killing of cows so that the Hindu population of the country may have respect and good relations with him.
3. You should never demolish the place of worship of any religion.
4. He may always ignore the differences between the Shia and Sunni sects because such difference shall weaken Islam.
5. The propagation and spread of Islam is better achieved by kind treatment and favours than by unjust and coercive ways.
6. You may consider different characteristics of his people as different seasons of the year"[1]

Despite his secular and physical perfection and characteristics, Babar was very regular in his prayers and fasting. Historian Farishta stated that: "Babar belonged to the Hanfi school of Islamic jurisdiction. He never missed his prayers and regularly kept a fast on every Friday.[2]

Humayoun:

After the death of Babar, his empire was divided among his sons. Humayoun, the eldest son was given the rule of Delhi; Kamran got Afghanistan and Punjab; the two sons were made governors of provinces under Humayoun. Due to rivalry of his brothers, Humayoun could find no peace of mind and kept dealing with internal dissension. Although the Afghans had been defeated,

---
1. Chashma-e-Kausar, P.358
2. Tareekh-e-Farishta, Vol.2, P.227

yet Sher Shah Suri had gathered forces in Bihar. He conquered Bengal and declared his independence.

Humayoun was busy with an expedition in Gujrat where he was informed that Sher Shah Suri had conquered Bengal. He, therefore, left for the East. In 1593 A.D. armies of Humayoun and Sher Shah Suri confronted each other at Baksar. Peace talks were going on when the Afghan army attacked the Mughal army treacherously. Due to sudden and unexpected attack, Humayoun's army was un-nerved and there was great turmoil in the battlefield. Humayoun fled for his life and reached Aagra where started fresh preparations for the second bout. In 1540 A.D. at Qannouj the two armies fought each other. Unfortunately, Humayoun got a crushing defeat and he sought asylum with the king of Iran, Shah Tehmasop together with his entire family. During this period of unrest and his fortune, in 949 A.H. 1542 A.D. Jalal ud Din Muhammad Akbar was borne of Humayoun's wife Hameeda Bano Begum.

Sher Shah Suri and His Fmaily:

After his victory at Qannouj, Sher Shah Suri reached Delhi and declared his ascension to the throne as a king. The original name of Sher Shah Suri was Farid Khan son of Hassan Khan. He belonged to an Afghan clan called Roahi.[1]

Farid Khan was brought up in Jampur where he received education from a large group of religious scholars gathered there. He had read Persian language and important books like Gulistan, Bostan, Sikandar Nama and Qafia. He had read both prose and poetry and had good knowledge of history. He had good administrative genius and, by dint of his great qualities, he rose from the ownership of an ordinary estate to the kingship of Delhi. He ruled as a king only for 5 years from 1540 A.D. – 1545 A.D. during which he was constantly engaged in warfare. Yet he introduced such administrative reforms and gave such a wonderful revenue

---

1. Roah is the long stretch of low mountains running from Hassan Abdal to Kabul. Suri is one of the tribes of the Roahi clan. Tareekh-e-Farishta, Vol.2, P.250

system to his kingdom that even Akbar, the great followed his reforms.

Shaikh Muhammad Akram, ICS wrote: "Sher Shah Suri had divided his country into districts. Every district was further divided into Pergnas. Every Pergna had one military officer, one treasury officer, one judicial judge and two accountants who maintained two registers of accounts – one in Persian and the second in Hindi. The whole land was measured. Revenue was fixed according to the area and quality of the land. Even the Revenue System of the British India was based on the pattern of the Sher Shah Suri. Akbar, the great followed Sher Shah Suri's system and his capable minister of Revenue, Shah Mansoor, added two years settlement system of land

Sher Shah Suri also paid attention to improvement of the trade for the benefit of peasants. He abolished the octroi tax and all such taxes which hindered the progress of free trade. He built a large network of roads for the transport of merchandise. One road ran from Attock to Dacca, a second road ran from Aagra to Burhanpur, a third road ran from Aagra to Chittor and the fourth long road ran between Lahore and Multan. Shady trees were grown all along the long roads and public inns were built up for both Hindus and Muslims.[1] The situation of law and order was exemplary during the reign of Sher Shah Suri. According to the Historian Farishta, the travelers were free to travel, peacefully and there were no cases of highway robbery.

Sher Shah Suri, originally Farid Khan, was an employee of Sultan Muhammad Khan, governor of Bihar. Once he hunted a lion despite being on foot. He was given the epithet of Sher Shah Suri on being the king of India he took the title of Sher Shah. In 1545 A.D. when Sher Shah Suri had laid siege to the fort of Kalinger, he met a sudden accident in which he received grievous injuries. But the army kept fighting under his order. As soon he heard the happy news of the fall of Kalinger fort, he suddenly died.

---

1. Mauj-e-Kausar

Successors of Sher Shah Suri:

After Sher Shah Suri, his second son, Islam Shah, generally known as Salim Shah, came to the throne. He largely maintained the tradition and ways of his father. He even made more progress in every way. He ruled over India for a period of 9 years, and died in 960 A.H. corresponding to 1553 A.D. After him, his brother-in-law, Mubaraz Khan ascended the throne and ruled under the name of Muhammad Shah Aadil. He was a most incapable and evil minded man who, only 3 days after the death of Salim Shah, entered the palace and killed the small child son of Salim Shah whose name was Feroze Khan. He performed this tyranny to ensure his seat on the throne. He did not listen even to the mother of the child who was his real sister. He was an extremely mean and diabolical person and was given to worship of evil desires. Historian Farishta wrote about him: "Due to his mean nature, he handed over key posts of the kingdom to evil minded men and always helped the undeserving persons".

He appointed Hemoo Baqqal, a low caste Hindu, as the Kotwal (administrator) of the city. This inferior man gradually rose to the office of Prime Minister. Adil Shah known in the public as Adli was in general in pleasure and wine day and night and the whole administration was in the hands of Hemoo Baqqal. The Afghan chiefs disdained to accept the suzranity of a low caste Hindu. There was rebellion on all sides but the Hindu Prime Minister was successful in quelling the rebellion.

Humayoun was then in Iran and he kept himself well informed of the events in India through the king of Iran. He had already captured Kabul and in 1555 A.D., he found a good chance to attack India. He defeated the governor of Punjab, Skindar Khan, and advanced towards Delhi. He was able to capture Delhi without much resistance. Then, after 12 years of deprivation, he was again on the throne of Delhi. However, only 6 months of his ascension to the throne, on 7th Rabi ul Awwal, 963 A.H., he went up to his library room where he sat for brief while. He was coming down the stairs when he heard the call to prayers. Out of reverence, he sat on a stair. After the call to prayer had finished, he began to climb down the stairs case when his foot suddenly slipped and he came down the stairs, trembling and hurting himself. His injuries were grievous and he could not survive. On the 11th of Rabi ul Awwal, he died. The date of his death is calculated from the line:

همایون بادشاه ازبام افتاد

i.e. the king Humayoun fell from the roof.

Humayoun was a paragon of courage, gentleness, valour and good manners. His brother Mirza Handal and Mirza Kamran always did injustice to his course and tried to injure his interests. But Humayoun always forgave and connived. The cruelty and unjust action of Kamran had reached such a limit that some of Chughtai chiefs associated with Humayoun advised his killing. But Humayoun did not agree to slay his real brother. However, he was constrained to get him blind folded.

The most authentic narration about the events of Humayoun's life in the book: "Humayan Nama" written by his sister, Gulbadan Begum. She has called him a most tenderhearted, forgiving and tolerant person with courage and bravery suiting any difficult occasion. His religious bias in amply proved by the incident of his death. Historian Farishta wrote that: "Humayoun was always in a state of purity due to his frequent ablution (Wazoo). He never uttered the name of God without Wazoo". Once he called his Prime Minister Mir Abdul Hayee as only "Abdul" and explained after a while: "I could not utter your full name because I was without ablution (and God's name Al-Hayee was left over)".[1]

---

1. Tareekh-e-Farishta, Vol. 2, P.311, 312

THE REIGN OF MUGHALS

The Mughal period of rule over India started with the second time ascension to the throne of Delhi by King Naseer ud Din Humayoun in 1555 A.D. he did not himself rule for many days but the foundation of the Mughal rule was certainly laid down by him.

When Humayoun returned from Iran, a great team of Iranian scholars and men of letters accompanied him besides a large army of Iranian soldiers. The result was that Iranian culture and civilization had a deep impact on the Islamic civilization of India. A strong relationship was built up between the two countries on grounds of sentiments and aptitudes exchanged with each other. It had a lasting effect on the future course of history.

Jalal ud Din Muhammad Akbar:

At the death of Humayoun, Akbar was engaged in the expedition of the Punjab along with his teacher and loyal commander of Humayoun, Bairam Khan. He was then only 14 years of age. He had seen the rough and troubles of life with his father. The education and training imparted by Bairam Khan had shaped his character and made him fit for the rulership of India.

After the death of his father, Akbar came upon the throne and appointed Bairam Khan as his Chief Minister. For two years Bairam performed the duties of Regent and Chief Minister of Akbar. For unknown reasons the relations between Bairam Khan and Akbar became strained and Bairam Khan prepared to proceed on Haj pilgrimage but he was unfortunately killed by an Afghan. In 1560 A.D. Akbar proclaimed that hereforth he would rule in person and only his orders would be lawfully obeyed.

Akbar continued the process of conquests so that his empire stretched in the North and the West to Kabul and Qandhar and in the East to Bengal and Orissa, and in the South to Ahmad Nagar. He did not leave the conquered territories to their fate but consolidated his administration over every inch of the land he annexed. The empire was divided by Akbar into 15 provinces each under a governor who had been invested with both civil and military powers. He was responsible to the central government at Delhi for all his acts of omission and commission. For this assistance of the governor, one military attachment and one judicial officer called "Mir-e-Adl" was appointed. In a big city a Police Officer, "Kotwal" was appointed. The rural areas were administered with the advice of the local elders.

As for the revenue and administration, Akbar followed the reforms of Sher Shah Suri. Raja Todar Mal was incharge of revenue and finances. Under his guidance, the cultivable land was measured every ten years and the quantum of revenue was fixed in accordance with the quality of the land and the produce it yielded. All details of the revenue system are clearly mentioned in the book: "Aa-in-e-Akbari". The period of Akbar's rule was considered to be successful. The law and order situation was good and there was complete peace and mutual understanding among various classes and sects.

Religious Innovations of Akbar and the Downfall of Islamic Values:

The peaceful co-existence with the non-Muslim population was obtained by sacrificing many Islamic laws and injunctions. In this keenness to win the sympathies of Hindu Rajputs, Akbar married Hindu ladies and got his son Jehangir married to a granddaughter of the Raja of Jodhpur. He appointed Hindus to many key posts of the state. The result of all this pro-Hindu activity was that Hindu influence began to dominate the private life of the emperor in his palace. His own inclination was divided to Hindu customs and rituals.

For 30 years Akbar lived like a staunch Muslim and was strongly inclined to mysticism and respected the Muslim saints. He went on foot from Aagra to Ajmir to pay homage to Hazrat Moeen ud Din Chishti. He was so much enamoured of Hazrat Shaikh Saleem Chishti that he sent his pregnant wife to him for blessings. The Chief Minister objected to his Hindu-like saffron dress and he did not minded. In his internal parlour for worship "Ibadat Khana", he was busy for hours in meditation and prayers. After 20 years, his mind was so much changed towards Hindu religion that Hindu rituals were freely being observed in the Mughal Palace by the Hindu queens for whom even temples were built up inside the palace. To appease the Hindu ladies in the palace, slaughter of cows was made unlawful. The Muslim tax of Jizya levied on non-Muslims was abolished. Akbar's mind was so much perverted that he did not hesitate to bow in reverence before the sun or the fire or the statue of Virgin Mary.

The causes of great mental change in Akbar may be attributed, on one hand, to his free mind dealings and marriages with Hindus and Non-Muslims, and, on the other hand, to the congregation in his court of Muslim scholars who loved nothing but worldly gains and positions and were always quarrelling with one another on petty religious interpretations. Scholars of all religions were gathered in the royal court and discussions on religious topics were freely held to which Akbar attended intently. The result of all scholarly quibbles and quarrels was that Akbar lost his original pristine faith in Islam. He was influenced by every one and his mind became totally confused as to what was right and what was wrong. His whimsical attitude made him announce the promulgation of "Din-e-Ilahi" – a new religion which incorporated points of all the religions Akbar respected. The tragedy of the situation was that Akbar considered himself to be an authority in matters of faith also and had became proud of his versatile knowledge. Some of his actions and orders were funny and one was driven to laughter at his mental condition. This state of affairs continued till one year before the death of Akbar.

This was a most troubled period for Islam. But for the reformatory efforts of Hazrat Mujadid Alf-e-Sani (R.A.), Islam would have become a strange religion in India and Hindu religion would have gained supremacy.

The Last Days of Akbar:

Due to the idiosyncracies of his sons the last days of Akbar were full of trouble. In 1599 A.D., prince Murad died of over drinking. In 1601 A.D. prince Saleem raised a banner of rebellion with the support of religious elements who disposed the religious policy of Akbar. Akbar quelled the rebellion of Saleem but, instead of any reprimand or punishment, appointed him as governor of Bengal and Orissa. Saleem did not change his attitude. He continued his playful activities at Ilah Abad and kept planning against his father. He got Abul Fazal a favourite minister of Akbar, killed.

Akbar was very grieved at the murder of Abul Fazal. After this event, prince Danial also died of extreme drinking. Apart from these disturbing events, the royal palace had become an arena of conspiracies. Some people advised Akbar to bypass Prince Saleem and appoint his son, Khusrao, as heir-apparent. Akbar called in Saleem and, after patching up his relations, made his successor. After this, Akbar died in 1605 A.D. corresponding to 1014 A.H.

Noor ud Din Saleem Jehangir:

After the death of Akbar, his eldest son Saleem ascended the throne. He took the title of Jehangir. Akbar had appointed the best teachers for the education of Prince Saleem, the most important of them was Maulana. Mir Kalan Hervi who was a famous scholar of his time. Apart from this scholar, persons like Shaikh Ahmad, Qutbud Din Muhammad Khan, Abdur Rahim Khan-e-Khanan, who were all scholarly elders – were associated with the training of Prince Saleem. The Prince Saleem was so well educated that he became proficient in Persian, Turkish and Hindi languages and could write prose and compose verses.

A lover of beauty as he was, fond of music and pictures. He was visually impressed at the sight of beautiful flowers and water falls.[1]

Due to his extraordinary comforts and delicacies in which Prince Saleem was brought up in childhood, he could not develop a strong character. He was unstable in his temperament and very

---

1. History of Jehangir by Deni Parsad, P.20-23

simple in his mental approaches. The Hindu bias in the royal palace and the promulgation of Din-e-Ilahi in the country had made Saleem a very superficial personality who could not wait the pros and cons of any situation. Akbar, however, believed in his capabilities to work as a successful monarch and nominated him his successor.

In the year 1605 A.D. Saleem sat upon the throne at an age of 35 years. Burden of responsibility reformed Saleem and he decided to follow the foot prints of his father in all government matters. His regime gradually came to be famous for justice and fair play. In religious matters, however, he continued to be wayward like his father, and could not tolerate the reforms of Hazrat Mujadid Alf-e-Sani (R.A.) who was imprisoned by Jehangir in the Gawaliar fort. But the spiritual powers of Hazrat Mujadid Alf-e-Sani (R.A.) manifested itself and Jehangir, not only freed him but sent his son, Prince Khurram to greet him and got him invited in the royal palace with the great respect and adoration. Hazrat Mujadid Alf-e-Sani (R.A.) availed the opportunity and put up the following demands before Jehangir:

1. The custom of bowing the prostration before the king must be abolished.

2. Slaughter of cow must be made lawful for the Muslims.

3. The king and his courtiers must regularly say their prayers in congregation.

4. The departments of Justice and Accountability must be revived.

5. All innovations and legally prohibited institutions must be abolished.

6. All laws and canons derogatory to the teachings of Islam must be abolished immediately.

7. All repairable and demolished mosques must be reconstructed.

The king immediately agreed to all the above points and passed orders for their implementation. The Muslims heaved a sigh of relief after nearly half a century when they had lost all hope for the revival of Islam, its loss and its institutions.

Hazrat Mujadid Alf-e-Sani (R.A.) reformed the entire structure of religious thought which had been polluted by the admixture of Shia trends due to the advent of strong Shia elements with the Humayoun and the Hindu elements due to waywardness of Akbar.[1] It was a monumental task which Hazrat Mujadid Alf-e-Sani (R.A.) performed with great courage and wisdom.

---

1. The name of Hazrat Mujadid Alf-e-Sani (R.A.) was Sheikh Ahmad, his epithet was Badar ud Din, his surname was Abul Barakat. He was born in the year 971 A.H. (1564 A.D.) at Surhind. The name of his father was Shaikh Abdul Ahad who was a disciple of Hazrat Shaikh Abdul Qadoos Gangohi and was himself a great scholar. Shaikh Ahmad completed his religious education at the age of 17 years and began to deliver lectures on the Holy Quran and Hadith. He pledged bai'at at the hands of Hazrat Baqi Billah in 1008 A.H. he died in 1034 A.H. and was buried in Surhind.

THE EAST INDIA COMPANY

A very important event which took place during the regime of Emperor Jehangir was the advent of the English traders in India. The contemporary ruler of England, James I appointed Sir Thomas Roc as an Ambassador to the great Mughal Jehangir in 1615 A.D. Sir Thomas was a very wise diplomat and he succeeded in winning great concession from Jehangir for the East India Company for trade. The East India Company was established in England in 1600 A.D. In India, the Portuguese were very powerful rivals of the English and there were many fights between the two rivals for establishment of their trading centers in India. At long last the English were successful in winning concessions from Jehangir for establishing of trading centers in Surat, Ahmad Abad, and Kumbay in 1613 A.D. Before the death of Jehangir, the East India Company had firmly established its centers in various places of India and had ousted the Portuguese from the land.

Death of Jehangir:

In 1627 A.D. the Emperor Jehangir visited Kashmir for improvement of his health. He was accompanied by Noor Jehan, Asif Khan, Sheharyar and Dawar Bakhshi. In Kashmir, his asthma did not improve and his companion Sheharyar also became ill. At the advice of the physicians he left Kashmir for Lahore. On the way he played hunting despite illness and weakness. Unfortunately, a soldier of his retinue fell down from a high mountain and lost his life. This event had a very sever effect on the mind of the King whose illness took a worse turn. He passed away on 27th Safar, 1037 A.H. corresponding to 1627 A.D. in the morning hours. He was buried in Lahore. He was only 58 years of age and had ruled over India for 22 years.

Emperor Shah Jahan:

Prince Khurram who succeeded Jehangir as Emperor Shah Jahan was in Deccan at the time of Jehangir's death. On hearing the news of father's death, he left for Aagra along with Mahabat Khan.

Prince Sheharyar was also a claimant to the throne with the support of Noor Jehan. Fortunately, Asif Khan, a strong supporter of Prince Khurram was at the headquarters. He was the father-in-law of Khurram. Before Prince Khurram arrived at Aagra, Asif Khan had arrested Sheharyar with the help of a heavy force. On reaching Aagra, he ascended the throne without any opposition. The first act of cruelty he performed on assumption of authority was to get Sheharyar and two of his own nephews killed for fear of their claim to the throne.

Shah Jahan ruled for 31 years from 1627 A.D. to 1658 A.D. during which his kingdom flourished. The state of Deccan which was rebelling, all of them became skirmishers. His minister, Saad Ullah Khan was a wise and prudent statesman. He introduced the monetary and revenue reforms of Akbar and Sher Shah and the country made economic progress. There was affluence and prosperity everywhere.

Shah Jahan had a fine taste for art and culture. He built grand and beautiful buildings in Aagra and Delhi. A comparison of the buildings constructed by Akbar and Jehangir would reveal that the Hindu trends had swayed the two rulers strongly. The period of Shah Jahan's rule was of peace and prosperity throughout the country and outside. Yet he himself was faced with troubles of grave nature towards the end of his life. The main cause of his troubles was his own sons, Dara Shakoh, Shujah, Aurangzeb and Murad who had great rivalry against one another for the capture of Delhi throne. When Shah Jahan came to know their rivalry, he tried to placate each one of them. He appointed Dara Shakoh as governor of Multan and Kabul, Shuja as governor of Bengal, Aurangzeb as governor of Deccan, and Murad as governor of Gujrat. But the plan turned to become a weapon against Shah Jahan himself because each of the four princes began to arm themselves for a decisive battle for the throne.

In 1657 A.D. Shah Jahan fell seriously ill and rumors spread that he had died. All the four princes became active to capture the throne. Shuja left Bengal for Aagra to punish Dara Shakoh who (as put by Shuja) had poisoned his father. Murad declared his kingship while staying in Gujrat. Dara Shakoh mustered his strong army and sent his son, Suleman Shakoh and Raja Jay Singh at the head of that army to cope with Shuja. Fighting took place near Banars and Shuja went back to Bengal. Aurangzeb joined hands with Murad and their common forces advanced towards the North to meet Dara Shakoh. There was a battle near Sam Garh/Fateh Garh in which Dara Shakoh was defeated and ran away. Murad and Aurangzeb advanced towards the capital.

On reaching Aagra, they found that king Shah Jahan was alive but was convalescing from illness. The system of the government had been shattered and there was every fear of Dara Shakoh coming to the throne, as he was the eldest prince and a favourite of his father. His capture of power and authority would result in the revival of Hindu influence which had ruined the Muslims during Akbar and Jehangir's rules. It seemed prudent in the interest of the country and Islam to capture power in the life time of Shah Jahan who was imprisoned by Aurangzeb. On a pretext prince Murad was also arrested and sent to Gowaliar fort. Prince Shuja fought with Aurangzeb but was defeated and ran away to Arakaan (Burma). Dara Shakoh reassembled his army and fought with the army of Aurangzeb near Ajmir but was badly defeated. He took shelter with an Afghan chief on account of his former good relations. But the Afghan betrayed him and handed him over to Aurangzeb who got him slain for apostasy.

Aurangzeb Alamgir dealt with all claimants to the throne effectively. He got some of his nephews killed while sent others to the Gowaliar fort. He did not spare his own son, Sultan Mahmood who was imprisoned along with his uncles and cousins in the Gowaliar fort for conspiring against his father.

Aurangzeb Alamgir:

Having dealt effectively with all opposition, Aurangzeb declared his assumption of power as Emperor of India in 1658 A.D. he took the title of Alamgir. He was born in Dohad on 24th October, 1618 A.D. when Jehangir was returning from Gujrat with Shah Jahan, Mumtaz Mahal and others. Aurangzeb had great love for his place of birht and wrote to his eldest son Muhammad Azam to be kind and considerate to the people of Dohad because the place happened to be his birth place.[1]

Aurangzeb and Dara Shakoh had been taken as hostages by Jehangir when Prince Khurram had revolted against his father Emperor Jehangir and were kept under supervision of Queen Noor Jehan at Lahore from 1626 A.D. to 1627 A..D. they rejoined their mother Mumtaz Mahal at the death of Jehangir, on 26th February, 1628 A.D. in the presence of Asif Khan.

Education and Training:

At the age of 10 years Shah Jahan appointed Sadullah Khan, his famous minister and Hakim Muhammad Hashim Gilani (a famous scholar who was subsequently made the Chief Minister) as the tutor of Aurangzeb. He was intelligent and well behaved and, under the training of capable teachers, he attained proficiency in various branches of religion and secular sciences. He had deeply studied the Holy Quran and the Traditions of the Holy Prophet ﷺ. Sir Jadu Nath Sarkar wrote "Aurangzeb used to speak and write Arabic and Persian like a Research Scholar". He was also well versed with the Hindi language. In the course of his stay in Balkh and Qandhar, he had picked up working knowledge of Chughtai Turkish language in which he could speak freely. He was a perfect calligraphist of the Nasakh writing style. He wrote quite a few copies of the Holy Quran with his own hand and sent them to Makkah Mukarma as gifts. Like some of the ladies of the palace he was also a Hafiz of the Holy Quran.

He was fond of study and used to study the explanation and commentaries of the Holy Quran and the Tradition frequently. He also kept study of jurisprudence and the work of mystical personalities like Hafiz Sherazi and Shaikh Saadi. He was fond of the company of the great scholars.

Muhammad Saqi Mustaid Khan wrote that Alamgir was a rigid follower of Islam and believed in the Sunni school of

---

1. Ruqaat-e-Alamgiri, No.3

jurisprudence. He was staunch follower of the teachings of Islam. He was regular in congregational prayers and did not miss even voluntary form of prayers like Ishraq, Chasht, Tahajud. He also kept fast regularly in Ramzan, paid his Zakat tax regularly and kept up the remembrance of God in so many ways as taught by the Holy Prophet ﷺ of Islam. He also observed ritual of Aitikaf (secluded worship during the last ten days of the Holy month of Ramzan).

Administration of Law and Justice:

He was so keen of doing justice to his people that every day he thrice appeared before the public to hear their petition which he decided on the spot. He used to ignore and connive at indifferent utterances and words of the common people who did not know the protocols. He was neither against the Hindus nor he was unjust and tyrannical towards them. Maulana Shibli and Maulana Akbar Shah Khan Najeebabadi have explained and nullified the baseless objections of Hindu historians against Aurangzeb. As a matter of fact Hindus had been appointed (like Muslims) to great positions of trust and responsibility in his time. There was also Trustees created by the Aurangzeb government for some important temples of Hindus.

Moral and Administrative Reforms:

To achieve political stability and good law and order in the country, Aurangzeb introduced moral and administrative reforms in the country. He made the drinking of wine and gambling unlawful. The prostitutes were asked either to get married or leave the country. In 1664 A.D. he declared the custom of Sutti (burning of alive women with the dead bodies of their husbands) as unlawful. He prohibited the sale of young children as slaves or earaches. All extravagant expenses on state functions were controlled. All taxes against Islamic laws were cancelled. It is said that as many as 80 such taxes were made unlawful and cancelled for the relief of the general public.

The East India Company

Codification of Islamic Laws:

Aurangzeb respected and appreciated the scholars of Islam. He gathered all prominent scholars of his time and asked them to collect and codify all the Shariat laws and rules into a comprehensive volume. "Fatawa-e-Alamgiri" was prepared at a cost of 200,000 rupees.[1]

Bravery and Fearlessness:

Fond of useful knowledge, Divine worship and obedience as he was, Aurangzeb was also a fearless warrior and did not hesitate to face the most difficult situations. During an encounter at Balkh against Abdul Aziz Khan, he got down his horse for the prayers and, despite caution of his army commanders, he said his regular prayers amidst hard fighting and was not scared of death or injury. He completed his prayers peacefully to the surprise of his opponent Abdul Aziz Khan, ruler of Bukhara who commented: "To fight with such a person was tantamount to putting ourselves in ruin".[2]

Alamgir ruled for more than half a century. All his life he fought against the enemies of Islam, particularly the Rajputs and Marhatas and always subdued their rebellions.

After subduing the insurgent elements in the South, Alamgir was smooth monarch of a vast empire which stretched to Tanjore in the South. Practical enough, despite great success in the battlefields and full maintenance of law and order in the country, the decline of the Mughal empire started in the days of Aurangzeb. Alamgir was a very determined ruler. Whatever he did, he did with a firm mind and unwavering heart. He had revived and guarded Islamic institutions. The cause behind the downfall of the Mughals was that, in contrast with the marry-making days of Jehangir, the period of Aurangzeb was noted for moral rigidity and governmental high handedness for the formal introduction of moral reforms. The Hindus regarded Alamgir as their avowed enemy while the common Muslim looked

---

1. Maasir-e-Alamgiri (Urdu translation, P.387)
2. Ibid, P.388

upon him as a perfect "Mulla", unfit for secular matters and for rule.

Unfortunately, Aurangzeb ruled entirely on religious scholars and jurisprudence who were pure extroverts and had no deep insight into the moral values of Islam. They did not recommend soft and friendly attitude to the non-Muslims. The author of "Maasir-e-Alamgiri" writes with great pride: "That non-Muslims were, as far as possible not appointed to position of trust and responsibility. In the courtiers under the Mughal control, place of worship of the non-Muslims were gradually demolished and a great number of mosques were built up in their places. Jizya (non-Muslims's tax) was imposed by Aurangzeb".

The scholars have failed to inculcate a sense of moderation in Aurangzeb which Islam taught strictly. The type of scholars who were associated with Aurangzeb were all lovers of worldly pomp and glamour and Aurangze did not like them. His own teacher, as Burnier wrote, came to him for a high post of authority. Aurangzeb took him to a secluded apartment and addressed him thus:

"Mulla Ji! You wish me to raise you to the rank of high ranking chiefs of my court. I know your demand would have been justified if you had given me useful education. You taught me that England was a small island where King was at first the governor of Portugal, then he became the king of Holland and now he is the king of England. About the rulers of France and Spain, you taught me that they were like the ordinary Rajas of one land, and that the emperors of India were greater than those 'petty' rulers among the great rulers of India, Humayoun, Akbar and Shah Jahan were prominent. You told me that Iran, Kashghar, Tartar, Peru, Siam and China used to tremble on hearing the names of the Mughal emperors. What a great knowledge you had of geography.

You should have taught me the various characteristics of nations in the world, the products of all countries, the military preparations of all nations, their modus Operandi in the battlefield, their customs and usage, their likes and dislikes, and the causes of rise and fall of nations.

You should have told me events and circumstances which can produce big revolution. You taught me baseless knowledge of logic and philosophy syntax and prosody which have had nothing to do with practical life. You should have taught me those branches of knowledge, which develop the mind and which enable the heart and enlighten the soul. Had you taught me the secrets of the human nature, or the conditions obtaining in different parts of the world and the social and political systems of the regions, you would have done my greater good than Aristotle did to Alexander, the Great and I would have appreciated your personality".[1]

The above rather lengthy speech of Aurangzeb would reveal that he had deep insight into the affairs of life; yet, unfortunately he kept following the councils of the scholars of the type who had approached him for a high political position. Another important cause of the down fall of the Mughals was that there was wide spread moral degeneration in the Muslims. All big political figures had no moral integrity and they could be purchased with power or money. Even the Mughal princes could be sold or purchased. Prince Kaam Bakhsh, a son of Aurangzeb, was about to side with the Marhattas on an occasion when Amir Zulfiqar Khan and his father, Asad Khan, detected his betrayal, arrested the Prince and sent him to Aurangzeb was purchased by the Marhattas for not interrupting their supply line. The fort which had only two months' provisions could not be captured even in a long period of six months due to constant supply of provisions under connivance of Prince Azam.

Even a person like Mir Jumla who was reported to have rendered great military services for the Mughal was not considered above suspicious by Aurangzeb who wrote to his son on his death: "You are mourning a kind father but I am mouring a friend who was at once powerful and dangerous".

After having ruled over a vast empire for more than fifty years, Aurangzeb died at the age of 91 years in 1706 A.D. at

---

Rood-e-Kausar by M. Akram I.C.S., P.286-288

Aurangabad (Deccan). His tomb is situated at a distance of eight miles from the city of his name.

General Conditions of India at Alamgir's Death:

After Aurangzeb there was wide spread anarchy and turmoil in the great and vast empire of the Mughals. As put by Shaikh Muhammad Ikram, ICS. "Every Marhatta peasant was a soldier who had become a torture for the Mughals under the minor successor of Seva Ji or some ambitious Marhatta Rani. The revival of the Hindu religion was widely spoken about. The movement of Hindu revival had become strong in Punjab, Rajputana and S. India. The British and the French were powers to count with as they were weaving the texture of future India. They had captured many factories along with coast of the Indian ocean. Forts had been constructed in Madras and Bombay. In the presidencies of big cities the local government was functioning under the British nationals of the East India Company. They realized the taxes and decided disputes in the courts.

The East India Company which was in the beginning a trading corporation was now coming out in its true colours, building forts in all important coastal cities of India and establishing their local government. The French also were trying since 1604 A.D. to set up trading companies in India. In 1664 A.D. the French succeeded in establishing their East India Company on a sound footing. Two years later in 1666 A.D. they obtained a large piece of land from the Bijapur State wherefrom they set up the town of Pondi Cherri.

The condition in India was such that people coming from seven seas across were taking firm roots in the soil of India. The Muslims could not hold their own due to internal dissensions and rivalries for power and position.

Successors of Aurangzeb:

Judging the circumstances of the country Aurangzeb divided his empire among his sons, hoping that they would remain contented and would not fight one another. His hopes were futile. Prince Azam and Moazzam both were in the Deccan when Aurangzeb died.

The East India Company

They left for the capital when Kaam Bakhsh, the youngest prince, assembled force to fight any one who captured the capital. There was a severe battle between Azam and Moazzam in which Azam was killed.

Moazzam ascended the throne in 1707 A.D. with the title of Bahadur Shah. He was a cool-headed man and loved peace. His younger brother, Kaam Bakhsh declared independence in the Deccan. Commander Zullfiqar Khan immediately proceeded to Deccan and arrested Kaam Bakhsh. Bahadur Shah made peace with the Marhattas and the Rajputs. But in the Punjab the Sikhs had created great uproar under the leader Banda. They molested Muslim women, burnt the mosques, burnt religious scholars alive and, in every way, tortured the Muslims. Bahadur Shah had a large army in 1710 A.D. to punish the Sikhs in the Punjab. He inflicted a crushing defeat on the Sikhs who took refuge in the mountains. This was his last great achievement. He was already 70 years old and died at Lahore in 1712 A.D.

Bahadur Shah had in 1708 A.D. handed over the Marhatta government to Sahoo, a grand son of Siva Ji. His uncles and cousins opposed him and internal fighting took place. Bala Ji Bishwa Nath was a capable Marhatta. He took over as the Chief Minister reducing Sahoo to the level of a tool. Bala Ji reorganized the Marhatta and made the part of Chief Minister (Paishwa).

Afterr Bahadur Shah, Jahandar Shah became the king. He was not capable and Zulfiqar Khan became the de-fecto ruler. He was a good military commander but lacked capacity of a good ruler. There was widespread corruption in the country.

After a year, Syed Hussain Ali, governor of Bihar and Syed Abdullah, governor of Ilahabad conspired against Zulfiqar Ali and brought Farrukh Syer as the Mughal successor and claimant to the throne. In 1713 A.D. there was a battle near Aagra in which both Jahandar Shah and Zulfiqar Khan were arrested and then killed. Farrukh Syer became the Mughal King. Farrukh Syer ruled for 5 years but the real power was in the hands of the Syed Brothers. Syed Hussain Ali was made the governor of Deccan. The Marhattas declared war and Hussain Ali had to enter upon a humiliating peace in which Mughal king Farrukh Syer was compelled to accept the suzeranity of Marhatta Sahoo. It was a slur on the Mughal dynasty.

In 1716 A.D. an event of importance took place which made the foothold of the British strong in India. A deputation led by Hamilton (a good civil surgeon) called on the king Farrukh Syer to complain against the governor of Bengal who was a harsh task master in realizing the government dues from the British subjects. Farrukh Syer was seriously ill and the local physicians had failed to cure him. Dr. Surgeon Hamilton cured him completely and he was very happy to regain his normal health. As a reward, Farrukh Syer accepted the petition of Hamilton for exemption for royal taxes on the British not only but granted them a few village estates around Calcutta.

In 1719 A.D. Syed Hussain Ali, governor of Deccan advanced upon Delhi with a 10,000 force of Marhattas. Bala Je (Paishwa) was the commander of Marhatta army. Chan Qulak Khan a great military general also joined the advancing army on the way to the capital. Farrukh Syer was arrested and later on assassinated. This was the first attack of Marhattas on Delhi when they were able to see Mughal weakness.

The Syed Brothers selected a Mughal prince for the throne who died after 3 months. Another prince replaced him who also died within one year.[1] In 1719 A.D. the Syeds put prince Roshan Akhtar on the throne of Delhi under title of Muhammad Shah. In between Farrukh Syer and Muhammad there were two kings named Shamsuddin Rafi-ud-Darojat and Rafi ud Daulah.

Muhammad Shah:

The fate of Syeds was not eclipsed. Chan Qulaij Khan and Sa'adat Khan jointly conspired (with the connivance of Muhammad Shah) and killed Syed Hussain Ali. His brother Abdullah Shah was

---

1. Shams-ud-Din, Rafi-ud-Darajaat and Rafi-ud-Dula are the kings also succeeded within one year after Farrukh Syer upto Muhammad Shah.

The East India Company

defeated near Aagra and the superemacy of the Syed brothers came to an end. Chan Qalaij Khan made the Chief Minister Muhammad Shah. He was given title of Asif Jah and Nizam ul Mallik. Sa'adat Khan was made the governor of Oudh. He declared independence, and Deccan continued to function as an independent state for 130 years. Sa'adat Khan was now head of the Deccan state with Hyderabad as its capital. Every succeeding ruler of Hyderabad Deccan was since Sadat Khan known as the Nizam.

In 1720 A.D. Bala Ji Paishwa died. His son Baji Rao led the Marhattas whose power became four folds under his guidance. In 1736 A.D. they attacked Delhi. the weak Mughal government was powerless and the Marhatta looted the city recklessly. At night they went to the shrine of Khawaja Qutbud Din Bakhtiar Kaki. Next day (a Wednesday) they again came to Delhi plundered and burnt the shops of the Main Bazar. On their retreat they looted the famous villages of Rewari and Patodi.

Attack of Nadir Shah:

During those days Nadir Shah captured Faris and then Afghanistan. He blamed the Mughal king, Muhammad Shah that he had failed to behave and act like a Muslim king and had actually degraded Islam by paying the Marhatta Tax "Choth". On this pretext he came to the Punjab through the Khyber Pass and, after plundering the Punjab he mashed upon Delhi when some of his soldiers were killed by the citizens of Delhi. This infuriated Nadir Shah and he ordered his army to plunder and ransack the whole city and to kill every body who came in sight of his army soldiers. The massacre of the citizens continued from morning till evening besides loot and arson. Muhammad Shah was very sad to see his people being butchered on a large scale. He came to Nadir Shah and placed his cap on his feet to request stoppage of massacre. Nadir Shah agreed and the mass killing was stopped. Nadir Shah collected all the wealth which had been deposited with the royal families since the arrival of Babar. He took away the Peacock Throne of Shah Jahan, his crown, precious jewelry of the royal princesses, the best of the horses, cannons, most precious velvet cloth and brocade and the precious Muslim cloth. Nadir Shah took away all the wealth in 1738 A.D.

After the attack of Nadir Shah, the Delhi Sultanat was tottering. Deccan, Malwa, Gujrat, Rajputana and the Punjab had refused to acknowledge the central government of Delhi. The Rohillas had captured Rohail Khand. The Sikhs and Rajputs were making concerted efforts to capture Delhi. The Marhattas were advancing from South India like a tornado. After a short period, Bengal, Bihar, Orisa and parts of the Punjab had already seceded from the central authority.

That the government of King Shah Alam was only from the city of Delhi to the airport of Delhi (Palace), came true. Under these circumstances, Ahmad Shah Abdali who had established his rule in the Punjab, launched a terrific attack on Delhi in September, 1756 A.D. and ravaged the city. Then he went to Mathra, where there was widespread loot and arson. Then Abdali left for his own country.

Battle of Panipat:

The central government of Muslims had become so weak that governor of each province had declared independence. On the other hand, the Marhattas had become so powerful that they had a firm hope of establishing Hindu Raj or Hindu imperialism in India. They had openly declared their intention which was widely known to all including the Muslim rules. The Muslims were awakened and began to think how to face the menace. The Rohilla chiefs, the Nawab of Oudh and the Afghans forged a united front to fight the Marhatta menace. Both the opposite forces (force of Islam and force of Hinduism) confronted each other in the vast ground of Panipat in the first month of 1761 A.D. The Marhattas were 270000 cavalry and infantry whereas the combined Muslim forces were less than 90000 in numbers. The Marhattas launched a fierce attack on the Muslim armies so that they were un-nerved and were about to be defeated. But Ahmad Shah Abdali kept up courage and himself led his army against the Marhattas. The Hindu forces despite numerical superiority, were routed and took to their heels. Their most famous chiefs, Wiswas Rao was killed in the battlefield. The fleeing

The East India Company

Marhattas were chased by Afghan soldiers who killed as many as they could. The battle of Panipat demolished the Marhatta's ambition of establishing Hindu Raj in India. Ahmad Shah Abdali did not play the role of a self-seeker or a plunderer of wealth. The great victory at Panipat was entirely due to his courage and statesmanship. He did not usurp the throne of Delhi which he could easily do. Instead, he handed over government to King Shah Alam, the minister-ship to Shuja ud Daula and the chieftain-ship to Najeeb ud Daula and himself left for Qandhar. The Muslims had a good opportunity to revise their political position on solid grounds. But nature had, perhaps, planned otherwise. The British (future rulers of India) were advancing to the entrance from the North and the South East coastal areas of India.

Siraj ud Daula:

In 1756 A.D. Ali Wardi Khan, governor of Bengal died and according to his will, his grandson, Siraj ud Daula succeeded him at the age of 25 years. He was a shrewd and wise ruler who had the foresight to realize that the English East India Company was gaining political power and they could create political difficulties in the near future. He made efforts to check their political activities which the English did not like. There was a small battle between the two in which the English were badly defeated. Lord Clive was assigned the responsibility of avenging the defeat of the English at the lands of Siraj ud Daula. He left England at the head of a well equipped army and a naval force headed by Admiral Wilson. This force reached in December at Calcutta and they recovered all their colonies which Siraj ud Daula had captured earlier. There was a pitched battle. Seeing the odds against him, Siraj ud Daula entered into peace with the English. Some of his army chiefs, most notable among them was Mir Jafar, began to conspire with the English. A Hindu Omi Chand was playing the role of go between the English and Mir Jafar. He somehow informed Siraj ud Daula of the grand conspiracy. There seemed no alternative but to fight.

On 17th June, 1757 A.D., the English under Lord Clive met the army of Siraj ud Daula who was defeated due to the betrayal of Mir Jafar. The English were now the masters of Bengal. The disloyal Mir Jafar was made the Nawab of Bengal, Bihar and Orisa. Siraj ud Daula was killed by Mir Jafar and his dead body was displayed on the back of an elephant and circulated in the streets of Murshidabad.

Deewani Rights for East India Company:

After the defeat of Siraj ud Daula, Lord Clive approached Siraj ud Daula and King Shah Alam for the grant of rights to the East India Company for collection of revenue in the three provinces of Bengal, Bihar and Orisa. The king and the minister had no alternative but to accept the request which in fact was a kind of order. The Farman was issued where the revenue of these provinces was fixed as 2,400,000 out of which 40,000 were fixed for the expenses of the administrator stationed in Bengal.

After Muhammad Shah – till the end of the Mughal government, the following kings succeeded one after the other,

Ahmad Shah	from 1748 A.D. to 1754 A.D.
Alamgir-II	from 1754 A.D. to 1759 A.D.
Shahalam-II	from 1759 A.D. to 1806 A.D.
Akbar-II	from 1806 A.D. to 1837 A.D. and
Bahadur Shah-II	from 1837 A.D. to 1857 A.D.

These were five kings. They were kings only in name but actually they were paid stipends or pension by the East India Company who had become the real ruling authority. All administrative matters were decided with and through the agents of company. About Shah Alam, it was a common saying that the government of Shah Alam worked only from Delhi to Palam (the airport of New Delhi). Outside the red fort of Delhi, the king had no say in the administration. As a matter of fact even the expenses of the repair in the red fort, the king had to seek approval of the directors of the East India Company. He could not deal even with the servants of the red fort in accordance with his own wishes. This state of affairs continued till 1857 A.D. when there was a fighting between the English usurpers and the supporters of Shah Alam. The

The East India Company

English rulers called it Muting whereas the Indian patriots called it the war of independence. This indeed was the last effort for getting rid from the foreign rulers.

The Indian armed struggle to oust the foreign rulers and to achieve liberty from their yoke failed desperately. The family and the person of Bahadur Shah Zafar had become like the scattered petals of a rose lying before a strong wind. Many princes were killed. Bahadur Shah was captured and tried before a court of law. Consequently he was imprisoned in Rangoon (Burma). Now onward the English had become the regular rulers of India.

After the fall of the Mughal empire, two important questions pose themselves before the thinkers:

1. From 1707 A.D. to 1857 A.D. i.e. from the death of Aurangzeb Alamgir to the last day of Bahadur Shah Zafar, a period of 150 years was a long period during which the Muslims of India made no tangible effort to reform themselves morally and politically?

2. The moral corruption among the Muslims was parallel and equal to the political corruption – how did the Islam survive as a faith and a religion in India?

These two important questions will be answered briefly in the following paragraphs.

Hazrat Shah Wali Ullah of Delhi:

The events obtaining in India during the Mughal period and the personalities born and active during this period go a long was to prove the Divine intention that Islam as a faith and a religion must continue in the land of India. When apostasy spread in the days of Jalal ud Din Akbar, Hazrat Sheikh Ahmad Mujid Alf-e-Sani of Sarhind came to the forefront and held up the tottering mansion of Islam. Similarly, after the death of Aurangzeb Alamgir, Hazrat Shah Wali Ullah of Delhi and his entire family came up as the defenders and saviours of Islam.

Hazrat Shah Wali Ullah was born in Delhi on 21st February, 1703 A.D. His father, Shah Abdur Rahim was a great scholar and a mystic. He took special pain in the education and training of his son.

At the age of 15 Hazrat Shah Wali Ullah had completed his education and then he became a disciple (Mureed) of his father who gave him spiritual training. When he was 17, his father died. For 12 years he taught in the fashion of his father. Twice he performed the Haj pilgrimage. He obtained a certificate of proficiency in Hadith from the famous Scholar, Shaikh Abu Tahir Bin Ibrahim of Madina. When he was in Araiba, the Marhatta turmoil was at its height and his friends advised Hazrat Shah Wali Ullah to stay on in Arabia. As such, he left Arabia in 1145 A.H. and reached Delhi on 14 Rajab, 1145 A.H.

On reaching Delhi, he devoted most of his time to writing books and to preaching in public meetings. The teaching activity was limited to the lessons of the Hadith. The political and moral degeneration of the Muslims had tremendous effects on the sensitive and thinking mind of Hazrat Shah Wali Ullah. His famous book: "Al-Tafheematul Ilahia" minutely pinpoints all the various defects, shortcomings and vices which had taken roots in various sections of the Muslims. His aim was to destroy the rotten moral building and to reconstruct a new mansion over it. He bluntly wrote in one of his writings: "I have arrived to destroy every old system in region at present".

The most monumental task he performed was the translation of the Holy Quran from Arabic into Persian which was the spoken language of Muslims in India of his time. His aim was that educated Muslims may have direct access to the meanings of the Holy Quran without dependence on the scholars who had opposed his reformatory measures. The short sighted Ulema once gathered

---

1. But he had seen a dream in Makkah Mokarrma when the Holy Prophet ﷺ gave him the glad tiding that in the Divine Scheme of things, he was to organize the scattered elements of the Muslim Ummah.

around him in the Fatehpur Mosque in Delhi and wanted to kill him for his "sin" of translating the Holy Quran into Persian. But he continued to work dauntlessly till he had completed his job. This effort of Hazrat Shah Wali Ullah was so much liked and appreciated by Almighty Allah that the Holy Quran came to be translated into many other languages. And in our modern time, there is no important language of the world into which the Holy Quran has not been translated. The great advantage of this Persian translation that the Holy Quran came to be read and understood in every educated Muslim home. Every man and woman, old and young was now conceived that the Holy Quran demands to be understood and to be acted upon.

Apart from the Holy Quran, Hazrat Shah Wali Ullah also wrote authentic books on Hadith (traditions), the principles of Hadith, Tafseer, (commentary of the Holy Quran), and on mystical subjects. But the most popular of his books was "Hujatul Baligha". This wonderful book explains how Islam is fit and suitable for all races, countries and people of the world and how successfully it solves the social, moral, economic and political problems of the human beings.

If any one wishes to work for the worldwide moral reforms of mankind, he would be well advised to seek full help from the works of Hazrat Shah Wali Ullah. He died in Delhi in the year 1176 A.H. corresponding to 1762 A.D. In Delhi, behind the central jail, there is a vast ground and a graveyard known popularly as "Mehindin Ka Khitta" which contains in it the grave of Hazrat Shah Wali Ullah and his progeny.

The family of Hazrat Shah Wali Ullah:

Hazrat Shah Wali Ullah was fortunate in having sons who were great scholars and God fearing men like himself. His eldest son, Shah Abdul Aziz was born in 1159 A.H. and died in 1238 A.H. corresponding to 1823 A.D. At the age of 17, he had become an accomplished scholar and began to teach like his father. For 60 years he continued to teach and preach Islam. The blessings of his knowledge of Hadith had reached every nook and corner of Indian sub-continent. Because of his versatile genius, he had the deserving title of "Ayatullah" i.e. a sign of God.

The second son of Hazrat Shah Wali Ullah was Shah Rafi ud Din. He was born in 1163 A.H. and died in 1233 A.H. His scholarly qualities may well be judged from the fact that, when Shah Abdul Aziz had become too old to teach, he passed on this responsibility to Shah Rafi ud Din. Among the works of Shah Rafi ud Din, his Urdu translation of the Holy Quran is most well known.

The third son of Hazrat Shah Wali Ullah was Shah Abdul Qadir. He was born in 1167 A.H. and died in 1230 A.H. He was also a big scholar but by his nature, he loved solitude, he spent his whole life in a secluded room of Akbar Abadi Mosque. He also did not much attend to literary writings. However, his Urdu translation under title of "Moozih ul Quran" was his monumental achievement which is recognized by scholarly circles.

His forth son was Shah Abdul Ghani. He was a saintly person. His son Shah Ismail Shaheed was a unique personality who had combined in himself all virtues of scholarly and mystical personalities.

Due to sincere and dedicated efforts of Hazrat Shah Wali Ullah and his illustrious sons the banner of Islam kept flying over the Indian sub-continent despite decline and fall of the Mughal empire. In Spain, the faith of Islam disappeared with the disappearance of the Muslim rule. Many Muslims were killed and many survivors were converted to Christianity. In India, however, the intention of the British Christian government did not realize and Muslim India did not convert to the faith of the ruling people despite missionary efforts of the British government who spent millions of money on missionary activities and arranged lectures, debates and seminars to propagate their faith. The failure of the British government in converting the Muslim India to the Christian faith was largely due to the concerted and dedicated efforts of Hazrat Shah Wali Ullah and his noble family.

Hazrat Syed Ahmad Shaheed:

The pro-Islam missionary activities of Hazrat Shah Wali Ullah and his family were not confined to preaching, writings, and production of Islamic literature and teaching. He also undertook struggle at arms to establish a truly Islamic government on the basis of "Khilafat-e-Rashida" i.e. truly guided government on the lines of the first four Caliphs of Islam. Although Hazrat Shah Wali Ullah was not personally involved in the struggle at arms, yet his son and grandson had led the struggles due to the spiritual force infused by Hazrat Shah Wali Ullah. Hazrat Syed Ahmad Shaheed, was trained by Hazrat Shah Abdul Aziz, and Shah Abdul Qadir. He spent most of his time with Shah Abdul Qadir in the Akbar Abadi Mosque.

In his holy war against non-Muslims, particularly the Sikhs, Shah Ismail Shaheed, a grandson of Hazrat Shah Wali Ullah, was the right hand associate of Hazrat Syed Ahmad Shaheed. With the martyrdom of Syed Ahmad Shaheed and Shah Ismail Shaheed at Balakot, the movement for the Islamic polity did come to a stand still. The movement remained active in North. Bengal and in N.W.F. Province for the revival of Islamic polity and the ascendancy of Islam.

According to Maulana Obaid Ullah Sindhi, Hazrat Shah Wali Ullah was the founder of a glorious movement for the revival of Islam in its old pristine form. Although the movement could not succeed in establishing a truly Islamic government, yet it had the effect of keeping the Muslim alive as Muslims. The religious condition of the Indian Muslims was far better than their counterparts in other countries. There is full-fledged religious activity in Indo-Pakistan where Islamic institutions are working and growing, Islamic literature in many languages is being produced and published and there is a wide sense of Muslim brotherhood which is being actively shared by other Muslim countries.

REVIEW OF THE PAST AND PRESENT AND CAUSES OF THE RISE AND FALL OF MUSLIMS

The story of our decline and fall started with the end of Khilafat-e-Rashidah i.e., that with the end of the truly guided government of the four caliphs of Islam. It would be a mistake to consider that there is no difference left in our past and present. The past of the Muslim nation was decidedly much better and much more hopeful than our present. It would be useful to analyze the causes of our decline in order to assess rightly our existing abysmal fall and decline.

During past years when Muslims were a ruling nation, the one single factor that they were the rulers, was a great positive factor. Despite moral degradation of the common Muslims and the sinful lives of the Muslim rulers, no body could tolerate the insult or mockery of the institutions of Islam. The rightly guided and pious scholars of Islam were present during all periods of our past history. They were not apathetic to the propagation of injunctions and prohibitions of Islam and had the courage to speak out the truth before the Rulers and government functionaries. Some of our great scholars like Hazrat Shaikh Ahmad Sarhindi and Hazrat Shah Wali Ullah brought about silent revolution in the body politics of the Muslims and force the rulers to accept their reforms to bring the public life in conformity with the dictates of Islam.

Reformatory Activities of Muslim Scholars:

Many events in the history of Muslims indicate that the Muslim scholars changed the course of history by their influence and guidance of the ruling classes of Islam. During the Umayyads, Sulaiman Bin Abdul Malik wanted to make his son, the heir-apparent. But Imam Hazrat Raja Bin Haiwah advised him to appoint Hazrat Umar Bin Abdul Aziz (the nephew and son-in-law of Sulaiman Bin Abdul Malik) as his successor. Sulaiman agreed to his proposal.

The name of Hajjaj Bin Yousuf is notorious for tyranny and high handedness. Once the name of Hazrat Imam Hussain was mentioned in his presence to which he retorted: "He was not included in the progeny of the Holy Prophet ﷺ". Perchance the famous scholar of Islam, Imam Yahya Bin Yamar was present in that meeting. He at once spoke out: "You are telling a lie, O Hajjaj! Hajjaj said: "Prove your assumption from the Holy Quran or else I shall get you assassinated". Hazrat Yahya Bin Yamar recited this verse "And from his progeny arose David and Solomon". According to this verse, Prophet Jesus Christ ﷺ is included in the progeny of Hazrat Adam ﷺ through his mother. Then how can you deny that Hazrat Imam Hussain ؓ is not included in the progeny of the Holy Prophet ﷺ through his mother Hazrat Fatima (Radhi-Allahu-Anha)". Hajjaj was a hot headed man but he was constrained to admit that Hazrat Yahya spoke the truth.

Another event involving Hazrat Yahya Bin Yamar took place. Once Hajjaj asked him: "Do I commit any mistake of accent in my recitation of the Holy Quran? Hazrat Yahya gave a very eloquent reply. He said:

$$ترفع ما يخفض وتخفض ما يرفع$$

i.e. you read out the vowel sign Kasra (i) in place of Rafa'a and you readout Rafa'a in place of Kasra(i). This laconic text also means: "You are unjust and cruel. You raise to position the persons who deserve to be down-graded; and you demote and down-grade persons who deserve to be raised to high positions"

Historian Ibne Khalqan said that Hajjaj was so much pleased at this utterance of truth that he appointed Yahya as Qazi (Judge) of Khorasan.

Imam Auzai was a religious leader of Syria. Once Abdullah Bin Ali, an uncle of the caliph Saffah Abbasi, asked him: "What is your opinion about the blood shed of the Banu Umayyads at our hands?" Imam Auzai tried to avoid a reply. But when Abdullah insisted on a reply, he said: "By God, it was unlawful for you to shed the blood of the Banu Umayyads ". Abdullah Bin Ali was a very hot-tempered man. On hearing this reply he was red with anger. He said: "What did you say so?" Imam Auzai replied: "The basis of what I said is the saying of our Holy Prophet ﷺ i.e., the blood of any Muslim is unlawful except under the following three conditions:

1. he should be guilty of fornication despite being married,

2. he may have assassinated any body without lawful provisions, and

3. he should be an apostate and guilty of forsaking his Islam".

Again Abdullah Bin Ali asked: "Is not our government a religious government?" The Imam put him a question: "How is it?" Abdullah replied: "Did not the Holy Prophet ﷺ make a will for Hazrat Ali ؓ ?" The Imam replied: "Had any will been made, Hazrat Ali ؓ would not have asked for an arbitrator". After this talk the learned Imam was sure that he would be beheaded. Abdullah Bin Ali was in a bad mood and he made the Imam leave his court. However, as an after thought, he sent him a bag full of Dinars (gold coins) to Imam Auzai which the Imam immediately distributed among the deserving people.

Once the Abbaside Caliph, Haroon-ur-Rashid and the princes went to hear the lectures of Imam Malik. He said to the Imam: "I shall recite the Hadith and you may hear. But you send away the common people from in front of you." The Imam said: "If the commoners are deprived because of the very important persons, even the VIP, shall not benefit". The Imam asked one of his pupils to recite the Hadith, which he began. The caliph had to keep quiet.

Such events of outspoken truth and courageous conversations in face of man of authority are numerous. Those scholars who were pious and dauntless kept up the practice of timely criticism of un-Islamic or anti-Islamic actions and orders of the men of authority. That was conducive to limiting the lawful influence of these despotic rulers.

The Abbaside caliph Hadi desired to nominate his son as his successor before his death. He called for a meeting of the dignitories of the state to obtain their approval. This decision would have deprived Haroon Rashid, his brother, of the office of caliphate. The dignitories kept quite and withheld their opinion. But Harsama Bin Aa-Yein, a religious scholar, made courage and spoke out the truth boldly, saying: "O Caliph! Your proposed step is wrong. Your father had made you and your brother Haroon Rashid – both successors – one after the other. Now that you are disregarding the will of your father to bestow caliphate on your son and deprive your brother, what guarantee is there that your wrong decision will not be altered after your death?" Hadi was so much impressed by the candid speech of Harsama Bin Aa-Yein that he addressed the audience in anger and said: "Woe to you all who have decived me. Only my master (Harsama) has expressed the truth and has been my well-wisher." The out-spoken-ness and dare of Harsama had saved the Ummah from a great political turmoil.

Incidents taking place between Caliph Mamoon Rashid and Qazi Yahya Bin Aksim are quite well known. Once Mamoon dictated a state circular to the effect that "Hazrat Moawaya Bin Abi Sufyan may be cursed". Qazi Yahya immediately interferred and the state circular was cancelled. Similarly the Shia doctrine of Muta'a (marriage for a fixed brief period) was being promulgated by Mamoon who was inclined towards Shiaism. Qazi Yahya immediately appeared before the audience of Mamoon and told him tactfully that there was no difference between fornication (Zina) and Muta'a (temporary marriage) under clear injunction of the Holy Quran. Mamoon at once admitted his mistake and the institutions of Muta'a (temporary marriage) was made unlawful.

The positive corrective role of the religious scholars was not confined to the Banu Umayyads and Banu Abbas caliphs. The truthful and bold scholars of Islam played a constructive role in all the countries when Muslim rulers held the government. The famous Egyptian King Rukn ud Din Baibris was very majestic and glorified. On one occasion he called upon the Muslims to pay more money for the Jehad (Holy War) than was normally fixed under the Rules.

Allama Nowi, famous commentator of the "Sahih Muslim" opposed the king tooth and nail and said to him: "I know that you were a slave purchased by Amir Band Qadaar and you did not own a single penny. Now that Allah, the Almighty, has granted you kingdom, you have purchased thousands of slaves, whose ornaments are made of gold. In your palace there were 100 maid servants who are laden with jewelry. Until I am convinced that you have taken away all the gold and all the jewelry from your slaves and your maid-servants for the expenses on Jehad, I cannot write a Fatwa in your favour to extort money from the poor Muslims in the name of Jehad". Baibris was infuriated at the daring speech of Allama Nowi and exiled him from the capital city. Later on he realized his mistake and cancelled the order of exile against Allama Nowi and asked him to return and settle in Damascus. But the great Allama rejected his offer and said: "I shall not return till Baibris is alive". Only a month later Baibris died.

During the caliphate of Abbaside caliph of Egypt, Mustakfi Billah, the non-Muslim subjects put in a petition requesting for the cancellation of certain peculiar laws applicable only to the non-Muslims. They offered to pay him 700,000 Dinars every year for this favour. The caliph and his minister both were inclined to agree. But Allama Ibne Timiyyah intervened and said: "The injunctions of the Shariat Law of Islam cannot be sold away for any amount". The caliph had to agree to the 'Fatwa' issued by the Imam, much to his dislike. He rejected the petition of non-Muslims.

In the Usmani dynasty, Sultan Salim I was the first monarch. Once he called upon the Grand Mufti of his empire, Shaikh Jamali and asked him: "Is it better to conquer more lands or to convert the non-Muslims to Islam?" The Shaikh replied: "To make people embrace Islam is a better act". After this verdict the Sultan gave general orders that whosoever did not embrace Islam, he shall be killed. On knowing about this proclamation the Mufti at once went to the Sultan and told him that his proclamation was against the Holy Quran. The non-Muslims should be left with liberty about their faith if they pay the Jizya Tax. The Sultan cancelled his proclamation and the Muslims were saved from great sin and tyranny. Sultan Sanjar used to follow guidance of Imam Ghazali in all matters. Shahab ud Din Ghouri had great respect and dedication for Imam Fakhruddin Razi. Haji Al-Dabeer has written a detailed account in his historical book "Zafar ul Wala Ba Muzaffar-Wa-Alihi" which indicates that Imam Razi had corrected many mistakes in points of faith of Shahab ud Din Ghouri. The rightly guided scholars of Islam not only criticized and corrected the rulers of their times, they also wrote books and constitutions for the permanent guidance of the rulers. Qazi Abu Yousuf wrote "Kitab ul Khiraj" for Haroon Rashid. A useful constitution for the rulers was written by Abul Mukaffa. Imam Abu Ubaid ul Qasim wrote a voluminous book "Kitab ul Amwal" for the same purpose. In the first chapter of his book, the Imam discussed the mutual rights of the rulers and the subjects. A treatise written by Imam Malik is also well known. It was a letter addressed to Caliph Haroon Rashid in which useful counsels were given.

Apart from corrective actions for the reformation of the ruling classes, the scholars of Islam also kept vigilant eyes on the causes of error in dogma and action created by foreign influences. When waywardness and open lewdness and disobedience to divine injunctions increased in Baghdad, Khalid Rawaish set up a reformatory association to meet the challenge of mischief mongers. A similar body was constituted by Sahal Bin Salam Al Ansaari. The aim and purpose of both the reformatory bodies was to eradicate the causes of mischief and evil in the Muslims and to provide them an effective bulwark against the forces of disintegration. The role of the Hunbalies in effectively curbing the menace of the evil sects of their time can not be over-praised. Our great scholars like Imam Malik, Imam Ahmad Bin Hunbal and Imam Abu Hanifa steadfastly bore all hardships of whipping and imprisonment to save positive Islam from pollution.

Mamoon Rashid as his nature was very tolerant and moderate in his religious views. Yet he could not bear the activities of the apostates. He dealt with them as harshly and as effectively as caliph Mehdi had done.

Reformatory Activities of Mystics:

Apart from the well guided scholars of Islam, a group of mystics of Islam were also silently working to convert to non-Muslims to Islam and to reform the misguided Muslims to follow pristine Islam both in dogma and ritual. The dissemination of Islam in India, Africa, China, Far East Islands, Java, Sumotra, Malay, Borneo, New Guinea, Slippese, and Philippines was largely due to the missionary activities of the mystics of Islam, who had reached into the above countries with small companies of their dedicated and sincere followers and disciples. Hazrat Khawaja Moeen ud Din Chishti lit the candle of Islam in Rajputana whereas Hazrat Khawaja Qutbud Din Bakhtiar Kaki and Sultan Nizam ud Din Aulia lit the candle of Islam in Delhi and areas around Delhi. Hazrat Shaikh Ali Hajweri lit the candle of Islam in Punjab. The population of Muslims now touches the lofty figures of 90,000,000 in the Indo-Pak sub-continent which is an achievement of our Sufi Mystics mentioned above.

In North Africa, the call to the Muslim prayer owes itself to the concerted efforts of Shaikh Abdullah Bin Yasin, Muhammad Bin Ali Alsanoosi and the "Jamat – e – Falaheen". The echo of Tauheed (monotheism) in Sumotra, Malay, and Java is due to the sincere missionary activities of Shaikh Abdullah Arif, Syed Burhan ud Din, Shaikh Abdullah Alyamni, Maulana Malik Ibrahim, and Shaikh Noor ud Din.

Blessings of Islamic Government:

All blessings which Islam showered on Muslims and non-Muslims were largely due to Muslim governments which were headed by Muslim rulers. Even if the Muslim rulers were not quite pious and God fearing, yet they had a feeling for Islam and a sense of defencive against anti Islam forces. Their swords were frequently used against forces which wanted to undo Islam.

Among the Muslim rulers, there were some extremely pious, wise and God fearing monarchs like Mansoor, Noor-ud-Din, Salah ud Din Ayyubi, Ghias-ud-Din Balban, Shamsud Din Altamash and Aurangzeb Alamgir who respected and followed the institutions of

Islam. Even those monarchs who were given to life of ease and luxury, did respect the injunctions of God. Haroon joined the gambling bouts yet he said 100 prostrate on every night. Similarly Jehangir himself did drink wine yet his prohibition order was widely obeyed. The legal suits and disputes were decided in accordance with the Shariat Law strictly. The mosques were full of praying public. Everywhere there was numerous religious institutions which imparted knowledge of Quran and Sunnah on systematical lines. Religious scholars and mystics worked diligently for the teaching and preaching of Islam. The society in general was inclined towards goodness and virtue and evil pursuits of life were discouraged. The Muslims were independent and could breathe in an atmosphere of liberty. The books on jurisprudence mention all types of problems except the thorny questions as to how should the Muslim lives as Muslims if they are to live as subjects of non-Muslim rulers.

The mischievous seditions like the "Qaramta" and the "Batnia" were faced with courage by the scholars of Islam. But they could not have been extirpated except with the help of Muslim governments. The conquests of Muslim rulers, even if they were for secular ends, yet they paved the way for effective propagation of Islam, dissemination of Arabic Language and widespread acceptance of Muslim culture and civilization in the world.

Final Comments on Rise and Fall of Muslims:

In the preceeding pages of this book we have read a brief account of the rise and fall of Muslims through different centuries since the advent of Islam. The point worthy of notice cannot ba escaped any reader that our palmy days were those when we strictly followed the principles of Islam which have a direct bearing with the nature of man. We began to decline and fall gradually when the true spirit of Islam declined in the collective body of the Muslims. The decline has always been gradual. Every moral fault or every sin has a definite effect which must manifest itself. The greatest sin of a government is that its Ruler or monarch should become a despot, a tyrant and a cruel power who has no heart, no spirit to look after the welfare of his people and his own concern is to live himself a life of ease and luxury. If this sin, this moral concern takes hold of a Ruler, he may be a Muslim or a non-Muslim, his government gradually moves towards its natural death. If a ruler is not forgetful to the welfare of his people despite his personal life of luxury and is keen and serious in doing justice to his people, Nature may connive at his faults and his doomsday may be postponed or averted. But a cruel, selfish, and arrogant government has never been tolerated by God who has always punished the Rulers in different ways and they lost their authority.

Our history is in fact a mirror for our own good or bad deeds. In the preceeding pages of this book, despite any can not to exaggerate, I have made a candid and correct criticism of the deeds of our Muslim Rulers. The purpose was not to give others a chance to laugh at our apathy or our self-created downfall, but impress upon the readers that the law of nature was always impartial. Muslims or non-Muslims, the cruelty or tyranny of any ruling authority cannot go unpunished.

The degeneration and the widespread misfortune which we Muslims are facing today is the result of our past misdeeds through the past centuries of our palmy days. The sins of any Muslim government or Muslim ruler are not sins of an individual. They are collective sins. We may have the good reason to understand and realize that we are desparately in need of sincere repentance, and to pledge that we shall, henceforth, individually and collectively change all aspects of our lives and make a covenant with God that we shall strictly follow His injunctions and prohibitions as laid down in the Holy Quran and the teachings of the Holy Prophet ﷺ and the sayings of the Holy Prophet ﷺ:

لن يصلح اخر هذاالامــة الا بماصلح به اولها

"The reformation of the latter generation of this Ummah shall be possible only in the same ways in which the beginning generations had attained their reformation".

INDEX

A

Aagra: 240, 241, 242, 244, 245, 249, 254, 255, 256, 263 and 265
Aamooriah: 65
Aaram Shah: 197 and 199
Abaqa Khan: 104 and 106
Abbasi Caliph Mansoor: 71, 85 and 107
Abdul Aziz Khan: 259
Abdul Aziz Zararah: 64
Abdul Malik Bin Marwan: 57, 59, 60, 71, 74, 79 and 150
Abdul Momin: 160
Abdul Qadir Jilani: 131
Abdul Rehman bin Ash'ath: 60
Abdullah Al Zaghal: 164, 165 and 166
Abdullah Bin Aamir: 179
Abdullah Bin Abbas: 34, 36 and 63
Abdullah Bin Ali: 79,275 and 276
Abdullah Bin Saba: 33 and 48
Abdullah Bin Umar: 49 and 63
Abdullah Shah: 264
Abdur Rahim Khan-e-Khanan: 242 and 251
Abdur Rehman Al-Nasir: 151
Abdur Rehman Bin Hisham: 154
Abdur Rehman III: 149
Abraha: 193
Abu Abdullah: 161, 164, 165, 166, 167, 168, 169, 170, 171, 172 and 173
Abu Basr Muhammad Bin Abdul Malik: 101
Abu Jafar Mansoor: 107, 151 and 185
Abu Marwan: 161
Abu Muhammad Jamhoor Bin Muhammad Bin Jamhoor: 155
Abu Muslim Khorasani: 77
Abu Nawas: 110
Abu Qasim Abdul Malik: 168

Abu Rafey: 25
Abu Raja Farsi: 30
Abu Shahma: 25
Abu Tayyab Mutanabbi: 103
Abul Fateh: 188
Abul Fazal: 251
Abul Mukaffa: 279
Abul Qasim Ahmad: 111
Abyssinia: 214
Acca: 98 and 100
Adam: 25, 26, 44, 192 and 275
Admiral Wilson: 267
Adrianople: 66
Afghanistan: 121, 143, 195, 208, 243 and 265
Afirca: 50,51,58,60,74,78,84,87,108,132,144,146,147,151,156,157,160,166,167,169,17,178, and 280
Afrinos: 120
Afzal: 97 and 99
Aghliba: 113
Ahmad Abad: 254
Ahmad Bin Khalid: 154 and 155
Ahmad Bin Mustakfi: 112
Ahmad Khan: 106
Ahmad Nagar: 248
Ahmad Pasha Qayudan: 140
Ahmad Shah Abdali: 266 and 267
Ainul Jaloot: 103
Ajmir: 186, 188, 190, 194, 195, 200, 249 and 256
Ajnedain: 41
Akbar Khan Khanan: 209
Akhtal: 56
Ala Bin Mughis: 151
Ala-ud-Din II: 114
Alauddin Khilji: 211, 213, 215, 216, 217,

218, 220, 222, 223, 224 and 233
Ala-ud-Din: 202
Albania: 117, 125 and 130
Aleppo: 98, 101, 102, 104 and 126
Alfanso: 157, 158, 159 and 160
Alghou Khan: 220
Algiers: 129
Al-Hakam: 179
Al-Hamra: 163, 166, 168, 170, 171 and 172
Aligarh: 218
Allama Abdul Wahid of Morocco: 159
Allama Blazri: 53 and 185
Allama Ibne Khaldoon: 151
Allama Ibne Timiyyah: 278
Allama Jalal ud Din Sayyuti: 105
Allama Nowi: 278
Almiriah: 161
Al-Morabitoon: 160 and 163
Almustaeen Billah: 152
Al-Mustazhar Billah: 154
Al-Qadir Billah: 190
Altamash: 199, 200, 201, 202, 203, 204, 205 and 208
Al-Tughral: 114, 121 and 122
Amir Band Qadaar: 278
Amir Ismail: 187
Amir Khusrao: 211, 226 and 229
Amir Mo'awiya: 34, 36, 37, 38, 39, 40, 41, 52, 46, 47, 50, 51, 52, 53, 54, 58, 60, 63, 64, 74 and 79
Amir Qalaoon: 104
Amir Sabukta-Gin: 186, 187 and 188
Amir Shakaib Arsalan: 169, 170, 173 and 175
Amir Umar Al-Kalwazi: 110
Amir Zulfiqar Khan: 261
Amr Bin Al-Aas: 40, 41, 42 and 48
Anand Pal: 188, 189 and 193

Ananda Sultan: 106
Anarkali: 197
Antakia: 96, 97 and 105
Arabian Sea: 242
Arkat Khan: 213
Arl Tughral: 122
Armada: 39 and 51
Armail: 181
Ashbilia: 151, 152, 153, 154, 156, 157, 158, 159, 161, 162 and 163
Ashtar Nakh'i: 37
Asif Jah: 265
Asif Khan: 254,255 and 257
Auf-al-Azdi: 63
Aurana: 116
Aurangzeb: 255, 256, 257, 258, 259, 260, 261, 262, 269 and 280
Austria: 97, 98, 100 and 119
Auzai: 71,72,275 and 276
Ayesha: 37, 48, 49, 53 and 172
Ayub Ansari: 63, 64 and 125
Azarbaijan: 27

B

Bab ur Rohlah: 177
Babar: 67, 241, 242, 243 and 265
Badayun: 197, 205, 219 and 240
Baghdad: 67, 84, 87, 88, 89, 101, 102, 103, 105, 109, 113, 131, 142, 153, 161, 190, 193, 201, 203, 204 and 279
Bahadur Shah: 263,268 and 269
Baheara Rai: 188
Bahlol Lodhi: 240
Bahman: 182 and 233
Bahrain: 84 and 179
Bahram Shah: 202 and 203
Bairam Khan: 248
Bait-ul-Muqaddas: 97, 98, 100 and 113
Baji Rao: 265
Bakhtiar Khilji: 195

Index

Bakhtishoo: 107
Baksar: 244
Bala Ji: 263 and 265
Balakot: 273
Balban: 203, 204, 205, 206, 207, 208, 209 and 280
Balkan Peninsula: 116
Balkh: 187, 257 and 259
Balniah: 152
Banars: 256
Banda: 263
Bannu: 179
Banu Aftas: 156
Banu Azmari: 156
Banu Hamood: 156
Banu Jamhoor: 156
Banu Zarin: 156
Banu Zinoon: 156
Bargz: 186
Barqa: 129
Barusa: 114 and 115
Basar Bin Artat: 63
Bashaar Bin Bardaas: 110
Basphorous: 63
Basra: 35, 48, 79, 84 and 110
Basta: 165
Ba-Yazid Sani: 125
Ba-Yazid: 115, 117, 118, 119, 120, 121, 122, 125, 134, 136, 137, 167 and 168
Bazantine: 65
Beeja: 116
Begum Malika Jahan: 212 and 213
Bengal: 199, 207, 229, 236, 239, 244, 248, 251, 255, 256, 264, 266, 267, 268 and 273
Berlin: 140
Bharoouch: 179
Bhatia: 188
Bhatinda: 194 and 204
Bhim: 189

Bibi Maahak: 223
Bibi Nalah: 235
Bihar: 195, 240, 242, 244, 245, 263, 266 and 268
Bishop Mandora: 175
Black Sea: 114
Blazri: 29, 30, 53, 181 and 185
Bolunsia: 161
Borneo: 280
Bosnia: 117, 118, 123 and 130
Bova: 130
Bowa: 119
Budail Bin Tahfah Al-Bijli: 180
Budhan Brahman: 241
Bughra Khan: 207
Bukhara: 242 and 259
Bulgaria: 65, 116, 117, 118, 119, 130 and 137
Bultaji Muhammad Pasha: 139
Burhanpur: 245
Burnier: 260

C

Cairo: 111 and 112
Castilla: 157, 163, 164, 165, 166 and 169
Chan Qulaij Khan: 264
Chan Qulak Khan: 264
China: 33, 39, 62, 78, 102, 134, 136, 162, 165, 231, 260 and 280
Chittor: 213, 214, 218 and 245
Constantinople: 62, 63, 64, 65, 66, 68 and 90
Cordova: 147, 148, 149, 152, 153, 154, 155, 161, 162 and 163
Count Tandal: 172
Crete: 51, 60 and 142
Culcutta: 264 and 267
Cyelon: 180
Cyprus: 39, 51, 113, 130, 140 and 142

D

Daghistan: 121

Daibal: 179, 180 and 181

Damascus: 36, 37, 64, 77, 99, 100, 103, 106, 145, 146, 148, 150, 184 and 278

Dara Shakoh: 255,256 and 257

Daulat Khan: 241

David: 275

Deccan: 218, 219, 221, 232, 233, 239, 254, 255, 262, 263, 264, 265 and 266

Delhi: 122, 186, 188, 189, 193, 194, 195, 196, 197, 199, 200, 202, 203, 204, 206, 207, 208, 209, 211, 212, 213, 215, 217, 218, 219, 220, 221, 226, 227, 228, 229, 231, 232, 233, 234, 235, 238, 239, 240, 241, 243, 244, 246, 248, 249, 255, 264, 265, 266, 267, 268, 269, 270, 271, 280

Dev Garh: 217, 231, 232 and 233

Dispenia: 137

Doctor Tara Chand: 183

Dohad: 256 and 257

Dorais: 120

Dr. Ishtiaq Hussain Qureshi: 206

Dr. Tripathy: 198

E

East Bihar: 242

Eastern Europe: 63, 115 and 116

Eliriah: 165 and 166

Emarah bin Shahab: 35

Emperor Louis IX: 101

England: 97, 98, 100, 119, 122, 140, 141, 254, 260 and 267

Ethiopia: 129

Eve: 192

F

Faiz Be Nastrullah: 101

Fakhuruddin Mubarak Shah: 198

Farid Khan: 244 and 245

Farishta: 186, 187, 189, 190, 191, 193, 201, 202, 203, 204, 205, 207, 212, 213, 215, 216, 218, 219, 220, 221, 222, 223, 224, 225, 227, 230, 232, 237, 238, 240, 243, 244, 245, 246 and 247

Farrukh Syer: 263 and 264

Fateh Garh: 256

Fatehpur Seekri: 242

Ferdinand: 163, 165, 166, 167, 168, 169, 170, 171, 172, 173, 174, 176 and 178

Fossais: 120

France: 64, 97, 98, 100, 141, 145, 149, 160 and 260

Francisco Shcemens DeSeosoz: 175

Frazdaq: 55

Froland: 162

Fuzaila Bin Obaid-al-Amin: 63

G

Geli Poli: 115

Germany: 97 and 123

Ghayas-ud-Din Abul Fath Ghazi: 99

Ghazi Malik: 226

Ghazni: 186, 187, 188, 189, 190, 191, 193, 194, 195, 197 and 198

Ghias-ud-Din Tughlaq: 226, 227, 228, 229, 235 and 238

Ghilen Bin Yunes: 75

Ghour: 113, 126, 194, 206 and 279

Gowaliar: 188, 199, 202, 222, 223 and 256

Granada: 120, 147, 161, 162, 163, 164, 165, 166, 167, 168, 169, 170, 171, 172, 173, 174, 176 and 178

Gujrat: 195, 204, 213, 221, 222, 224, 239, 244, 255 and 266

Gulbadan Begum: 247

H

Habenah: 73

Habib Bin Al-Mohallab: 184

Hadi: 277

Hafiz Ibne-e-Temiyya: 52

Index

Hafiz Shirazi: 257
Haji Al-Dabeer: 279
Hajjaj Bin Yousuf: 57, 180, 182, 183 and 275
Hakeem Sanai: 190
Hakim Bin Jablah Al Alvi: 179
Hakim Muhammad Hashim Gilani: 257
Halaku Khan: 103, 104 and 106
Hamdan: 84, 88, 102 and 126
Hameeda Bano Begum: 244
Hamid Bin Zararah: 170
Hamilton: 264
Hardwar: 120
Haroon-ur-Rashid: 276
Harsama Bin Aa-Yein: 277
Hassan Khan: 244
Hassani: 154
Hazrat Abdullah Bin Umar: 49
Hazrat Abu Bakar: 23
Hazrat Ali Bin Musa Raza: 193
Hazrat Ali: 22, 24, 25, 26, 33, 34, 35, 36, 37, 38, 40, 41, 42, 43, 47, 54, 55, 121, 179, 193 and 276
Hazrat Amr Bin Aas: 26
Hazrat Ayesha: 37, 48, 49 and 53
Hazrat Baqi Billah: 253
Hazrat Eisa: 72
Hazrat Fatima: 25 and 275
Hazrat Hozaifa Bin Al-Yameen: 138
Hazrat Imam Hussain: 54, 55, 60, 81 and 275
Hazrat Khawaja Moeen ud Din Ajmiri: 199
Hazrat Khawaja Moeen ud Din Chishti: 200 and 280
Hazrat Khawaja Qutbud Din Bakhtiar Kaki: 199, 200, 201, 226, 265 and 280
Hazrat Majadid Alf-e-Sani: 250, 252 and 253
Hazrat Nai'la: 36
Hazrat Nizam ud Din Aulia: 216, 218, 219 and 224
Hazrat Shah Wali Ullah: 269, 270, 271, 272, 273 and 274
Hazrat Shaikh Abdul Qadoos Gangohi: 253
Hazrat Shaikh Ahmad Jam: 223
Hazrat Shaikh Ali Hajweri: 280
Hazrat Shaikh Shahab ud Din: 233
Hazrat Talha: 33 and 37
Hazrat Usman: 22, 32, 33, 34, 36, 37, 38, 39, 40, 46, 63, 68, 81 and 179
Hazrat Zubair: 33, 35 and 37
Hazrt Umar: 22, 23, 24, 25, 26, 27, 32, 33, 38, 42, 46, 48, 54, 66, 68, 69, 70, 71, 72, 73, 74, 75, 81, 108, 138, 179, 184 and 274
Hemoo Baqqal: 246
Henry: 100
Hisham Bin Abdul Malik: 54, 74, 75, 79, 80 and 184
Hisham Bin Amr-Al-Tughalbi: 185
Hisham Bin Hikam: 153
His-nul-Lait: 157
Holland: 260
Honiaday: 123
Humayun Khan: 238
Hungry: 98
Hyderabad: 265

I

Ibne Abee Amir: 152
Ibne Aqeel: 183
Ibne Batoota: 230
Ibne Khalqan: 275
Ibne Rameemi: 161
Ibne Rasheeq: 159
Ibne Zinnoon: 152
Ibn-e-Asad: 96
Ibn-e-Mas'adah: 50
Ibnul Aftas: 152
Ibrahim Bin Muhammad: 112

Ibrahim Lodhi: 241 and 242
Ibrahim Pasha: 139
Idrees Bin Ali: 153
Ilahabad: 251
Imad-ud-Din Rehan: 204
Imad-ud-Din Usman: 99
Imam Abu Hanifa: 131, 132, 197 and 279
Imam Abu Ubaid ul Qasim: 279
Imam Auzai: 71, 72, 275 and 276
Imam Ghazali: 94, 160 and 279
Imam Hassan: 42. 152 and 154
Imam Hazrat Raja Bin Haiwah: 274
Imam Malik: 276 and 279
Imam Yahya Bin Yamar: 275
Imam Zain-ul-Abideen: 55 and 56
Imran Bin Moosa: 185
Inbe Hood: 152 and 161
India: 120, 121, 138, 179, 186, 192, 19, 194, 195, 199, 208, 211, 213, 214, 233, 236, 238, 239, 242, 245, 246, 248, 250, 254, 256, 260, 262, 266, 267, 268, 269, 270 and 272
Iraq: 33, 34, 38, 40, 41, 57, 59, 60, 61, 66, 75, 77, 79, 99, 104, 111, 129, 150, 179, 180, 182, 183, 204, 214 and 229
Iraq-e-Ajam: 77
Islam Shah: 246
Island of Sicily: 51, 60, 96, 100 and 120
Isphahan: 77 and 84
Italy: 97 and 127
Izzuddin Bin Abdus Salam: 111

J

Jabai-ut-Tariq: 144
Jahandar Shah: 263
Jaisha: 184
Jalal ud Din Khilji: 207, 208, 209, 210, 211, 213, 220 and 224
Jaloola: 29
James I: 254

Jamia Azhar: 99
Jampur: 239, 240, 241 and 244
Jarjan: 187
Java: 280
Jerusalem: 97, 100 and 119
Jesus Christ: 275
Jhelum: 195
Jiaan: 161 and 162
Jingiz Khan: 195, 208, 214, 220 and 239
Jokhta: 106
Junaid: 74 and 185

K

Kaam Bakhsh: 261 and 263
Kabul: 186, 187, 241, 242, 244, 246, 248 and 255
Kad Bano: 235
Kalinger: 186 188, 190 and 245
Kalsidon: 63
Kamil: 100, 101, 144, 190, 192, 193 and 196
Kantakozin: 137
Kareej: 29
Karoona: 154
Kasoda: 117, 120 and 123
Katbagha: 103
Khalid Bin Abdullah Al-Qasir: 75
Khalid Bin Walid: 38
Khalid Rawaish: 279
Khalida Adeeb Khanum: 133, 135 and 140
Kharasan Mawra un Nahr: 214
Kharza: 145, 153, 154 and 156
Khawaja Jahan: 238
Khawaja Usman Harwani: 199
Khizar Khan: 221, 222, 224, 239 and 240
Khorasan: 58, 62, 76, 77, 79, 84, 88 and 275
Khusrao Khan: 225, 226, 227 and 228
Khwarism: 62 and 191

Index

King Lazar: 117
King Louis VII: 97
King of Qustailah: 160
King Phillip Augusts: 98
King Richard: 98
King Shah Alam: 266, 267 and 268
Kishlu Khan: 204
Koofa: 35, 37, 48, 61, 70, 79, 80, 81 and 87
Kotwal Alaul Malik: 214
Kumbay: 254
Kurdistan: 101

L

Lahore: 179, 186, 197, 204, 219, 245, 254 257 and 263
Lakka River: 145
Lala shaheen: 116
Lebanon: 142 and 143
Libya: 143
Locrais: 120
Lohkot: 189
Lord Bishop Scheemens: 176, 177 and 178
Lord Clive: 267 and 268
Losha: 164

M

Ma'raj-un-Noman: 96
Madain: 29 and 138
Madina: 37, 40, 42, 45, 48, 57, 61, 76, 77, 79, 105, 128, 131, 149, 235 and 270
Madrasa Fateh: 140
Madrasa Sulemania: 140
Madrasa-e-Nizamia: 102
Mahabat Khan: 254
Mahmood Lodhi: 241
Makhdoom Zada Abbasi: 235
Makkah: 35, 37, 42, 45, 46, 76, 79, 85, 126, 128, 131, 142, 157, 190, 242, 257 and 270

Makran: 179 and 180
Malay: 280
Malik Aadil: 99, 100 and 101
Malik Afzal: 99
Malik Ahmad: 208 and 209
Malik Aziz: 100
Malik Jhajju: 209
Malik Kafoor: 221, 222 and 223
Malik Khasro: 223
Malik Lagheeq: 205
Malik Mansoor Noor ud Din: 103
Malik Mansoor Saif ud Din: 106
Malik Muzaffar: 103 and 104
Malik Qahir: 104
Malik Saifuddin Abu Bakr: 100
Malik Salih Najmuddin: 101
Malik Suleman: 240
Malik ul Umara Fakharuddin: 207
Malik Zahir: 99, 104, 105 and 106
Malika: 153, 161, 164, 165, 210, 212, 213, 221 and 222
Mallo Iqbal: 239
Malwa: 185, 204, 239 and 266
Mamoon: 89, 90, 107, 155, 185, 194, 277 and 279
Mansurah: 185 and 186
Maqam-e-Hanfi: 128
Maqdoos: 117
Marj-e-Wabiq: 96
Marquis: 105
Marwan al Himar: 185
Marwan Bin Abdul Aziz: 161
Marwan: 54, 57, 59, 60, 68, 71, 74, 75, 76, 77, 79, 150, 161 and 185
Maseera: 61
Masood: 57, 61, 72, 194 and 203
Masoodi: 57, 61 and 72
Mathra: 190 and 266
Maulana Akbar Shah Khan Najeeb Abadi: 120 and 150

Maulana Fakhruddin: 232
Maulana Malik Ibrahim: 280
Maulana Mir Kalam Hervi: 251
Maulana Najam ud Din Dimashqi: 205
Maulana Obaid Ullah Sindhi: 273
Maulana Shamsuddin Yahya: 232
Maulana Sirajuddin Sanjri: 205
Mausil: 77, 84 and 88
Mawalis: 57 and 155
Mediterranean: 39, 51, 113, 125, 129 and 130
Mehdi: 109, 110, 160, 233 and 279
Mercia: 86 and 159
Mir Abdul Hayee: 247
Mir Jafar: 267 and 268
Mir Jumla: 261
Mirza Handal: 247
Mirza Kamran: 239
Mo'ta'mid: 155
Mo'tazid: 155
Moazzam: 85,262 and 263
Morocco: 150, 156, 159, 160 and 173
Mosseu Leban: 175
Mossil: 142
Motamid Ibne Ibad: 156
Motasim Billah: 121
Motasim: 155
Motawakkil: 155
Motawaqif: 155
Mr. Aziz: 115
Mu'izuddin Muhammad Bahauddin Sam: 205
Mubarak Khan: 222 and 223
Mubaraz Khan: 246
Mufti Dahlan: 128
Mughira bin Sho'ba: 34 and 38
Mughira: 34, 36, 38, 49 and 179
Muhammad Ali Pasha Khadyu: 139
Muhammad Azam: 257

Muhammad Bin Abdur Rehman: 154 and 155
Muhammad Bin Abi Bakr: 37
Muhammad Bin Ali Alsanoosi: 280
Muhammad Bin Qalaoon: 112
Muhammad Bin Qasim: 29, 62, 67, 68, 74, 180, 181, 182, 183 and 184
Muhammad Bin Tomert: 160
Muhammad Saqi Mustaid Khan: 257
Muhammad Shah Aadil: 246
Muhammad Tughlaq: 230, 231, 232, 233, 234, 235 and 236
Muiz Jashenger: 103
Muiz ud Din Baharam Shah: 203
Mukhtar Bin Obaid Saqfi: 60
Multan: 92, 120, 182, 183, 186, 188, 199, 209, 212, 232, 238, 242, 245 and 255
Muqtadir: 83, 86, 132, 155 and 156
Murabiteen: 156
Murad II: 123
Murad III: 137
Murtaza River: 116
Musa Bin Nusair: 144, 145, 146 and 182
Muslimah Bin Abdul Malik: 65 and 66
Mustafa Kamal Pasha: 142
Mustafa: 134 and 142
Mustakfi Billah: 83,112 and 278
Muta-Wakkil Ala-Allah: 119
Muzir: 76 and 84

N

Nabluna: 152
Nadir Shah: 265 and 266
Nagar Kot: 188, 189 and 194
Najeeb ud Daula: 267
Nankopollis: 119
Nasar Bin Omar: 162
Nasibain: 139
Nasir ud Din Mahmood: 202, 203 and

Index

204
Nasir ud Din Muhammad: 238
Neem Rose: 191
Nehr-Wan: 41
Neko Dar Oghlan: 106
Neshapore: 187, 191, 197 and 204
New Guinea: 280
Nizaar: 76
Nizam ud Din Ahmad: 201, 202, 208 and 228
Nizam ul Malik: 265
Noman Bin Moqran: 29
Noor Bano: 138
Noor Jehan: 254, 255 and 257
North Africa: 50, 51, 60, 74, 144, 146, 160 and 280
Nusrat Khan: 238

O

Obai Bin Ka'b: 26
Obaidullah: 35 and 57
Omi Chand: 267
Oor Khan: 114, 115, 116, 137 and 222
Orissa: 248, 251
Oudh: 195, 265 and 266

P

Paishwa: 263, 264 and 265
Palam: 268
Palestine: 61, 76, 77, 98, 103, 105 and 142
Panipat: 241, 266 and 267
Pattan: 190
Peshawar: 186, 187, 188 and 189
Pharos: 221
Philadelphia: 118
Philippines: 280
Podolia: 130
Poland: 117, 123
Pondi Cherri: 262

Pope Innocent, the VIII: 175
Portugal: 97 and 260
Prince Azam: 261 and 262
Prince Danial: 251
Prince John: 172
Prince Khurram: 252, 254, 255 and 257
Prince Murad: 250 and 256
Prince Sheharyar: 255
Prithvi Raj: 194
Professor Kurd: 177
Professor Sadev: 146 and 148
Punjab: 186, 187, 189, 193, 194, 203, 204, 207, 208, 213, 226, 232, 240, 241, 243, 246, 248, 262, 263, 265, 266 and 280
Pyranese Mountains: 145

Q

Qabqan: 179
Qadam Bin Mazoon: 25
Qadsia: 30, 52 and 53
Qaffal Maroozi: 67
Qahtaba: 77
Qaiqabad: 207 and 208
Qairwan: 151
Qais Bin Sa'd: 35 and 37
Qaisaria: 105 and 106
Qaiser Cantakozin: 116
Qaiser of Rome: 72, 118, 120 and 121
Qalij Khan: 208
Qandhar: 194, 248, 257 and 267
Qannuj: 186
Qara Yousuf Turkman: 120
Qari Hasheem: 108
Qarrabou: 180
Qashnala: 152
Qasim Bin Hamood: 153
Qasr-e-Feeroze: 191
Qawam-ud-Daula Kabuqa: 96
Qazi Abu Yousuf: 279

Qazi Fakhuruddin Abdul Aziz Al-Kufi: 197
Qazi Mughis: 214, 216, 217, 218 and 219
Qazi Yahya Bin Aksim: 277
Qonia: 101 and 114
Qous: 112
Qublai Khan: 106
Queen Catharine: 139
Queen Izabella: 167, 1 9, 170, 172, 175 and 176
Queen Zuhra: 149
Qutaiba Bin Muslim: 62 and 67
Qutbud Din Aibak: 195, 196, 197, 198, 199 and 226
Qutbuddin: 200 and 201
Qazi Taj ud Din: 111

R

Rafi ud Daulah: 264
Raiy: 77
Raja Chach: 183
Raja Dahir: 180, 181, 182, 183 and 184
Raja Jai Chand: 194 and 195
Raja Jay Pal: 186 and 190
Raja of Jodhpur: 249
Raja Rana Mal Bhatti: 235
Raja Todar Mal: 249
Rajab: 234
Rajputana: 213,239,262,266 and 280
Ramehwaram: 206
Rana Sanga: 241 and 242
Ranthambore: 199, 210 and 213
Raziyya: 201, 202 and 203
Rhodes: 51, 125, 129 and 130
Roderick: 144 and 145
Roha: 97 and 98
Rohail Khand: 266
Romania: 98
Ruknud Din Feroze Shah: 201

Ruknuddin: 104, 201, 203, 212 and 213

S

S. P. Scott: 157 and 158
Sa'atat Khan: 264 and 265
Sa'd Bin Abi Waqqas: 29
Saadat Khan: 238
Sadr-e-Jahan: 234
Sadullah Khan: 257
Saeed Bin Aslam: 180
Sahal Bin Salam Al Ansaari: 279
Sahara: 129
Sahl Bin Hanif: 35
Sahoo: 263 and 264
Saif Ud Daula Abul Hassan Ali Bin Abi Haija: 102
Saif ud Din Mahmood Qatoozi: 103
Sajasmund: 118 and 119
Sakhrah: 163
Salamah: 73
Salih Bin Abdur Rehman: 183
Salim Shah: 246
Salman Farsi: 45
Sam Garh: 256
Samiyyah: 53
Sarqastah: 152
Saudi Arabia: 143
Seena: 117
Serbia: 116, 117, 118, 119, 123, 130, 136 and 137
Sesman: 137
Seva Ji: 262
Sewas: 121 and 122
Shadi Khan: 222
Shah Abdul Aziz: 271,272 and 273
Shah Abdul Qadir: 272 and 273
Shah Abdur Rahim: 270
Shah Alam: 266,267 and 268
Shah Ismail Safwi: 126

Index

Shah Ismail Shaheed: 272 and 273
Shah Rafi ud Din: 272
Shahab ud Din: 194, 195, 196, 197, 222, 223, 226, 23 and 279
Shah-e-Turkaan: 201
Shaikh Abdul Ahad: 25
Shaikh Abdullah Alyamni: 280
Shaikh Abdullah Arif: 280
Shaikh Abdullah Bin Yasin: 280
Shaikh Abu Tahir Bin Ibrahim of Madina: 270
Shaikh Bashir: 224
Shaikh Burhanuddin Bilji: 205
Shaikh Mahmoodi: 112
Shaikh Muhammad Akram: 219 and 245
Shaikh Najmuddin: 223
Shaikh Naseer ud Din Chiragh Delhvi: 232 and 235
Shaikh Noor ud Din: 280
Shaikh Saadi: 257
Shaikh ul Islam Jam Zinda Peel: 233
Shajrat ul Dur: 101
Shams ud Din Altmush: 197
Shamsuddin Rafi-ud-Darojat: 264
Sharif-e-Makkah: 128
Shazoona: 145
Sheikh Qutbi: 128
Sheikh ul Islam Mufti Jamali: 129
Sher Khan: 204
Sher Shah Suri: 244,245,246 and 249
Shuja: 255 and 267
Sibta: 153
Sindh: 180, 182, 183, 184, 185, 186, 199, 239 and 273
Sir Thomas Roe: 254
Siraj ud Daula: 267 and 268
Slippese: 280
Solomon: 275
Som Nath: 190 and 192
South India: 233, 239 and 266

Spain: 13, 62, 64, 68, 74, 78, 84, 87, 97, 120, 127, 144, 145, 146, 147, 148, 150, 151, 152, 153, 154, 156, 158, 159, 160, 161, 162, 166, 167, 168, 169, 170, 172, 173, 174, 175, 176, 177, 178, 182, 260 and 272
State of Vijya Nagar: 233
Sudan: 129 and 143
Sulaiman Bin Abdul Malik: 64, 65, 66, 67, 68, 150, 183, 184 and 274
Suleman Pasha: 115, 116 and 118
Sultan Abdul Hamid: 140 and 141
Sultan Abdul Majid II: 115 and 139
Sultan Ahmad: 120 and 121
Sultan Alauddin Bin Sultan Muhammad Shah: 240
Sultan Alp Arsalan: 101 and 102
Sultan Feroze Shah Tughlaq: 234, 235 and 236
Sultan Hassan: 163 and 164
Sultan Mahmood: 186, 187, 188, 189, 190, 191, 192, 193, 194, 196 and 256
Sultan Murad: 116, 117, 118, 123, 124, 137, 138 and 139
Sultan Noor-ud-Din Zangi: 97, 98, 99 and 101
Sultan Salah-ud-Din Ayyubi: 98, 99, 100, 101, 105 and 113
Sultan Saleem I: 113
Sultan Sikandar Shah: 238
Sultan Tooman Bay: 126
Sultana Saffiya: 138
Sumotra: 280
Surah-I-Feel: 193
Surat: 184,254
Surhind: 253
Syed Burhan ud Din: 280
Syed Hussain Ali: 263 and 264
Syed Mubarak Ghaznawi: 205
Syedi Maula: 211
Syria: 34, 35, 36, 38, 39, 50, 51, 55, 61, 63, 66, 76, 77, 80, 84, 88, 96, 98, 99,

100, 103, 104, 105, 106, 107, 113, 119, 126, 127, 142, 143, 149, 150, 180, 182, 204, 214 and 275

T

Tabook: 35
Tabrani: 31
Tabriz: 126
Taghan: 186
Tagsi: 144
Tahmasap: 134
Taimoor, the lame: 239
Talhat: 181
Talsman: 167
Tana: 179
Tanjah: 153
Tariq Bin Ziad: 144, 145 and 182
Temur: 106, 120, 121 and 122
Thanseer: 189
Thatta: 180 and 181
Theodora: 116 and 137
Thrace: 115 and 117
Tigris: 30 and 108
Tirmzi: 44
Tolado: 96
Tolaiha bin Khowalid: 35
Tona: 147
Toos: 193
Toran Shah: 101
Trimz: 187
Tripoli: 39, 107 and 129
Tughlaq Shah: 238
Tunis: 129
Turgi: 218
Turkistan: 13, 62, 187, 203, 204, 214 and 215

U

Ubaid Ullah Bin Nabaan: 180
Ujaib Bin Marrah: 185
Ujjain: 185 and 231
Umar Bin Abdul Aziz Al-Hibari: 185
Urkely Khan: 212
Usman Bin Abil Aas: 179
Usman Bin Hanif: 35
Usman Khan: 114, 131 and 136
Utba Bin Farqal-al-Salmi: 27

V

Valley of Aash: 165 and 166
Vennice: 138
Venus: 137
Vienna: 115 and 123
VISHNU: 206
Volteer: 178

W

Wadi-ul-Kabir: 144
Wahid Bin Abdul Malik: 62, 144, 145, 180 and 182
Walachia: 117, 118, 119 and 123
Walansa: 147
Walid Bin Abdul Malik: 59, 62, 144, 145, 180 and 182
Walid: 24, 35, 38, 62, 64, 68, 75, 76, 144, 145, 146, 180 and 182
Wameek: 195
Waran: 219
Wardi Khan: 267
Wasit: 88 and 183

Y

Yahya Bin Ali: 153 and 155
Yaqoob Pasha: 117
Yazd Gard: 29
Yazid Bin Abi Jaisha: 183
Yazid Bin Abi Kabsha: 29
Yazid Bin Malik: 71
Yazid: 29, 53, 54, 58, 63, 71, 73, 74, 75, 76, 115, 117, 118, 119, 120, 121, 122, 125, 134, 136, 137, 167, 168, 183, 184

Index

and 239
Yeni: 114 and 139
Ymen: 35, 86, 125 and 130
Yousuf Bin Tashfein: 156, 157, 158, 159 and 160
Yuleen: 144
Yushina: 164

Z

Zaab-e-Aala: 77.
Zahak: 221
Zahir Bi-Amirullah: 111
Zaid Bin Abi Sufyan: 53
Zaid Bin Abihe: 53
Zaid Bin Thabit: 26
Zain ud Din: 104 and 112
Zakaria Bin Wasiq: 112
Zakirya Bin Abee Hafas: 160
Zalaka: 156, 157, 158 and 159
Zawia: 199
Zia ud Din Barni: 211, 225, 229 and 234
Ziada-tullah Aghlabi: 113
Zul Qadria: 126

اَللَّهُمَّ رَبَّ هَذِهِ الدَّعْوَةِ التَّامَّةِ وَالصَّلَاةِ الْقَائِمَةِ آتِ مُحَمَّدًا الْوَسِيلَةَ وَالْفَضِيلَةَ وَابْعَثْهُ مَقَامًا مَحْمُودًا الَّذِي وَعَدْتَهُ